Tara,

You pick the links

I'll choose the hotel

P1 will deliver the car

Let's attempt to get round 18

quality links courses in 2008.

Fun, love + competative spirit included,

Love Alex xV.

JOURNEY THROUGH THE LINKS

BY DAVID WORLEY

First published in the UK 2007 by
Aurum Press Limited
7 Greenland Street
London NW1 0ND
www.aurumpress.co.uk

A catalogue record for this book is available from the British Library.

ISBN-10: 1 84513 295 5
ISBN-13: 978 1 84513 295 8

10 9 8 7 6 5 4 3 2 1
2011 2010 2009 2008 2007

Designed by Graphic Partners, Melbourne, Australia
Printed in China through The Australian Book Connection

Front cover photo: The European, Ireland

SEASIDE GOLF

How straight it flew, how long it flew,
It clear'd the rutty track
And soaring, disappeared from view
Beyond the bunker's back –
A glorious, sailing, bounding drive
That made me glad I was alive.

And down the fairway, far along
It glowed a lonely white;
I played an iron sure and strong
And clipp'd it out of sight,
And spite of grassy banks between
I knew I'd find it on the green.

And so I did. It lay content
Two paces from the pin;
A steady putt and then it went
Oh, most surely in.
The very turf rejoiced to see
That quite unprecedented three.

Ah! Seaweed smells from sand caves
And thyme and mist in whiffs,
In-coming tide, Atlantic waves
Slapping the sunny cliffs,
Lark song and sea sounds in the air
And splendour, splendour everywhere.

John Betjeman

CONTENTS

FOREWORD BY PETER THOMSON

Photo courtesy Eagles Nest Publishing

We golfers are an extraordinary bunch. Never mind that we are gullible when it comes to technology, and easily blinded with science, when it comes to the arenas on which we play our game, we are peculiar indeed.

We are absolutely intolerant of the slightest imperfection of our home club fairways – no unfilled divots permitted, greens must be as smooth as a sheet of glass, and our sand bunkers raked impeccably to facilitate escape without punishment. Our home course must be manicured like a catwalk model's nails. How then can we explain our fascination, even reverence, for seaside links, and inland "bracken and gravel", "heather and pine" courses, which are anything but the comely insistence we indulge in playing at home.

It doesn't make a lot of sense but that is how it is. We love to experience the tackling of a wild course of unkempt nature left as it was before golfers intruded on its territory, even if it is merely visual. And what a rich tapestry there is if we look hard enough!

The game of golf in its early years was started on the fringe of villages and small towns, where the course was easily accessed by a short walk. The territory was usually Common Land shared with shepherds and dairymen. These interests fused together to everyone's benefit and acceptance. The animals kept the grass eaten short and the golfers got their maintenance free.

There were side benefits too. The beasts found the shelter of sand-blows if the ground was close enough to the coast, and their persistence led to defined bunkers. This mutual co-habitation created the wild coastal courses we worship today.

An example of this is the Brora course on Scotland's Sutherland coast. A better piece of links ground I have yet to find. The 18 holes features two cross burns, the water of which a little higher up makes a superior malt whisky! The course though is kept playable by five men and a hundred sheep and cows. In consequence the local golfers who love their course pay a very modest annual subscription.

Yet there are other courses inland and some high in the hills that have their own beauty. A seaside links is not automatically better than an inland one. Its merit or otherwise depends on its basic attributes. Who can say with authority that Muirfield is a better course than Sunningdale? Is Royal County Down above Walton Heath? I wonder.

This book does not explain the phenomenon of our capture by wild and woolly courses scattered along exposed coasts, but it illustrates it beautifully. David Worley's second odyssey, (his first sortie into the world of golf produced "Fairways in Heaven, Bunkers from Hell"), takes us on a wider, deeper trail of courses in their natural settings which makes us envious and footloose. Would we not, all of us, like to go off wandering where our golf clubs lead us, meeting interesting people of like mind, and some glorious courses all welcoming the traveller from a far place.

The book is a pictorial and textural encyclopedia of all that is best in golf touring, which makes it possible to go "travelling" with your fingers and never leave home. It also makes it clear to us that the more famous courses have no more to offer in interest and pleasure than the less known ones. The former owe their fame to the fact of being championship venues over a long long period, and if they have a reputation for confounding the champions, the more familiar they become.

Golf is now a fast growing worldwide sporting phenomenon. New courses are being put together in far-flung places. Many of them will be replicas of what is presented in this collection, but I doubt that the new will ever replace the old; that is if the old is preserved in its pristine state. Some of these courses are world treasures.

Peter Thomson

Peter Thomson and the author at Commonwealth GC Melbourne, November 2005

AUTHOR'S NOTE
In a career that started in 1947, Peter Thomson has almost 100 tournament victories. His achievements in the British Open have been nothing short of legendary status. Over a 21 year period, commencing at Royal Portrush in 1951, Peter achieved a finish in the top 10 no less than 18 times. In a golden period from 1952 to 1958 he was never placed lower than second. The end result saw him winning five Open Championships – 2 at Royal Birkdale and single victories at St Andrews, Royal Lytham & St Annes and Royal Liverpool.

We are indeed fortunate that Peter's great depth of knowledge of golf and golf courses has been left as a legacy for all through his involvement in course design which at this stage numbers in excess of 200.

INTRODUCTION

To quote from the words of a Paul Kelly[1] song: "From little things, big things grow". On November 17th 1995 my wife Irene presented me with a rather unique 50th birthday present – a ticket for a round at Carnoustie in May of the following year. This was the beginning of my love affair with links golf, and I am happy to report that the love is growing with a burning passion.

"Journey through the Links" has been ten years in the making. The 1996 trip was five weeks of golf and one week at Wimbledon. The idea for a golf/travel book led to six weeks of non stop golf in 1998 after which I produced "Fairways in Heaven, Bunkers from Hell" which sold very well in my home town of Melbourne, Australia.

The first two trips had included a mix of links, heathland and inland courses. I knew that it was the genuine links that I wanted to experience so, with this book in mind another six weeks of non stop golf was planned for 2003 and this time to also include Ireland.

The more links courses I played, the more of them I discovered – often in rather remote areas. One such delightful spot was The Machrie on the isle of Islay which lies off the west coast of the Mull of Kintyre. From what I could see, there is nothing at Islay except for their great golf course and several whisky distilleries famous for the peat influenced taste. How could you ever forget approaching a green only to find it was already occupied by a hedgehog and three sheep all of whom are enjoying the momentary burst of sunshine? Islay is not exactly over-run with tourists – and I'm pretty sure the weather is a major factor. On one of our days there it was just too wet for golf so my wife and I organised for a taxi journey around the island. My other lasting memory of Islay is our driver whose sufficiently well proportioned stomach enabled him,

whilst driving, to balance on it his can of soft drink, chocolate bar and cigarettes.

Instead of just writing a review of some links courses I decided to go where no one has been foolish enough to set foot before. To play virtually every eighteen hole links course in Scotland, England, Wales and Ireland. Each week of research I discovered a new, and often relatively unknown links. When you tell someone you played golf in the far north of Scotland they will normally assume that Royal Dornoch or perhaps Brora is the end of the line. Well, there are two good links courses about 40-50 miles north of Brora, namely Reay and Wick. The next stop north of Reay is the Arctic Circle.

I had spent some time in Wales in 1998 but only Aberdovey and Royal St. David's had been on the agenda. My investigations concluded that there are sixteen good links courses in Wales – several of them extremely good. This is very under rated links country.

Ireland is not without some remote areas. Perhaps Rosapenna on the northern coast, Enniscrone in the North West and Carne on the Belmullet Peninsula are all a long way from the normal tourist route but each has fabulous dune land golfing terrain. Every new course meant an extra day or two would be needed if I was to visit and I was determined to get to every links.

The 2006 journey required playing or walking (mostly playing), 97 courses in 90 days. Starting from Northern Scotland my wife and I travelled clockwise around the whole of the coastline of Britain with the exception of North West Scotland where there are no seaside links. For the second time I travelled the complete coastline of Ireland, in an anti-clockwise direction starting at Royal

County Down and finishing with the group of links from Dublin to about forty miles north.

I estimate that in these four trips I have driven 26,000 miles. My golf has been spread over the months of early May to early September. In the first three trips, we encountered some of the wettest spring and summer weather ever experienced in the UK. Then in 2006 we had the complete reverse with July being the warmest ever recorded in England. The day Irene and I played Rye it was 39 degrees Celsius. The fairways were burnt to a crisp and there were no drinking taps in sight.

The reviews of each course are as objective as is humanly possible with no influence from weather, attitude of the people there etc. "Journey" contains many hundreds of photos to help you experience what I have been fortunate enough to do. Where possible, I have taken all the photos myself. But sometimes the weather was just so poor I have had to call upon outside help.

My book is meant to be of very high 'coffee table' quality. You may wish to use it as a guide for a journey of your own so I have deliberately listed the courses more or less in the geographic order you would come across them if you travelled clockwise around Britain and anti-clockwise in Ireland.

Don't be confused by the occasional change from yards to metres. Most descriptions are in yards but I have adopted the measurements used by each individual course on their score cards.

The selection process as to which courses could be defined as a 'links' was of necessity rather difficult. I have attempted to define 'what is a links course' in the chapter that follows.

My original, somewhat fixed, concept was expanded from the simplistic seaside links type of course to include a wider variety of the species. Some examples may help. The seaside links that are on flat land and sandy soil are quite obvious. The second category I have included is that of 'cliff top links'.

Some cliff top courses have sand based fast running fairways and yet others have heavier soil and do not play like a true links. Nefyn in Wales is an example of cliff top that is links. On the east coast of England the fairways at Sheringham were such that it made my list but nearby Royal Cromer had heavy soil and was thick with trees and bracken and did not qualify.

The only course that is included that is more than a short distance from the sea is Ganton which is eleven miles inland from Scarborough. This selection may surprise you but I have outlined the reasons for its qualification in the individual course review. This land was once covered by the sea so Ganton is the only participant that I have categorised as 'inland links'.

The fourth category I have labeled is heathland links. These are courses that are very close by the sea but may have nine holes of the genuine seaside links style and nine holes that is more heathland in appearance. Examples are Golspie in northern Scotland and Scotscraig at Tayport just north of St Andrews. I have also included a few that have at least nine holes of links but the balance may even have a few parkland holes due to the presence often of a nearby river estuary – Hesketh is one such example.

In all there are 155 courses for you to savour, and they are all different. How can we not enjoy the challenge of links golf when there are such stark contrasts as the flat terrain at St Andrews, the spectacular pyramid like dunes at Enniscrone and the extraordinary cliff top experience at Old Head near Kinsale in southern Ireland.

Enjoy your "Journey through the Links".

1.   Paul Kelly is a well known contemporary Australian song writer and
     performer.

Towering pyramid dunes at Enniscrone

Photo courtesy Gary Prendergast

WHAT IS A LINKS COURSE?

A TRUE LINKS COURSE SHOULD NOT ONLY LOOK LIKE A LINKS BUT IT SHOULD ALSO PLAY LIKE ONE.

My non-golfing friends are constantly bemused by my excitement of playing a course for the first time. But, "aren't golf courses all the same?" is their usual retort. Others among the non golfers have seen the television portrayal of the US Masters at Augusta and the stark contrast with the courses used for the Open Championship in Britain. They then comment that the links courses often look less interesting and easier because there appear to be fewer obvious hazards, namely trees and water.

One has to play the links courses to appreciate just how much Mother Nature, in the form of wind, is frequently the major hazard. Because of the continuous wind, links courses usually have smaller but deeper bunkers which can be the ruination of a stroke round. After a wet spring the rough can be ridiculously long and distinctly inhospitable, but conversely, when the fairways are running fast and the dry summer has burnt off the rough then many a golf ball has run into unplayable territory in the gorse bushes (whins). Wind varies in response to temperature changes. An on-shore breeze can quickly change to off-shore because the sands warm up more rapidly and cool down more slowly than water.

Wind direction is affected by changes in the tide. I was informed by the manager of the links at Carnoustie that some zealous locals study the tide times and then book a tee time that may give them the advantage of playing most holes with the wind. This is far more relevant on the traditional links which were usually designed for a narrow piece of land necessitating 9 holes out and 9 holes back.

My golfing companions who have not been lucky enough to play in the United Kingdom or Ireland always ask me to define what is meant by a 'links' course. This enquiry is normally prefaced by their own observation that a links course has no trees and is situated beside the sea.

The Oxford Dictionary defines the word 'links' as "level or undulating sandy ground near sea-shore, with turf and coarse grass." Some say that the word 'links' is originally derived from the Old English 'hlinc', which referred to a ridge or parcel of unploughed land. The land was uncultivated for the very reason that it was a wasteland. These swards of land are often no more than two fairways wide so this largely explains why so many of the original links courses have their necessary 'out and back' configuration.

To say that links land is simply the link between arable land and the sea ignores what is really a very complex ecosystem. After the last ice age, sands were blown in from the beaches and, together with small particles of shell derived from previous marine life; this led to the formation of dunes. Free draining and with little in the way of nutrients other than bird droppings, this gave rise to a very special variety of flora. Marram grass and native fescues grew and helped preserve the dunes from further wind erosion. These knee high grasses may mean a lost or unplayable ball for the golfer, but without them the links land could not have survived.

Based on my own experience of playing links courses, I would stress that the type of soil is one of the key elements. The sandy soil that drains well and is conducive to the springy turf with its coarse grass is absolutely essential. It stands to reason therefore that these locations will be beside the sea or where this land was once covered by the sea. Whilst this soil is ideal for a golf course, it is usually

considered unsuitable for any kind of farming other than grazing livestock. When golf became popular in the second half of the nineteenth century many of the early courses were virtually already there. Sheep and rabbits had kept the grasses short, and since initially greens were not cut, then little needed to be done to make the course playable.

The lack of trees is generally not due to man. Rather it is a result of the constant winds, salt spray and soil that is not high in the nutrients necessary for deeper rooted vegetation.

But that is not to say that all seaside courses are genuine links. There is no doubting that Cruden Bay in North East Scotland is the real thing. But even here there are several holes early in the back nine that lie on what was probably once a small river floodplain with the resultant richer farm land type soil that has been deposited over the centuries. These holes have an unmistakingly different feel underfoot.

Carlyon Bay in Cornwall and Portpatrick in south west Scotland are right on the waters edge but their heavier downland or farmland soil immediately removes any suggestion of them being a links.

To add further to the confusion, there are some inland courses – best described as heathland – that also have that almost unique springy turf feel from which it is a joy for the golfer to hit down upon and squeeze the ball into the air. Walton Heath near Gatwick is a prime example. It is no-where near the sea and has heather lined fairways surrounded by trees and neighbouring farmland. It is not a links course but you could not pick a better place to practice the links type of shot making before venturing to the wind affected seaside courses. In his biography entitled James Braid, the doyen of golf writers Bernard Darwin sums up Walton

Heath by saying that it… "is and always will be one of the great inland courses, big fierce and exacting, blown upon by mighty winds, and having to my mind some indefinably seaside quality in the problems it sets the golfer".[1]

There are stands of fir trees at Carnoustie on the central east coast of Scotland, and Formby, near Liverpool, has holes that play through thick pines. Royal Lytham and St Anne's is not beside the sea and is surrounded by houses and yet these three courses are fine examples of links with two of them being on the rota of The Open Championship which can only be held on a links course.

Some links, for example Troon on the Ayrshire coast of Scotland, are quite flat and may be considered by many as being relatively unattractive. Others, such as Royal County Down at Newcastle in Northern Ireland, are quite hilly and have spectacular views both within and from outside the course itself. Beauty is not always immediately recognisable. I recall spending a relatively windy afternoon sitting in complete isolation in the natural grasses between the fairways at Machrihanish. What may have first appeared as a harsh landscape soon became a scene of great natural beauty with waving grasses blending imperceptibly with distant fairways and the only sound being that of seagulls, oystercatchers (this bird is part of the Machrihanish Golf Club logo) and the occasional distant golfer. In short, the true links represent an endless variety of battlefields.

You will often find hazards on links courses that are far less common on their inland counterpart. Blind shots over dunes are a regular occurrence and add a sense of what Bernard Darwin delightfully describes as "pleasurable uncertainty". Whilst this is normally reserved for the tee shot, at The Machrie on the island of Islay (west of the Mull of Kintyre) the blind shots are frequently those to the green.

St Enodoc in Cornwall contains a church, once buried by sand, in the middle of the course together with a bunker so large that there is a ladder up the face to help you retrieve your ball. It is the only example of which I am aware whereby you can take a penalty of one and drop outside the bunker. Stone walls can be common place and in the case of Pit, the 13th at North Berwick West, the wall is right in front of the green.

The links courses were, in most cases, built before the age of the motor car. This probably explains the very close proximity of railway lines to many of them. So much so that they have often become integral hazards, especially when the wind is blowing. Some well known examples occur at the 1st hole at Prestwick, the 16th at Aberdovey, the 11th at Troon, the 4th at Irvine and the 16th on The Old Course at St Andrews where the train used to run by. Nothing strikes terror into the golfer's soul more than out of bounds running along side the fairway. The awareness of this danger is surely heightened by the presence of railway tracks.

Every now and then grazing animals can be an unusual hazard on the links. Sometimes small electrified fences are necessary to protect the greens from their incursion but, from my experience, they rarely cause problems. The fairways at Aberdovey are home to a number of very large cattle. I have seen cattle and horses grazing peacefully at Westward Ho! Wild ponies graze at their leisure at Pennard in Wales. Lahinch is famous for its goats, and in the far north of Scotland at Brora the sheep usually outnumber the golfers. At Tralee we were closely followed round the back nine by a fox which felt at home enough to even venture into the Pro shop. But perhaps the most lasting image I have is the 7th at The Machrie where my wife and I could not putt out until the hedgehog and three sheep quietly departed from their positions in the centre of the green.

The older links courses have a natural look about them because that is precisely what they are with often only the teeing ground and greens being the result of man's intrusion. Designed before mechanical earth movers existed, the dunes and original hazards were left largely intact. The first bunkers came about from sheep and cattle eroding the hillside whilst sheltering from the harsh wind and rain of the Scottish winter. Fairways were wide with often no strict definition between holes running side by side. Nowhere is this better exemplified than at St Andrews. With few exceptions, over the past 40 years fairways on most courses have narrowed somewhat and have become more defined (and less natural in appearance) due to the introduction of watering systems. In recent times I have played some traditional old links courses that have lost some of the feel and the fun by being over-watered in summer. Oh for the days when foreign professionals playing at St Andrews would complain that the fairways were faster than the greens. After such a complaint was overheard by the green keeper he was purported to have said: "Aye, and if I could get them faster I would".

Part of the joy in experiencing a links course is best described by Peter Thomson in his book *Lessons I Have Learned*: " I have always regarded the bounce of the ball as the third dimension in golf… It is sickening to see the game reduced to something like archery or darts. Golf only becomes really difficult and challenging on hard courses. It is then that skill, not strength, counts for everything. If the ground is allowed to become firm by the natural processes of the weather, then the ball will bounce as it should and as it was intended to do".[2]

Playing on linksland requires the right mental approach and attitude. One must accept the vagaries of the bounce of the ball and there needs to be an appreciation of the natural landscape. I unhesitatingly suggest to you dear reader that unquestionably… Links golf is real golf.

There are probably only about 150-160 genuine 18 hole links courses in existence and, with but a few exceptions, are nearly all located in the United Kingdom and Ireland. Whilst there have been several magnificent newcomers in recent years, for example Kingsbarns near St Andrews,

Doonbeg in south west Ireland and The European on the south east coast of Ireland, conservation concerns for unspoiled coastal dunelands will make it practically impossible for many new courses to be built in the future.

 A number of the older links are under threat due to the constant bombardment of the sea and prevailing winds. Montrose and Troon nearly lost some of their early holes in heavy storms. The second fairway at Troon has been especially vulnerable. In January 1963 Felixstowe Ferry, on the east coast of England, lost an entire hole during a storm. According to their club history "the final installment to the sea wall was not completed until 1971, only just in time to prevent the loss of almost the whole course".

Three of the premier Irish links, Ballybunion, Royal County Down and Royal Portrush have each spent considerable sums to ward off the damage caused by wind and sea. One night in 1973 Ballybunion lost over 18,000 square feet of fairway and cliff during a violent storm. This led to their world wide appeal for help.

Let us hope that global warming and the resultant rise in sea levels does not further endanger these precious natural treasures.

1. *James Braid* by Bernard Darwin, first printed 1952, Hodder and Stoughton, reprinted Ailsa Inc, 2003.

2. *Lessons I Have Learned* by Peter Thomson and Steve Perkin, GSP Books, 2005.

Photo David Worley

Royal St George's in South East England possesses all the ingredients of a true seaside links – sandy soil, springy turf, coarse rough and some intimidating bunkers

SCOTLAND

1 Royal Dornoch
2 Reay
3 Wick
4 Brora
5 Golspie
6 Tain
7 Skibo Castle
8 Fortrose and Rosemarkie
9 Nairn
10 Nairn Dunbar
11 Hopeman
12 Moray (Lossiemouth)
13 Spey Bay
14 Strathlene
15 Cullen
16 Inverallochy
17 Cruden Bay
18 Royal Aberdeen
19 Murcar
20 Montrose
21 Carnoustie
22 Panmure
23 Monifieth
24 St Andrews – Old
25 St Andrews – New
26 St Andrews – Jubilee
27 St Andrews – Eden
28 St Andrews – Castle (Course No 7)
29 Kingsbarns
30 Crail – Old/Balcomie
31 Crail – New/Craighead
32 St Andrews Bay – Torrance
33 St Andrews Bay – Devlin
34 Lundin Links
35 Leven
36 Elie
37 Scotscraig
38 Nth Berwick West
39 Muirfield
40 Gullane No 1

41 Gullane No 2
42 Gullane No 3
43 Kilspindie
44 Luffness New
45 Craigielaw
46 Archerfield – Fidra
47 Archerfield – Dirleton
48 Dunbar
49 Eyemouth
50 Southerness
51 Turnberry – Ailsa
52 Turnberry – Kintyre
53 Prestwick – Old
54 Prestwick – St Nicholas
55 Irvine
56 Glasgow Gailes
57 Western Gailes
58 Dundonald
59 Kilmarnock Barassie
60 Royal Troon
61 West Kilbride
62 Machrihanish
63 Machrie

ENGLAND

64 Berwick-upon-Tweed
65 Seahouses
66 Newbiggin
67 Seaton Carew
68 Ganton
69 Seacroft
70 Royal West Norfolk
71 Hunstanton
72 Sheringham
73 Great Yarmouth and Caister
74 Felixstowe Ferry
75 Princes
76 Royal Cinque Ports
77 Royal St.George's
78 Littlestone
79 Rye

80 Hayling
81 Royal Jersey
82 Royal Guernsey
83 La Moye
84 Mullion
85 West Cornwall
86 Perranporth
87 Trevose
88 St Enodoc
89 Bude & North Cornwall
90 Royal North Devon (Westward Ho!)
91 Saunton East
92 Saunton West
93 Burnham and Berrow
94 Weston-Super-Mare
95 Royal Liverpool
96 Wallasey
97 West Lancashire
98 Formby
99 Southport & Ainsdale
100 Hillside
101 Royal Birkdale
102 Hesketh
103 Royal Lytham & St Annes
104 St Annes Old Links
105 Castletown
106 Silloth on Solway

WALES

107 Royal Porthcawl
108 Southerndown
109 Pyle and Kenfig
110 Pennard
111 Tenby
112 Ashburnham
113 Cardigan
114 Borth & Ynyslas
115 Aberdovey
116 Royal St David's
117 Porthmadog
118 Pwllheli

119 Nefyn
120 Conwy
121 North Wales
122 Prestatyn

IRELAND

123 Royal County Down
124 Royal Portrush
125 Portstewart
126 Castlerock
127 Portsalon
128 Ballyliffin – Old Links
129 Ballyliffin – Glashedy
130 Rosapenna – Sandy Hills
131 Rosapenna – Old
132 Donegal (Murvagh)
133 Co. Sligo
134 Enniscrone
135 Carne
136 Connemara
137 Lahinch
138 Doonbeg
139 Ballybunion – Old
140 Ballybunion – Cashen
141 Tralee
142 Dingle
143 Dooks
144 Waterville
145 Old Head
146 Rosslare
147 Arklow
148 The European
149 Royal Dublin
150 Portmarnock
151 Portmarnock Hotel and Golf Links
152 The Island
153 Laytown & Bettystown
154 Seapoint
155 County Louth

SCOTLAND

2

3

4

5

1, 7

6

8 9 10 11 12 13 14 15

16

17

18, 19

20

21, 22

23

37

24, 25, 26, 27, 28

32, 33

29

30, 31

34, 35

39 36 38

46

43 47

45 40

41

42

44

48

49

64

65

66

67

68

69

70 71 72

73

74

61 55

56, 57, 58, 59

60

53, 54

51, 52

63

62

50

106

NORTHERN
IRELAND

130, 131 128, 129

124

127 126 125

132

133

135

134

123

105

104 103

102

99, 100, 101 98

97

96 95

121

120 122

119 117

118 116

115

114

113

ENGLAND

WALES

111

112 109

110 107

108

94

93

75

77

76

78

79

80

IRELAND

154

153

155

152

150, 151

149

136

137

148

138

147

139, 140

141

146

142

143

144

145

91 92

90

89

88

87

85 86

84

CHANNEL ISLANDS

82

GUERNSEY

JERSEY

81

83

Photo courtesy Darren J Kirk at Scratch Design

SCOTLAND *Par 3, 8th hole Carnoustie*

SCOTLAND

1	Royal Dornoch
2	Reay
3	Wick
4	Brora
5	Golspie
6	Tain
7	Skibo Castle
8	Fortrose and Rosemarkie
9	Nairn
10	Nairn Dunbar
11	Hopeman
12	Moray (Lossiemouth)
13	Spey Bay
14	Strathlene
15	Cullen
16	Inverallochy
17	Cruden Bay
18	Royal Aberdeen
19	Murcar
20	Montrose
21	Carnoustie
22	Panmure
23	Monifieth
24	St Andrews – Old
25	St Andrews – New
26	St Andrews – Jubilee
27	St Andrews – Eden
28	St Andrews – Castle (Course No 7)
29	Kingsbarns
30	Crail – Old/Balcomie
31	Crail – New/Craighead
32	St Andrews Bay – Torrance
33	St Andrews Bay – Devlin
34	Lundin Links
35	Leven
36	Elie
37	Scotscraig
38	Nth Berwick West
39	Muirfield
40	Gullane No 1
41	Gullane No 2
42	Gullane No 3
43	Kilspindie
44	Luffness New
45	Craigielaw
46	Archerfield – Fidra
47	Archerfield – Dirleton
48	Dunbar
49	Eyemouth
50	Southerness
51	Turnberry – Ailsa
52	Turnberry – Kintyre
53	Prestwick – Old
54	Prestwick – St Nicholas
55	Irvine
56	Glasgow Gailes
57	Western Gailes
58	Dundonald
59	Kilmarnock Barassie
60	Royal Troon
61	West Kilbride
62	Machrihanish
63	Machrie

ROYAL DORNOCH

The lovely par 3, 2nd hole at Royal Dornoch

FOR ANY LOVER OF THE LINKS, TO PLAY AT DORNOCH IS SIMPLY A MUST. THE TOWN ITSELF HAS AN UNDERSTATED AMBIENCE AND THERE IS STILL A LOVELY FEELING OF UNSPOILT BEAUTY AND SERENITY IN THE WHOLE AREA.

Whilst golf at Dornoch can be traced back many centuries, it must be said that the modern Dornoch owes an enormous debt to John Sutherland who was appointed Secretary in 1883 at just 19 years of age and who guided the affairs of the club for almost 60 years. He also learned the art of green keeping and helped further refine the course laid out by Tom Morris in 1886.

Alec and Donald Ross were born in Dornoch and were exceptionally good golfers with Alec winning the American Open in 1907. Donald became one of the great golf course architects with Pinehurst No.2 generally regarded as his finest achievement.

Dornoch tests your golf in every possible way but it is also an undeniably fair course. But, be warned, you can be unlucky with the tide affected wind and you just may end up playing 16 holes into a decent breeze.

Looking across the 3rd green to the Dornoch Firth

Photo David Worley

You have to be on your game right from the word go. An accurate drive is required from the first tee and then you play to a typical Dornoch green that is slightly raised with bumps, hollows and bunkers adding to the challenge.

The second is a superb par 3 of 184 yards from the back tee. The green is raised and is quite exposed being one of the highest points at the clubhouse end of the links. There are deep revetted pot bunkers on either side of the green. Into even a slight breeze you can bet on most being short with their tee shot.

The next two holes are good par 4's of over 400 yards with a bank of gorse awaiting any shot pulled left.

The 5th is one of the best par 4's anywhere. It is only 354 yards long but precision is required with both the drive and approach. Trouble in the manner of thick rough and gorse runs the whole length of the left side. The fairway slopes to the right where six pot bunkers are waiting. The green is guarded by three deep bunkers at the front and a steep bank on the right hand side. Another bunker lies at the back for anything

too bold. Be pleased if you are on in two but then you realise the green is 54 yards long and a 3 putt is a real possibility.

Whinnie Bray, the par 3, 6th is one of my favourite short holes. It is frequently featured in postcards with the huge bank of gorse flanking the left and beyond. A bunker and steep bank lies on the right. The little pot bunkers on the left are frequent attractions and from them it can be a daunting task jut to keep your escape shot from running off the green.

For any lover of the links, to play at Dornoch is simply a must.
The town itself has an understated ambience and there is still a lovely feeling
of unspoilt beauty and serenity in the whole area.

The 7th is a long par 4 of 463 yards, on a plateau above the rest of the terrain. The 8th green takes us to the furthermost point from the clubhouse. Nine is a shortest par 5 but out of bounds and the beach is all along the left.

Both the 10th and 13th are par 3's of great quality with the latter being particularly well protected by no less than seven bunkers.

Foxy, the 14th, can play much longer than 445 yards would suggest. It is one of the hardest holes on the course despite having no obvious hazards.

A steep uphill drive can make the tee shot especially tricky on sixteen, particularly if you are trying to force the ball into a decent wind.

The 17th can be a lost ball scenario if you do not know exactly the line to take for your tee shot. You hit blind over a steep hill that sends anything slightly right of centre further in that direction and into very thick gorse. The green is raised and has two pot bunkers inset into the front apron.

The final hole is very long at 456 yards par 4 and uphill. Any errant shot here is likely to find gorse. When playing your second you need to be careful not to be fooled by the bunkers which are deceptively forward of the green so take one more club than your eyes tell you. For me, this is definitely the hardest hole on the links.

At 6679 yards off the championship tees, Royal Dornoch is quite a long par 70. Play there in late spring whilst the gorse is still in bloom, and if you get a balmy sunny day then you might just think you are in heaven.

The Club also has a second course, the Struie, which has recently been upgraded and in 2003 five completely new holes were added. It is much flatter in contrast to the Championship course. From the 10th green enjoy the lovely views across the Dornoch Firth and from the par 3, 12th you will see the town of Dornoch and the Cathedral from an entirely different perspective. The greens and fairways are excellent and it's a reasonable length at around 6300 yards.

Photo David Worley

'Whinnie Brae', the postcard par 3, 6th

REAY

THIS IS A CHARMING LITTLE COURSE OF 5831 YARDS AND DATES ITS BEGINNINGS RIGHT BACK TO 1893. REAY HAS THE DISTINCTION OF BEING THE MOST NORTHERLY LINKS COURSE ON MAINLAND BRITAIN. IN FACT, TO MY KNOWLEDGE, THE ONLY GOLF COURSE OF ANY DESCRIPTION THAT IS FURTHER NORTH IS THE LOVELY 9 HOLER AT DURNESS FURTHER WEST.

Situated in virtually the centre of the northern Scottish coast on the A836, Reay nestles in Sandside Bay with every hole providing views across the Pentland Firth. Reay is also somewhat unusual in that it opens and finished with a par 3.

Entrancing dunes and the par 5, 6th 'Braid's Choice'

The course is predominantly seaside links and as such the wind is often the most daunting of the hazards in addition to the burn which runs through the centre of the layout. At times the course takes on a hilly aspect and there is an area of lovely coastal dunes, especially along the par five, 6th hole which apparently was Braid's favourite when he advised on the layout of the course.

The 4th is the first of the par fives. At 581 yards it is a genuine 3 shotter as it winds towards a pretty green near the sea. The tee of the par 3, 5th is almost on the beach. Don't hook into an offshore wind or you will find yourself out of bounds and in thick marram grass beside the beach. Whilst 'Braid's Choice', the par 5, 6th, is only 477 yards it is rated index 9 due to the out of bounds along the left side and burn round most of the green.

The 7th is a super par 3 of 196 yards with a burn and steep bank at the front of the raised green. Its difficulty is borne out by the rating on the card of index 1.

Stand on the 16th tee and you will be tempted to drive the green on this short par 4 of only 314 yards. But first you must carry a deep and very penal bunker which is the only fairway bunker on the links.

If all is well at this stage of your round then there are still two stern tests remaining. The 17th can be an intimidating tee shot with the Reay burn to be crossed and out of bounds on the left hand side and a fairway that slopes to the right. This is also the most difficult of the greens.

The finishing hole is an uphill par 3 of 162 yards. The green is two tiered and is protected by deep pot bunkers. On the day I was at Reay this hole was into the wind and was playing very long which also brought the possibility of out of bounds into play for anything left of the back of the green.

Reay can be recommended as a good and enjoyable test of golf. The course has a very natural feel with not too many outside distractions other than the sea views. The clubhouse is modest but I love their welcoming brochure which says: "There are no strangers here, only friends you have not yet met".

WICK

WICK CAN TRACE ITS ROOTS RIGHT BACK TO 1870 AND WAS FOUNDED BY GEORGE DUNBAR. JAMES BRAID IS BELIEVED TO HAVE HAD SOME LATER INVOLVEMENT IN THE COURSE DESIGN. IN RECENT YEARS CHANGES HAVE BEEN MADE UNDER THE GUIDANCE OF RONAN RAFFERTY.

Photo David Worley

Looking back down the course from near the 18th tee

The course itself is about three miles north of the town of Wick in far north east Scotland and runs alongside Sinclairs Bay.

Whilst there is a line of dunes along part of the beach side, the course is basically quite flat. It is a good 'holiday' course with a traditional 9 holes out and 9 holes back design.

When I visited there, the course was well maintained but with only a few, generally small, pot bunkers. The greens appeared rather flat and uninteresting and seemed to be merely an extension of the fairway.

Some holes to look out for are the 5th, 9th and 12th.

The 5th is a par 4 of 423 yards and has a ditch running right across the fairway around 250 yards from the tee. It is rated the hardest hole on the course. The 9th is a par 3 of 150 yards alongside the River Wester. The green is small and is nestled amongst the dunes. Twelve is another par 4 of over 400 yards, index 2, with the second shot to a green with a narrow entrance guarded by a bunker on the right hand side and a mound on the left.

Wick will provide you with old fashioned golf amongst friendly members.

BRORA

ALTHOUGH BRORA WAS ESTABLISHED IN 1891 IT WAS INITIALLY 9 HOLES. IT BECAME 18 IN 1897 AND WAS REDESIGNED IN 1910. THE COURSE OF TODAY IS LARGELY THE COURSE THAT ENSUED FOLLOWING JAMES BRAID'S IMPROVEMENTS IN 1924.

For many visitors this is the end of the line when it comes to golf. This is understandable as Wick and Reay are quite a distance further north and are not as good as Brora. Here is a traditional links course where most likely you'll not hear any sounds other than the sea or roaming sheep.

Bunkers are limited in number as the course is totally unprotected from the ever present wind. Brora has five par 3's hence its short length of 5872 yards, and each one runs in a different direction.

The opening hole looks relatively easy but don't be fooled into aiming straight for the green on this 297 yards par 4. Stay on the fairway for the best approach to the very tricky green which has a frighteningly severe slope from back to front. Anything short of the green may roll a fair distance back so many approaches finish at the back of the green with the consequential downhill putt.

The first 5 holes are all par 4's. The fourth is a real birdie opportunity being only 325 yards in length.

From here there are some interesting holes. The 5th hole is aptly named 'Burn'. The hole is bisected by the Clynelish Burn and a ravine behind the green adds to the danger of too strong a second shot.

Next is the first of the par 3's, 'Witch'. The slightly elevated tee gives a perfect view of the green with some lovely swales and guarded by a number of pot bunkers.

Eight and nine are the last holes beside the sea with the 9th green being the furthermost point on the course. The 8th is the only par 5 and the 9th is a delightful par 3 that plays to a green not far from the beach. Interestingly, as with the opening hole at Machrihanish, the beach is not out of bounds but is treated as a lateral water hazard.

The 13th is the shortest of the par 3's at only 125 yards. The tee shot is slightly uphill and over a valley with gorse and a wandering burn which seems to make distance harder to judge. It is easy to over club here and finish in one of the bunkers at the back of the green.

Fifteen and sixteen are par 4's which require very accurate drives, as does most of the back 9, and there is the added hazard of out of bounds on the right.

The 17th is possibly the best hole on the course. The view from the tee is exceptional whether you are looking forward, behind, or across the course towards the dunes and sea. This is a hole requiring two accurate draw shots and the avoidance of a nasty bunker almost in the middle of the fairway at 180 yards from the green.

Eighteen is a tricky par 3 of 201 yards with an elevated green and a large hollow at the front where the green slopes significantly back towards you. This is the right time for a good shot as you're bound to have at least a small audience in the nearby clubhouse.

Brora is a real fun course to play. My only criticism is that each time I have been there the greens have been rather slow, but maybe this is a necessary compensation for the ever present wind.

Photo David Worley

Brora's 17th fairway with the usual variety of four-legged spectators

GOLSPIE

Photo David Worley

Par 3, 10th hole, 'Locky'

GOLSPIE PROVIDES AN INTERESTING MIXTURE OF LINKS AND HEATHLAND. SITUATED BETWEEN DORNOCH TO THE SOUTH AND BRORA TO THE NORTH, THE COURSE PROVIDES WONDERFUL VIEWS OF THE DORNOCH FIRTH AND BEN BHRAGGIE WITH THE STATUE OF THE FIRST DUKE OF SUTHERLAND AT THE SUMMIT.

This quiet little part of the north can get very windy and was described to me once by a member as "the longest short course in Scotland".

The Club was founded in 1889 and owes its present design to James Braid who laid out some of the more wooded holes in 1926. Like nearby Brora, it has only one par 5 and five par 3's.

The first six holes are in the flatter more open part of the course with three, four and five running right along the beach. From the 7th hole the course moves towards the holes featuring heather and trees, however the fairways keep a true links feel.

Several holes from the 9th are known as 'paradise corner'. The 9th in particular requires accurate hitting to stay out of the heather on the 412 yard par 4. The 10th is a most attractive par 3, 'Locky', with two small ponds, heather and bunkers making the 148 yard sloping target seem just a little bit smaller.

The 11th is a lovely hole to observe and play. Pine trees, birches, gorse, heather, a mountain backdrop and usually complete solitude here in the heathland.

The par 4, 11th in late spring

Twelve and thirteen are two further par 4's needing straight hitting. The 14th is currently a par 4 of 425 yards but this may be lengthened to a par 5 in the future. A number of fairway bunkers here add to the difficulty.

The remaining holes are in the open around the club house. Whilst sixteen and seventeen are back to back par 3's, eighteen is a tough finishing par 4 of 335 yards. The green can not be seen from the tee and a fairly long and straight drive is required if you are to be approaching from the fairway rather than the rough.

Golspie is an enjoyable course punctuated by some interesting scenery. It also represents an interesting contrast to its nearest neighbours, Dornoch and Brora.

TAIN

TAIN WAS PART OF THE GOLF COURSE EXPLOSION LATE IN THE NINETEENTH CENTURY AND WAS FOUNDED IN 1890. DURING THE LAST 15 YEARS OF THAT CENTURY, OLD TOM MORRIS HAD A HAND IN DESIGNING NO LESS THAN 69 COURSES AND 52 OF THESE WERE IN SCOTLAND.

Photo David Worley

The 11th green from the 12th tee

Old Tom originally advised the club on 15 holes which were then briefly reduced to 12. By 1894 Tain was an 18 hole course. When John Sutherland remodeled the links he left 10 of Old Tom's holes intact and the par 3, 17th today remains one of the latter's best short hole designs.

In spring, Tain is a blaze of yellow, but, unlike most other courses, this is primarily due to the rather more friendly species, namely broom not gorse.

If it is your first time at Tain then the first hole may take you by surprise. It is a par 4, slightly uphill, of 382 yards. A road bounded by post and wire fencing runs across the fairway about 50 yards from the green. At first sight you can not see the green behind all this so you begin to wonder where on earth you should be hitting.

The 2nd hole may also catch you unaware as there is a burn running about 75 yards short of the green. Be accurate here as rough and broom is thick on both sides of the fairway.

Three is an excellent dog-leg left par 4 of 435 yards. A really bad tee shot may catch water on either side or a long drive can run out of fairway on the right.

For me, the stand out hole is the 380 yard par 4, 11th appropriately known as 'Alps'. The tee heads you towards the sea over a bumpy fairway then requiring a blind second shot to a seaside green set behind and below two large mounds. There is also a well hidden bunker just short of the mound on the right hand side. If your approach is too strong then you could well finish in the sea if the tide is in.

When the fairways are hard and fast then some of the par 4's may play a little short but, equally, you can be assured that any shot off line will run into trouble. The 14th is a good example with both sides lined with broom and thick rough, especially on the right.

You may have a good score going but don't celebrate too soon because the two par 3's at sixteen and seventeen can be potentially disastrous mainly due to the River Tain. At the 215 yard 17th hole it winds its way across the fairway twice and then flows along the length of the green on the right hand side. For many women this would be a difficult hole requiring a lay up tee shot to just short of where the river runs about 30 yards in front of the green.

Par 3, 16th with the River Tain close by

Tain is easy walking terrain but the fairways are interesting due to the many smaller undulations. In summer the course can get quite fiery, as any true links course should, so be prepared to land some of your longer approaches well short of the green.

SKIBO CASTLE (THE CARNEGIE LINKS)

18th green and castle in the distance

THE MAGNIFICENT CASTLE AND SURROUNDING ESTATE WAS COMPLETED FOR ANDREW CARNEGIE AT AROUND THE END OF THE 19TH CENTURY. IT EVEN INCLUDED A NINE HOLE COURSE LAID OUT BY JOHN SUTHERLAND, THE SECRETARY AT DORNOCH. IT REMAINED IN THE CARNEGIE FAMILY UNTIL 1981 WHEN ANDREW'S DAUGHTER, MARGARET, DUE TO HER OWN FAILING HEALTH INSTRUCTED THAT THE ESTATE BE SOLD.

Photo David Worley

Sadly it fell into disrepair but then in the early 1990's the new owner, Peter de Savary, embarked on a major repair and upgrade which included the building of a new 18 hole championship course in this stunning location regarded by Andrew as "heaven on earth".

The Carnegie Links was designed by Donald Steel and Tom Mackenzie and was first open for play in 1992. The course provides beautiful views of the surrounding treed countryside and has a number of holes beside the sea and Loch Evelix.

From my experience, the course plays longer than its 6672 yards. The fairways and bunkers were in very good condition, as you would expect, and the rough was thick but on the downside the greens were below par and extremely slow even though they had been cut reasonably short.

All of the par 3's were challenging with the 6th being particularly difficult to hold the raised green, especially if the wind is assisting. The 9th is very demanding at 215 yards from the back tee and has a large pot bunker guarding the front left of the green. The 13th and 15th each have water in play all along the right hand side. Thirteen has three large greenside bunkers but fifteen needs none as it employs clever use of an angled and raised green that will lead to anything short and even slightly faded to be headed towards a watery grave.

Photo courtesy Carnegie Club, Skibo Castle

Par 4, 8th alongside the Dornoch Firth

Photo courtesy Carnegie Club, Skibo Castle

Many of the par 4's and three of the par 5's are significant dog-legs. Care must be exercised as to how much of the corner to take on otherwise you are looking at thick rough and possibly a lost ball.

The 11th and 12th (index 3 and 1 respectively) are very tight driving holes, dog-leg right, with Loch Evelix at the fairway edge, particularly on the 12th.

The short 304 yard par 4, 17th (267 yards from the non championship tee) is one of the few genuine birdie opportunities. The green is not as close as it looks as you stand on the tee and contemplate how to avoid the five fairway and one greenside bunker. Best to hit down the centre of the fairway to about 90 yards short of the green unless you hit 280 yards in the air (243 yards from the forward tee) and carry the largest of the bunkers which is in the perfect line to the green.

The 18th is a picture perfect par 5 with a sharp dog-leg left. If you are left of the fairway with your drive then you are in the salt marsh. You then have an estuary from the Dornoch Firth all the way to the green. The stately baronial castle is nestled in the trees on the other side of the estuary. The green has just one bunker, at front right, but be warned that any approach left of centre will kick further left and into rough or water.

This is a challenging and enjoyable course to play, not withstanding the very average quality of the greens. Everything else at Skibo will provide you with memories for a lifetime, especially when the piper leads you to the dining room for the evening meal.

Photo courtesy Carnegie Club, Skibo Castle

Top left: par 4, 7th
Left: 8th green

FORTROSE & ROSEMARKIE

Photo David Worley

FORTROSE LIES AT CHANONRY POINT NEXT TO THE MORAY FIRTH ON THE CHANONRY PENINSULA. THIS IS ONE OF THE MOST CHARMING LOCATIONS YOU WILL EVER CHANCE UPON. THERE IS A RATHER UNIQUE FEEL HERE WITH A RELAXED ATMOSPHERE AND A SPORTY COURSE THAT WILL CHALLENGE DESPITE ITS SHORTNESS OF LENGTH.

Looking across to the 2nd green and lighthouse

The course is well presented with relatively small greens, ample gorse and well placed pot bunkers. The sea is in close proximity on eight of the holes.

A stroke round can be in disarray early if you hook any shots on the first hole which runs along the water's edge. The fourth is a standout hole. It is a par 5 of just 455 yards and yet it is rated the most difficult hole on the course. Accuracy is essential as you play towards the sloping green in front of the Chanonry Lighthouse. Dolphins also enjoy the shoreline.

The par 3, 9th is 196 yards in length and can require anything from a short iron to driver but beware of out of bounds which runs all along the left side. Ten and eleven are par 4's that will test your ability to avoid fairway pot bunkers that can spell ruin to any round if you are unlucky enough to finish against a steep revetted face.

The 17th fairway has a marker stone which is reputed to also be the location of the last burning of a witch in Scotland. The round concludes with a 212 yard par 3 and plenty of gorse, particularly left.

Pick a mild sunny day with the gorse in full bloom and, regardless of how you played, you will have fond memories of Fortrose.

Photo David Worley

Looking back to the clubhouse

NAIRN

Photo David Worley

Par 3, 14th with the Moray Firth providing a rich blue backdrop

NAIRN IS DEFINITELY ONE OF MY FAVOURITE COURSES IN SCOTLAND'S NORTH. ON A CLEAR SUNNY DAY YOU CAN NOT HELP BUT BE SEDUCED BY THE SIGHT OF THE RICH BLUE MORAY FIRTH ON ONE SIDE AND THE DISTANT HIGHLANDS ON THE OTHER.

The original layout is the result of the input from Old Tom Morris and Archie Simpson and, subsequently, in the 1920's alterations were made by James Braid.

The first seven holes each have the sea as out of bounds on the right hand side. When I played there with Peter Gordon, a well known member from the famous Gordon family, he advised me that over the years he had lost a ball to the sea on all seven holes, but one poor chap had the distinction of achieving this feat in the one round.

Most of the par 4's have well placed bunkers to catch any drive a little off line. The 2nd is a shortish par 5 from the championship tee, but from the medal tee it transforms into a very difficult par 4 of 474 yards. The 5th hole at 390 yards is not long, but bunkers are everywhere including the middle of the fairway.

The real challenge awaits at Nairn's version of Amen Corner – the 12th to 14th holes. Twelve requires an accurate drive and the avoidance of a fairway bunker on the left. The green is raised and anything off line will almost certainly finish in trouble. The 13th runs up a hill and with plenty of trees, gorse and heather for any indifferently struck ball. At 430 yards and the last part quite steep, it is deservedly index one. Allow yourself an extra few minutes on the tee of the picturesque 14th. A par 3 of 221 yards, it heads back downhill from the highest point on the course. The hole is framed by long grass and gorse on either side and the Moray Firth in the distance. Three bunkers at the front ensure that only a very lucky shot can reach the

The 5th at Nairn features a wide bunker in the centre of the fairway

Nairn, 15th green

green by any other than the aerial route. A hollow runs through the green so even being there with your tee shot is no guarantee of par. These three holes are rated 5, 1 and 7, so par them all and you have done exceptionally well.

The 15th is like the 8th, a relatively short par 4, but a precision shot is needed to hit and hold the green which is protected by a deep gully. You will have to decide whether you should play a high lofted approach or take your chances with a low bump and run.

The 17th green has the added danger of a narrow burn nearby. The final hole is especially tight if you play from the very back tee, but from the forward tee this is one of the few uninteresting holes on what is otherwise a super golf course.

Nairn is right up there in the highest echelon. Perhaps only Muirfield and Royal Aberdeen have better greens. If you are lucky, as I was, you might also get to enjoy a pink sunset over still waters and dolphins quietly diving in and out along the shoreline.

NAIRN DUNBAR

NAIRN DUNBAR IS OFTEN OVERLOOKED BECAUSE OF THE GREAT REPUTATION OF NEIGHBOURING NAIRN. HOWEVER YOU WILL NOT BE DISAPPOINTED BY A VISIT TO THIS UNDERRATED COURSE.

Thick rough alongside the 7th hole

Don't be fooled by the appearance from the first tee. The first few holes look fairly easy but things get decidedly tougher from the 448 yard par 4, 4th. This is the start of a stretch of four hard holes culminating with the 7th, 'King Steps', where thick rough, heather and the whins(gorse) lie in waiting if you don't keep to the fairway.

The 8th is a lovely par 3 with a green encircled by pot bunkers. The 10th turns back towards the clubhouse and can be a tough proposition, particularly into the wind, because you have a burn to the left and thick scrub all along the right.

When I played Nairn Dunbar I noted that the 11th, "a short par 3, was the only real weakness".[1] I am pleased to see that the Club has subsequently re-designed both the 10th and 11th holes. The 10th has an easier driving line and a more interesting approach shot whilst the 11th now has a new tee. This has added 50 yards and changed the visual perspective of the hole which is lined with gorse and silver birches.

The remaining holes are on flatter terrain with traditional links fairways. Twelve is an excellent Par 4 and the thirteenth is an equally good Par 5. Gorse aplenty awaits any stray shots on these two attractive holes. The last few holes are a good finish with a ditch in play on sixteen and seventeen. Although it is a short par 5 of 499 yards, the 18th is made more difficult by a semi-blind approach from lower ground to a green hidden behind a high mound.

There are no seaside holes or stunning Highland views, but notwithstanding this, Nairn Dunbar represents a good test of golf for all to enjoy.

1. *Fairways in Heaven, Bunkers from Hell* David Worley.

The well bunkered par 3, 8th

HOPEMAN

HOPEMAN GOLF CLUB IS APPROXIMATELY SIX MILES WEST OF LOSSIEMOUTH AND IS PROBABLY WORTH A VISIT JUST TO PLAY THE PAR 3, 12TH HOLE.

The approach to the course, like Spey Bay, is through a wooded area and then lush coastal fields. Hopeman became an 18 hole course as recently as 1985. Whilst a number of the holes are clifftop, the soil is certainly links-like and the fairways are hard and fast.

With a total length of just 5624 yards it is a short course, however constant wind and profuse gorse and broom ensures there is always a challenge.

Hopeman gets off to a fairly tough start with two uphill par 4's. The raised second green is a particularly difficult target with approaches often kicking into the bunkers on either side.

The 4th hole is the only par 5 and is a mere 517 yards. Nonetheless it is rated number 3 in terms of difficulty. A dog-leg to the left, it requires a good draw shot from the tee for right-handers. You then have to contend with fairway bunkers, gorse on the left and a sloping green.

The par 4, 6th is index one. This dog-leg left to right hole has internal out of bounds along the right of the fairway. The green is part of a double green with the third.

The eleventh can be a tricky par 4 with a very undulating fairway and gorse on both sides. The small fairway mounds on this hole unfortunately have a somewhat artificial look.

I am not overly fond of the expression "signature hole", but the twelfth (Prieshach) is certainly the stand out hole at Hopeman. It is only 150 yards long even from the medal tee, but the green itself is 100 yards below the tee. In front of the tee is a mass of wild red poppies, whilst in spring and early summer the hillsides are one giant blaze of yellow from the gorse. The Moray Firth provides the more distant back drop. The green has bunkers on both sides, plus the sea on the right, to add to the challenge of a hole that Paul Lawrie described as one of the best par 3's he has ever played.

The fifteenth is another attractive short par 3. Two pot bunkers are at the front of a green that slopes away and sends any over-hit shot tumbling towards the nearby sea-front. Seventeen is a long par 3 at 191 yards uphill. You have to hit over gorse bushes which protrude onto the fairway on the right and then you must avoid a stone wall that runs adjacent to the green on the same side.

The 18th hole is an extremely demanding finishing par 4 of 399 yards and requires you to make a number of decisions. The drive must carry a stone wall and two fairway bunkers. Out of bounds lies along the right side and heavy gorse awaits any wayward drive to the left.

Photo David Worley

The picturesque and challenging par 3, 12th

Next, you must choose whether to lay up short of the burn that runs across the fairway or go for the green which is hidden below fairway height as is the pond and bunker at the front. This last hole could dampen your mood in the clubhouse.

MORAY (LOSSIEMOUTH) – OLD COURSE

Top: par 3, 6th with the lighthouse in the background
Above: approaching 17th green with 18th green and clubhouse further back

THE MORAY GOLF CLUB AT LOSSIEMOUTH WAS FORMED IN 1889 AT THE END OF AN INCREDIBLE DECADE FOR GOLF COURSE CONSTRUCTION IN SCOTLAND AND ENGLAND.

As early as 1892 a lovely stone clubhouse was erected. It was enlarged in 1923 to what is essentially the building you see today.

The sandy soil and relatively mild climate meant that Lossiemouth quickly gained a very high reputation. A correspondent in the local paper "The Bulger" wrote in the summer of 1894:

> "The already famous golf course can hold its own with any on the eastern seaboard of Scotland. During summer and winter it is always dotted with players, but there is never the anxious rush, the drawing for places, the quarrel or discontent of the older links of St. Andrews or North Berwick. There are always players on the green, yet all goes with smoothness and good humour which speaks well for the organisation of the club, and the civility of its members." [1]

The front nine has a number of holes which can play quite long, especially into the wind. Moray is well bunkered for both tee shots and approaches to the green. The importance of accuracy to avoid bunkers and profuse gorse becomes apparent from the second, a par 5 of 494 yards with a V-shaped ditch right behind the green.

The par 3, 4th is long at 197 yards and has three bunkers in front of the green plus out of bounds running in close proximity to the rear. The fifth, seventh and eight are all long par 4's (the eighth is 474 yards) with the added hazards of either ditches or out of bounds. Most of this nine is furthest from the sea with holes from the New Course sometimes running along side.

The tenth is a short par 4 of only 318 yards and is a potential birdie opportunity. The key here is to ensure your drive is on the fairway and avoids the nest of three bunkers on the left side. The par 4, 11th can cause problems due to six fairway bunkers and a burn that runs across about 50 yards short of the green. The problem for first time visitors is that you can't see the burn when you are playing your second shot.

A draw from the tee on twelve and thirteen will help you achieve par on these two par 4's. The fifteenth is a super par 3 of 184 yards. There is thick rough and a bunker left of the green whilst the right has five bunkers and a grassy hollow. This is as near as you get to the sea which runs along the left.

Up until now, the greens have all been quite flat. The sixteenth and seventeenth however are quite different and feature large undulations.

The par 4, 18th is definitely one of the best finishing holes in Scotland. The tee shot is very tight partly due to a large rock which protrudes from the wall of a neighbouring property. This makes it virtually impossible to hit a draw if you are a right hander. Out of bounds runs the length of the hole on the right hand side and is also on the left as you near the green. The temptation is to hit your tee shot left but there are five fairway bunkers waiting for you. The green is elevated and sits just below the clubhouse. There is a big hollow at the front and to the left of this hollow is a deep bunker that is not visible from further back. You will need two very precisely struck shots to be on this green for two.

This really is an excellent test of golf. Tight, bumpy and well bunkered gorse lined fairways together with very good greens is pretty hard to beat.

The New Course is nearly as good. Twelve holes are mingled amongst the Old Course and six are at the far end as you play towards the lighthouse. The eighteenth green of the New is just behind the eighteenth tee of the Old so there is a bit of a walk when your round is completed.

The only negative aspect of Lossiemouth is the very close proximity of the RAF Station which is right next door. This was an important base for many World War II missions. Unfortunately the arrival of the jet engine has meant a big increase in noise levels.

Play Lossiemouth on a Sunday when the RAF Base is non operational and you will see why it quickly gained its deserved high reputation.

1. *The Moray Golf Club at Lossiemouth*, John McConachie

Photo David Worley

View from behind 18th green with 1st hole on the right

SPEY BAY

IN THREE PREVIOUS GOLFING TRIPS TO
SCOTLAND I HAD NEVER HEARD OF SPEY
BAY. YOU MAY NOT HAVE EITHER, BUT THIS
IS A REAL LITTLE GEM OF 6219 YARDS.

Y ou drive through wooded areas and lush fields to get to
the course which is located right on the sea about 10
miles east of Lossiemouth.

This is one of the few courses remaining that was designed
by the legendary Ben Sayers of North Berwick fame.
The opening in 1907 was apparently attended by thousands.
The front of the card features an historic photo of the then
Prime Minister, The Right Hon. James Macdonald,
presenting the prizes at The Spey Bay Golf Club's Annual
Tournament in August 1929.

Six holes run alongside the seashore on this traditional out
and back design. The course plays over the natural contours
of what was once a shingle bed, formed over thousands of
years. The greens are quite small and were originally square
in design.

Spey Bay fairways run fast and the many severe bumps and
hollows can knock a ball into the acres of heather and gorse
on either side of the fairway. Some of the fairways are quite
narrow and in parts are not far from others, although usually
running in the same direction.

One of the best holes is the par 5, 16th which is at the closest
point to the beach. Apart from the sea, there is gorse in
abundance so don't be wayward.

In recent years some work has commenced to get the links
back more to the original Ben Sayers design.

Photo David Worley

Above: 17th green, Spey Bay
Below: 18th hole from behind the green

*I was at Spey Bay on a lovely
Saturday afternoon in June
and the course was nearly
empty. You need go no further
if you want to rediscover old
fashioned links golf with a
minimum of fuss.*

Photo David Worley

STRATHLENE

Photo David Worley

Par 4, 17th hole appropriately named 'Gullies'

ORGANISED GOLF STARTED HERE, NEAR THE TOWN OF BUCKIE, AS FAR BACK AS 1877 WHEN STRATHLENE WAS A NINE HOLER. THIS CLIFFTOP LINKS DID NOT BECOME 18 HOLES UNTIL 1936.

The course has undulating fairways, deep gullies and exposed elevated greens. The last four holes (particularly the par 4, 17th) which are on the other side of a public roadway feature some interesting deep hollows just short of the green.

In total the course measures just under 6000 yards and is par 69. The only par 5 is the 515 yard 14th hole.

When I visited there the greens and fairways were in good condition. With any semblance of a sea breeze your play into the green will be given a good test. However, if you are in the area and you want a more traditional links then you might have to travel a few miles west to nearby Spey Bay.

CULLEN

THIS CERTAINLY TAKES THE AWARD FOR ONE OF THE MOST UNUSUAL 18 HOLE GOLF COURSES I HAVE EVER SEEN. CULLEN IS LOCATED IN THE NORTH EAST ON THE A 98 SITUATED ALMOST MIDWAY BETWEEN NAIRN TO THE WEST AND FRASERBURGH TO THE EAST.

Golf has been played here for centuries with the original first 9 holes laid out by Old Tom Morris in 1870. The links occupies a small parcel of flat sandy land bounded by high cliffs on one side and Cullen Bay on the other. Parts of these cliffs stand like sentinels of huge rocky outcrops in the middle of the course – the 80 foot high Boar Crag being the largest.

I have never seen a golf card before that has absolutely no hole distances whatsoever. The holes are given a stroke index but you will also have to work out what the par is for yourself. My research indicates that it is probably par 63 and the total length is just 4597 yards.

Amongst a plethora of unusual par 3's there is just the one par 5, the 510 yard 15th. The outward nine is closest to the cliffs with the inward nine near the beach. The par 4, 13th will intrigue you with a green located behind one of the large rock formations.

Strictly just for fun –
you be the judge.

Photo David Worley

Looking back to the 18th green and 1st tee

Photo David Worley

Rocky outcrops punctuate the fairways at Cullen

INVERALLOCHY

INVERALLOCHY IS JUST A FEW MILES FROM FRASERBURGH ALMOST AT THE VERY NORTH EAST CORNER OF SCOTLAND.

There is evidence of golf being played here as early as 1613. This is based on church records referring to an individual who was admonished for playing on the Fraserburgh Links on the Sabbath in that year.

Inverallochy Golf Club was officially established in April 1888 but it would seem that the present site was not used until the 1890's. Although it started as 18 holes, over time enthusiasm dwindled and it was reduced to nine holes until the club's fortunes were resurrected in the early 1950's. By 1954 Inverallochy once again had an eighteen hole links.

The course is rather short at just 5340 yards and featuring six par 3's. Nevertheless it is a traditional seaside links which provides views of the sea from every hole.

The opening holes, a par 4 and a par 3, each have out of bounds by way of the beach on the left. However, except for closer to the 2nd green, only a wild hook will reach the shore line.

Thick rough and bunkers are mainly at the left on the 376 yard par 4, 3rd hole. Just left of the green is out of bounds by way of the clubhouse car park.

The short par 4, 4th and even shorter 5th are both birdie prospects as long as you drive straight.

Index 1 at Inverallochy is the 6th which is the only par 5. Rough and low dunes run along the left side whilst on the south side of the fairway there is out of bounds which finishes at the Allochy Burn. If you try to keep away from out of bounds on the right then you may finish in one of the bunkers on the left side.

The 7th is a good par 3 of 198 yards. You can run your ball on to this green as the bunkers are at the sides. The 8th is also a par 3, but somewhat shorter at 142 yards. The green is raised and has one nasty pot bunker at the front and one at each side.

Nine is a very short par 4 of 278 yards, slightly uphill. A ridge running along the fairway will tend to send shots left into one of three bunkers or right into the rough.

Ten is also a short par 4 whilst eleven is a tricky short hole of 199 yards to a sloping green. One pot bunker guards the left and anything right will run into the rough.

The 12th and 13th are each par 4's with the beach along the right. The 12th is the longest and more difficult hole.

The par 3, 14th (156 yards) is downhill to a green in a hollow. A burn runs across the front of the green which is very narrow at the front and is also quite undulating.

Be careful at the 15th, a par 4 of only 316 yards as out of bounds is just one yard from the left of the green. The uphill par 3, 16th has out of bounds along the left so you can bank on many involuntary fades on this hole.

The Allochy Burn is a constant hazard on the 17th, a testing par 4 of 419 yards. The finishing hole is a good par 4 that runs uphill back to the clubhouse.

If you happen to be in this rather distant part of Scotland then you'll have an enjoyable, fun links experience if you visit Inverallochy Golf Club.

Approach to the 6th green, the only par 5 at Inverallochy

Photo courtesy Inverallochy GC

CRUDEN BAY

THE GOLF COURSE AT CRUDEN BAY WAS COMMISSIONED TO BE BUILT AT THE END OF THE 19TH CENTURY BY THE GREAT NORTH OF SCOTLAND RAILWAY. THE ORIGINAL DESIGN WAS BY OLD TOM MORRIS BUT A NUMBER OF CHANGES WERE MADE IN 1926 BY TOM SIMPSON AND HERBERT FOWLER.

Photo David Worley

10th - 13th holes from the 9th tee

Ironically, shortly after the end of the Second World War, the railway line to Cruden Bay ceased to operate and the course fell on hard times. This led to a foresighted group of local businessmen purchasing the course in 1950 for 2,750 Pounds which effectively marked a new beginning for the club. It is now, once again, one of the premier links anywhere in the United Kingdom with the improvements culminating in the erection of the new clubhouse which was completed in 1998.

The clubhouse is well appointed and affords wonderful views across the course from its high vantage point. To my mind, however, this has come at a cost as the entrance to the club is now through the housing development on the blocks that were no doubt sold to finance the construction of the clubhouse.

The first three holes are a reasonably gentle opening with the third being a particularly short par 4. The fourth is the first of the very good par 3's at Cruden Bay. The tee shot must carry a deep hollow to a slightly elevated green with Port Errol picturesquely framed on the left. This can be a long 193 yards into the sea breeze.

The fifth and sixth are interesting holes through the dunes with thick rough all along the coastal side. The shot into the plateau sixth green must avoid a burn which is very much in play.

The eighth is a picturesque short par 4 of 258 yards. There are no bunkers but the green is in a dell slightly to the right. Drive to the middle of the fairway and it is a birdie hole. However, due to the prevailing winds and the dog-leg fairway, many drives finish right and are in thick bracken on the steep dune side slopes.

When I first played Cruden Bay (in 1998) I thought the uphill 9th hole was the blandest hole on the course. The tee is now higher up and more above the eighth green and this has improved the hole considerably. The views from the 9th tee are stunning in all directions. Behind you is the dune land, sea and Slains Castle in the far distance. Ahead lies the few holes that have a slightly different feel as they are on an old flood plain.

A meandering burn is in play on the flatter tenth, eleventh and thirteenth holes but you then rejoin the dune land at 'Whins', the par 4, 14th. This is a fun hole, uphill to a narrow sunken green only yards from the sea and the raised fifteenth tee. Admittedly there was plenty of run when I was there again in 2003, but I can't understand how this hole deserves an index rating of number 2 on the card, especially as I was playing only a 9 iron to the green for my second shot. The fifteenth 'Blin Dunt' is a blind par 3 to a green hidden by the dune below the ninth tee. Into any sort of a breeze, this blind par 3 of 239 yards requires a slight draw around the dune so getting your ball to stop on the green can be difficult. The tee position could not be any closer to the adjacent beach.

Photo David Worley

The undulating fairway of the par 4, 14th

The sixteenth is also a par 3 and can be quite difficult despite being rated the easiest hole on the course. The hole takes the name 'Coffins' from the grassy hollows to the right and back of the green which slopes away from you.

The round finishes with two good par 4's, the seventeenth being the more difficult.

Photo David Worley

From the spectacular 9th tee looking to 15th green and 16th green

For genuine lovers of the links this is a fun course to play.
There is not the slightest tinge of monotony with every hole being different and
a delight to experience with enjoyment to be had regardless of your handicap.
Perhaps the greens are not quite to the high standards of Royal Aberdeen
to the south, but I can guarantee you will want to make the
trip to Cruden Bay more than once.

ROYAL ABERDEEN

An earth wall runs across the approach to the 14th green

ROYAL ABERDEEN GOLF CLUB WAS FOUNDED IN 1768 WHICH MAKES IT THE SIXTH OLDEST IN THE WORLD. THE CLUB MOVED TO THE PRESENT LOCATION OF THE BALGOWNIE LINKS IN 1888. EARLY DESIGN WORK WAS BY THE SIMPSON BROTHERS, ARCHIE AND ROBERT OF CARNOUSTIE. THE COURSE WAS LATER LENGTHENED AND RE-BUNKERED BY JAMES BRAID WHOSE DRAWINGS FOR EACH HOLE'S ALTERATIONS ARE ON DISPLAY IN THE CLUB HOUSE.

1st green with North Sea in the background

Photo David Worley

Royal Aberdeen is a traditional links course with the front nine predominantly along the seaside and dune land whilst the home nine is on a slightly higher inland plateau. Balgownie Links possess one of the best opening nine holes you will ever find.

The first hole heads straight towards the North Sea. The fairway is reasonably wide but shot making becomes a little more daunting when you see the huge expanses of forest-like gorse, especially on the right hand side. The approach area is a mass of mounds and is strictly bump and run territory. The 2nd is the longest hole on the course and suits a slight draw shot through the coastal dunes. The 3rd is a wonderful par 3 of 223 yards, but as it is usually played into the wind and there is no fairway whatsoever, this can be quite a demanding tee shot. With a length of 210 yards from the ladies tee, this is one of the toughest carries for the fairer sex.

By the time you reach the fourth, a par 4 of 423 yards, you realise that this course does not let up. The 8th is an entrancing par 3. It is only 147 yards in length but requires a perfectly executed iron as there are no less than ten bunkers surrounding the green.

Aberdeen does not have as many bunkers as other courses of similar quality but they are all strategically placed and are definitely to be avoided.

Be careful at the 9th because you could easily find yourself crossing over on to the neighbouring course, Murcar.

The 12th and 14th are rather reminiscent of courses like North Berwick West. The 12th green is guarded by a ridge which runs at 45 degrees and the green is perched on a plateau. There is a fair chance your second shot will either be deflected left or go through the green. The 14th has a burn at around 240 yards and then an earth wall angled across the approach to the green, this time running from left to right, the opposite of the mound on the 12th.

Standing on the tee of the 17th, a par 3 of 180 yards, you may well be confused as to which green is the correct target as the most visible green is part of Murcar. Sensibly, Royal Aberdeen uses white flags on the front nine, red flags on the back nine and Murcar has blue flags. The 18th can be a difficult finish at 434 yards uphill and with a green protected by five bunkers. To have any chance of being on for two it is essential that you hit a good drive that avoids the three fairway bunkers.

Unless you hit a really wild shot, the rough and gorse is not too intrusive at Royal Aberdeen. The fairways are all interesting and the greens are first class. The rough was no doubt more difficult when golf started here, for the "Society of Golfers at Aberdeen", as they were originally known, wisely in 1783 introduced the five minute rule when looking for balls.

Photo David Worley

The testing 3rd hole, a par 3 of 223 yards

Any opportunity for a round at the Balgownie Links should be eagerly accepted.

MURCAR

MURCAR'S BEGINNINGS ARE FAR MORE RECENT THAN ITS MORE HIGHLY REGARD-ED NEIGHBOUR, ROYAL ABERDEEN. THE CLUB WAS FORMED IN 1908 AND A COURSE DESIGNED BY THE THEN ABERDEEN PROFESSIONAL, ARCHIE SIMPSON, WAS OPEN FOR PLAY IN JUNE 1909.

This is a very interesting and under rated course. Currently a number of alterations are being made in the lead up to the club's centenary. Modifications and lengthening of some holes will be in accordance with James Braid's original design philosophy.

The opening hole is an ideal start and is a well bunkered par 4 of 322 yards. The view to the area behind the green is an attractive vista of gorse and dune land heading down towards Royal Aberdeen.

The 3rd green is in a dell, rather more reminiscent of Irish courses. The fairway is full of small undulations and provides a good indication of what lies ahead.

'Plateau', the 5th, is the first of the three par 3's. The green is up a steep hill and has bunkers to the right and at the rear. There is no fairway at all, so anything short can be a lost ball in gorse, heather or grassy mounds.

The 7th, 'Serpentine', is one of the most demanding par 4's you will ever encounter. From an elevated tee you hit over a burn which also runs in a wetland area along the right hand side between the fairway and the seaside dunes. There are high cliffs on the left with gorse covered banks.

When approaching the green you need to exercise great care as anything long or to the right is in trouble.

Eight and nine are both good short par 4's with tight fairways being the main feature. The 10th is very difficult and is index 1 on the card. The tee shot is uphill to a hole that dog-legs left. Thick gorse is not far from the back of the green.

The eleventh is another blind tee shot – again uphill. The marker post is not correctly aligned here as your ball will run hard right into impenetrable gorse unless you hit a strong draw a little left of the marker.

The 13th hole also requires a blind tee shot but this hole is not as hard as it first appears provided you drive straight. There are lovely views over the course from the top of this hill which features out of bounds along the right.

The tee on fifteen is elevated but has very heavy gorse right in front. The shot into the elevated green is a fun challenge as you play over a burn and steep bank.

The 16th hole is a good little par 3 of 160 yards. There is no bail-out zone anywhere here. You have to clear the burn and miss the two pot bunkers around the uphill green. The round finishes with two shortish par 4's but beware left on the 17th and out of bounds on the well trapped 18th.

Murcar is a real test and requires very accurate driving. My one criticism would be the number of blind tee shots on the back nine which are especially difficult for the first time visitor. There is never a dull moment here.

Top: the challenging 5th, an uphill par 3 of 162 yards
Centre: the dangerous par 4, 7th hole 'Serpentine'
Bottom: 7th green

MONTROSE (MEDAL COURSE)

Photo David Worley

Par 3, 3rd hole

SITUATED ON THE EAST COAST BETWEEN ABERDEEN AND CARNOUSTIE, THERE IS NO DISPUTING MONTROSE'S CLAIMS OF SENIORITY AS THERE ARE RECORDS OF GOLF BEING PLAYED HERE AS FAR BACK AS 1562. AT ONE STAGE MONTROSE HAD 25 HOLES. AT THE TURN OF THE CENTURY TOM MORRIS ADVISED ON ALTERATIONS TO THE PRESENT CHAMPIONSHIP (MEDAL) COURSE AND IN 1903 THE FINAL ALTERATIONS WERE IN ACCORDANCE WITH A DESIGN BY WILLIE PARK JUNIOR. THERE IS A SECOND COURSE AND, TO-GETHER, THREE CLUBS SHARE THE TWO COURSES WHICH ARE ADMINISTERED BY THE MONTROSE LINKS TRUST.

Photo David Worley

2nd hole alongside the beach where erosion damage can be clearly seen

Anumber of important events have been hosted by Montrose and it was selected as a final qualifying course for the Open Championship at Carnoustie in 1999 and 2007.

The layout is a little unusual for a traditional links. The first hole heads to the sea and then holes 2-9 run more or less parallel with the seashore. From the 10th to the 15th the course runs inland in a T formation before holes 16-17 are again adjacent to the coastline with the 18th returning inland beside the first. The front nine is rather more interesting because it is in the vicinity of the seaside dunes whereas the home nine suffers a little from rather flat and featureless fairways.

The 2nd and 5th are attractive driving holes with the beach a distinct prospect for any sliced tee shot on the 2nd. One of the best holes on the Medal Course is the 154 yards, par 3, 3rd. A very deep and wide gully lies between tee and green so there is nowhere to land your ball except on the putting surface. This hole can play a little longer than it looks and, being close to the shore line and with the green slightly raised, it is at the mercy of the sea breeze.

In terms of length, there are no demanding holes until you reach the 9th which is index 1 and a par 4 of 444 yards. On the back nine, the 11th and 14th and 17th are all par 4's of over 400 yards.

However, whilst many of the holes are tight off the tee, an accurate drive on these firm fairways will give you every chance of being on the green in regulation figures.

The Medal Course at Montrose has stood the test of time fairly well. A little extra length and a few bumps and swales on the home nine would make it even better.

CARNOUSTIE

18th with the Barry Burn along the right before it crosses the fairway again in front of the green

THE FIRST FORMAL ATTEMPT AT ESTABLISHING A COURSE AT CARNOUSTIE WAS IN 1842 WHEN THE ST. ANDREWS PROFESSIONAL ALAN ROBERTSON LAID OUT TEN HOLES. SOME TWENTY YEARS LATER OLD TOM MORRIS MADE CHANGES AND ADDED A FURTHER EIGHT HOLES. THE LINKS, AS WE KNOW THEM TODAY, HOWEVER ARE VERY MUCH THE WORK OF JAMES BRAID WHO CREATED NEW TEES AND GREENS AND ADDED MANY MORE BUNKERS.

Photo courtesy Darren J Kirk at Scratch Design

The Spectacle bunkers completely block the view of the green at the 14th

1st hole green, a good opening par 4

There are some who do not like Carnoustie. My personal view is that it represents a true test of championship golf and, although demanding, it is a very fair test. The beautifully presented revetted bunkers are perfectly positioned but are all there for you to see and contemplate before deciding upon your strategy and executing your shot. I have heard comments that the course is "dull". What on earth do they mean? Sure there are no towering dunes or holes beside the seashore, but every hole is different and I see beauty all around. Not being a straight out and back course there is the added challenge with the wind coming from all points of the compass.

You have to be thinking right from the outset. A tee shot left is best on the 1st hole, but a quick hook may find the burn. A par 4 of 435 yards awaits you at the second. The fairway dog-legs right and has four bunkers to snare the tee shot. A burn runs all the way along the left and then behind the narrow green which is 50 yards in length. Three and four are slightly easier par 4's but you simply must keep your drive in play to have any chance of par at Carnoustie.

The 5th hole is also the fifth consecutive par 4. It is aptly named 'Jockie's Burn' after the burn which crosses the fairway 300 yards from the championship tee. Holes two to five are all slight dog-legs to the right.

The 6th hole is an intriguing par 5, named 'Hogan's Alley' after the thoughtful way Ben Hogan played this dangerous hole in winning the 1953 Open, his only appearance at this event. Out of bounds lies all the way along the left. There is rough on the right and then a drainage ditch around 80 yards short of the green. The drive must also negotiate two bunkers that are right in the middle of the fairway. The angled green is well bunkered on both sides. You can feel very pleased to have made par here.

Like the Old Course at St. Andrews, there is no par 3 until the 8th hole. This is a very attractive hole, especially when the gorse is in full bloom or the heather is prominent. Just a few yards left of the green is out of bounds. With the wind behind you, this slightly raised green is hard to hold.

The 9th is one of the best holes on the course and was rated the most difficult during the 1999 Open. A par 4 of 413 yards, there are trees along the left and a ditch and rough on the right. There are seven nasty little pot bunkers on this classic hole.

The 10th, 'South America', is one of my favourite holes. It is a long par 4 at 446 yards from the Championship tee and 425 yards from the normal back tee. Four bunkers are waiting for any drive pushed a little right. Your shot to the green must first carry the Barry Burn 30 yards from the front and then the two bunkers at the front left. If you go too far right of the green then you may have to negotiate some trees or the burn again.

Index 1 at Carnoustie is the 14th 'Spectacles', a short par 5 of 483 yards from the back tee or a par 4 of 468 yards from the yellow. On a course that is long (6941 yards) it is interesting that a short par 5 is rated its hardest. The start of the fairway is narrow with gorse and rough very visible. There are four fairway bunkers to catch an errant drive. You must then clear the two Spectacle bunkers which are in the side of a large mound which completely blocks any view of the green 50 yards further onwards. The 14th green is a double green with the 4th so you may find yourself with a very long putt if your approach is too firm.

The remaining four holes would have to be the most difficult run home you will ever experience. The finish consists of three par 4's all over 430 yards and the par 3, 16th which at 245 yards is the longest one shotter on the Open rota. In two Open Championship appearances at Carnoustie, Tom Watson was unable to achieve par on the 16th.

You need to think very carefully before your tee shot on the 17th. The Barry Burn snakes through this fairway and, depending upon the wind, may be in play left, right or straight and too long. Land your drive over the first crossing and short of the second crossing of the burn, but even then you will still be playing a long second to a green with four bunkers, hollows and gorse protecting it.

Your drive on the final hole must avoid out of bounds all along the left and the Barry Burn which starts at about 150 yards from the back tee. It forms a U shape so it is also in play for anything left or right for the first 280 yards. Into a strong

headwind you can lay up with your tee shot onto a tongue of fairway to the right but you still have the burn on both sides of this section of fairway. Unless you are well over the burn then going for the green is out of the question as you are still about 230 yards from the green. The Barry Burn is wider than you think and you will be unlikely to get lucky and bounce over it. Especially if the flag is at the front then you would be wise to lay up with your second and try for a pitch and putt par 4.

I am sure there is no one who does not remember the adventures of Jean Van De Velde here in 1999 when he needed just six to win the 128th Open Championship. I will not join his list of critics for he was dreadfully unlucky. Out of bounds ran along the left of the green and anything right would get relief from the spectator stands in the nearby drop zone. Van De Velde's second shot went high and right, but instead of staying in the spectator stand it hit the metal scaffolding and ricocheted into the Barry Burn. The rest is history as he subsequently lost a play off, along with Justin Leonard to Paul Laurie.

Great golf courses usually produce great tournament winners. The first five Open Champions at Carnoustie were: Tommy Amour (1931), Henry Cotton (1937), Ben Hogan (1953), Gary Player (1968) and Tom Watson (1975).

Gary Player might be correct in describing Carnoustie "as the toughest course in the world" but it can still be lots of fun if you keep your head and play each hole sensibly.

Photo courtesy Alan C. Birch

The Open Championship 1999. Long par 3, 16th and to the right the 17th and the snaking Barry Burn

PANMURE

WHAT EVER YOU DO, DON'T MISS OUT ON PANMURE WHICH MUST BE ONE OF SCOTLAND'S BEST KEPT SECRETS. PANMURE IS LOCATED ADJACENT TO CARNOUSTIE, ON THE INLAND SIDE, TOWARDS THE TOWN OF BARRY. IT IS A QUALIFIER FOR THE OPEN AND RIGHTLY SO.

Photo David Worley

The approach to the green at the par 4, 12th hole at Panmure requires great care

Panmure dates back to 1845 and by 1880 had been extended to 18 holes. However, due to congestion on the original course at Monifieth, it was decided in 1899 to move to its present site at Barry.

Don't let your first view of the opening and closing holes fool you. The first two holes are quite flat and fairly easy and I am rather puzzled as to how the first, a par 4 of 289 yards, is rated index 9. As you walk up the second fairway there is a real feeling of the countryside and the smell of cow manure is guaranteed to clear the nostrils. Once you reach the 3rd, you are in a different world with stands of fir trees, gorse-clad dunes and fairways full of bumps and swales.

Length is not everything at Panmure, but accuracy and club selection certainly is. The 6th is a super hole and is rated index 1. When Ben Hogan practised here for the 1953 Open, it was this hole which really took his fancy. A draw is needed with the drive followed by a most difficult approach to this 387 yard par 4. You hit slightly up hill to an elevated green that is protected by a steep grass-covered dune on the front right. Behind the dune are bunkers on both sides of the front of the green. If you are too far through the back left side of the green, then out of bounds awaits you.

Photos David Worley

The clubhouse at Panmure looking back from behind the 1st green

Panmure has some first class par 3's. The 9th is 174 yards and has no fairway whatsoever

The tee shot on the eighth is semi-blind and if you haven't played Panmure before, then you're likely to take too much club and run out of fairway.

The 9th and 11th are excellent par 3's with the 11th green surrounded by 5 bunkers. The 9th has very little fairway in front but be careful as anything through the green may run into heavy gorse.

Hit two good shots on the 12th and it's an easy hole, but if you spray your second then watch out. First there is a

meandering burn that forms an S along the fairway commencing about 100 yards short of the green and then there is the elevated green with grassy humps and deep pot bunkers nearby.

Panmure is an underrated course. The holes from the 3rd to the 14th especially, are all well conceived and challenging for even the best of players whilst they are not impossibly difficult for higher handicappers. Strategy, rather than brute force, is the order of the day here, particularly from the tee.

The 14th and 15th have a railway line forming out of bounds. Similarly, the practice fairway beside the 18th also becomes out of bounds. Incidentally, you won't find many par 3's longer than the 15th which measures 234 yards.

Panmure is a course to which I would definitely return. Interestingly, the membership is restricted to only 500 to ensure the course is never overplayed and remains in top condition.

MONIFIETH

MONIFIETH IS A SMALL SEASIDE TOWN JUST FIFTEEN MINUTES FROM DUNDEE. THERE ARE TWO COURSES, THE MEDAL AND THE ASHLUDIE, THE LATTER BEING A SHORTER MORE COMPACT LINKS.

The Medal Course has been used as an Open qualifier for Carnoustie and, ironically, the leading qualifying score in 1999 was from Jean Van de Velde with two rounds of 67.

The course layout resembles the shape of an axe. Holes 1 to 6 and then 16 to 18 are the handle whilst holes 7 to 15 are in more of a square area furthest from the clubhouse.

The first 6 holes all run in a straight line away from the clubhouse and each has the railway very close to the boundary fence on the right hand side.

The first real challenge, in terms of length, comes at the 4th, a par 4 of 456 yards. In summer the fairways are extremely firm and fast running so even this hole does not play to its nominal length. The green is in an attractive setting backed by a stand of fir trees. If you push your second shot right you will be faced with a difficult chip over a large mound at the edge of the green. The par 3, 5th will test your accuracy. The hole is 191 yards to a narrow green with three bunkers on each side.

The 7th is much more testing when hitting into a stiff breeze. The main hazard to be avoided is a burn on the left which is in play for around 193 yards before it turns away in front of the 6th tee.

With the wind behind, you will be tempted to try to drive the 8th, a short par 4 of 284 yards. However a perfectly hit slight draw is required otherwise you will be playing from rough, especially if you pull your shot left.

The 9th is a very good par 5 that necessitates straight hitting. Ten is an attractive par 4 where the ideal tee shot is a fade. Anything too far left is a strong candidate for finishing in the large pond. Both twelve and thirteen are good par 4's in what is probably the most scenic part of the course. Anything too far right on the 13th is either in heavy gorse or out of bounds.

Be careful as you exit the 13th green because you have to walk past the 15th tee before you arrive at the 14th. I am embarrassed to say that my round consisted of only 17 holes as I had completed the 15th by the time I realised it was not the 14th! A good drive over the hill is essential on fifteen if you want to be on the green for two. Fourteen and fifteen are the only holes which run north/south with the other 16 all in an east/west direction.

The last three holes run in a straight line back to the clubhouse. All are well bunkered near the green with the 18th being a good par 5 finishing hole.

The Medal Course provides plenty of quality golf. Firm, bumpy and narrow fairways and very true greens. Most of the bunkers are situated so as to catch the approach to the green but there are far less to worry about from the tee. A minor criticism would be that on a number of holes there was quite a walk from the green to the next tee but that should not deter you from enjoying the links experience at Monifieth.

Top: approach to the green at the long par 4, 4th hole
Below: a slight fade is needed for the drive at the 10th

ST ANDREWS – OLD COURSE

"The more I studied the Old Course, the more I loved it;
and the more I loved it, the more I studied it." Bobby Jones

Looking back down the 16th from the Old Course Hotel

MUCH HAS BEEN WRITTEN ABOUT ST ANDREWS, AND PARTICULARLY THE OLD COURSE, SO I WILL ATTEMPT TO GIVE YOU A SLIGHTLY DIFFERENT PERSPECTIVE. IF YOU HAVE NEVER BEEN TO ST ANDREWS BEFORE THEN I WOULD HIGHLY RECOMMEND YOU ALLOW AT LEAST A FEW DAYS IN THE TOWN SO AS TO ABSORB SOME OF ITS WONDERFUL ATMOSPHERE. "IT IS THAT UTTER SELF-ABANDONMENT TO GOLF THAT GIVES THE PLACE ITS ATTRACTIVENESS." [1]

I am a great defender of the classic qualities of the Old Course and I do not believe it should ever be included in ratings lists. It should be set aside as a unique links – in fact the one by which all others may be judged. I have been lucky enough to play from the Medal tees on a sunny, calm afternoon. I have been just as fortunate to experience the Old Course with a cool wind blowing at 40 knots so that even 2 foot putts were no certainties and staying on the fairway was a major achievement.

I will have to admit to be coming rather agitated when, usually first time players there, dismiss it as being an overrated piece of flat ground. Bernard Darwin assesses the situation perfectly: "St Andrews provides the very best possible evidence that the greatest courses and the greatest holes are those which want knowing. The interesting course is one that the stranger, after his first round, denounces as unfair, and St Andrews does not yield up its secrets 'til after many rounds; indeed, it never yields them all, for there is ever something to learn there." [2]

I do not think there are any weak holes on the Old Course and the 1st, 11th, 16th and 17th holes are the standout ones for me. In places it can get a little confusing as to just where you are meant to be headed. For example, the par 4, 7th plays into the right hand side of a double green whilst the par 3, 11th crosses from the right side of the 7th fairway to the left hand side of the same double green. Not far from either end of this elongated green are the tees for the 8th and 12th holes. As you can imagine, when there is a strong cross wind there can be golfers and caddies going in all directions on this part of the course.

The 5th hole, the first par 5, encapsulates many of the features of the Old Course. Gorse is ever present down the right and the fairway is littered with bunkers, any one of which can be the ruin of a round. No less than 7 bunkers lie of the right side of this fairway between 240 and 300 yards from the tee. Anything near the left of them always finishes in the sand as Jack Nicklaus found in three of his four rounds when he first played there in the Open. When you reach the green you encounter one of the largest in the world, about one acre in size joined with the 13th green.

Two bunkers to be definitely avoided on the par 3, 11th are Hill and the tiny Strath. In major championships the flag is frequently set right behind Strath bunker. When the wind whips across the course the large Shell is always in play on the 7th. The 12th hole, Heathery In, has two nasty sets of little bunkers which are not really visible from the tee. The first are about 185 yards from the tee and the second two about 225 yards out. Many of these bunkers are set down below the fairway level so any ball nearby will funnel into them as if in a whirlpool. The 13th hole contains the Coffins at around 210 yards. You can avoid them by aiming right, but this means you are heading towards the gorse.

The 14th, appropriately called 'Long Hole', is a par 5 of 530 yards. If you are into the wind, then the huge Hell bunker looms right in the middle of the fairway about 410 yards from the tee. The general advice is to play left of Hell bunker with your second shot and approach the green from the 5th fairway.

The 15th is a par 4 of 414 yards. If you aim, as I did, towards the centre but slightly right to hit away from the gorse, then

8th hole, the first of only 2 par 3's on the Old Course

Hell Bunker on the 14th fairway

you will have the pleasure of a horrible little monster called Sutherland bunker. It was named after a member of the R & A who apparently frequented it so often that in 1885 he directed the Greens Committee to have it filled in. The golfers of St Andrews objected to this and under cover of darkness they restored the bunker. The 16th provides

17th 'Road Hole' green with 18th in background

View from the 18th fairway – note how close the Swilcan Burn is to the 1st green

similar dangers with three bunkers known as Principal's Nose being one of the worries on the tee. The other concern is out of bounds further to the right.

Until the 1950's, the train ran from Leuchars station and passed along the 16th fairway and close by the Road Hole green. What a brilliant sight it must have been seeing the Links from the slow moving carriages and observing "familiar friends plying their niblicks in familiar bunkers."[3]

The Road Hole, 17th, is one of the great par 4's and has influenced the result of many an event at the Old Course. When you first play this hole, there are two things that really stand out. Firstly, the dog-leg right is much greater than you realise, so unless you hit over the old railway shed in front of the hotel or you play a long fade then you will soon run out of fairway. You will only finish up in light rough, but your shot to the green is much more difficult as you bring the Road Hole bunker into play or you can easily go across the front of the green and on to the bitumen road. The second surprise is just how high the green is above the road. It is much harder to chip from the road or the grass near the wall by either bumping your ball into the bank or pitching to the green than appears the case when viewing this green on television. Furthermore, it is always possible to putt from the front left edge of the green and see the ball spiral left and into the bunker. Brian Barnes and Tommy Nakajima are just two of the players who have done this whilst in contention during the Open.

Links land is often public and frequently has to provide access to the beach for the locals and visitors alike. The Old Course has a pathway, now sealed with bitumen, known as Granny Clark's Wynd, which runs across the 1st and 18th fairways. It never ceases to amaze me how many people (presumably non golfers) casually stroll across here with not the slightest thought of looking to see if anyone is on the 1st or 18th tee. Obviously nothing much has changed with the passing of time. How wonderfully Darwin describes the

scene in the days of yore: "All day long there is a procession along it of motor cars, perambulators, children and old ladies and the golfer, learning perforce to be callous, drives over, round, or through them from the first and from the last tees. Mr. Horton in his box shouts 'Fore' at the people in a voice of thunder or rather he makes some horrific sound with no distinguishable consonants in it, but nobody pays any attention and, which is more surprising, nobody is killed."[4]

The 18th hole, 'Tom Morris', should be the easiest on the course. A relatively short par 4, the only visible hazard would appear to be out of bounds along the right of the fairway and at the back of the green. For the average golfer however there is also the mental pressure of knowing you will be putting on this green under the critical gaze of the constant throng of interested observers. When Bobby Jones putted out to win the Open of 1927 there was a conservative estimate of 12,000 people around the 18th green. In 1933 Leo Diegal had only a short putt to win the Open here. He missed the ball completely and then easily missed the hole with his next, which, had he sunk it would still have put him in a play-off.

The spirit of St Andrews is beautifully summed up by Peter Thomson in a 2005 interview. "When I first looked out in September 1954 it seemed like heaven. All my imaginings were proved true. There before me in the soft damp light of autumn lay this holy ground. So wide and keen was that first hole, sharing with the last the width of two cricket fields, and down at the end that dark surface ribbon that indicates the narrow burn. And over it, banking, the closer cut green with the flag straight out in the wind." [5]

1.   *The Golf Courses of the British Isles*, Bernard Darwin.
2.   *Playing the Like,* Bernard Darwin.
3.   *A Golf Writer's Revenge*, Bernard Darwin.
4.   *The Happy Golfer*, Bernard Darwin.
5.   *The Weekend Australian Magazine* – Aug. 27 2005.

ST ANDREWS – NEW COURSE

THE NEW COURSE DATES BACK TO 1895 AND IS JUDGED BY MANY TO BE MORE DIFFICULT THAN THE OLD. IT IS SANDWICHED IN BETWEEN THE OLD COURSE AND THE JUBILEE ON THE SEAWARD SIDE. IT IS TIGHTER AND HAS MORE GORSE LINED FAIRWAYS THAN THE OLD COURSE, HOWEVER THE HOLES ARE LESS MEMORABLE AND DO NOT CONTAIN AS MANY LITTLE POT BUNKERS. ON A WINDY DAY YOU CAN LOSE QUITE A FEW BALLS HERE IN THE THICK GORSE.

Photo David Worley

Left:
gorse in full bloom in spring,
1st hole New Course

The New starts with two par 4's and a par 5 all of modest length – par is not a problem if you are straight.

The 4th hole is considerably more difficult. A par 4 of 369 yards, it is a dog-leg left with thick gorse and rough all the way along that side. Three bunkers close together guard the front of the green.

If you are inclined to be a little inaccurate then the par 3, 5th will increase your anxiety levels. Almost all of the 180 yards is flanked by expanses of gorse on both sides of the fairway. You need to thread your way past the two greenside bunkers but don't over-club as there is also gorse not far from the back of the green.

Now that you are on the 6th tee and all you can see is a narrow fairway again bordered by gorse on both sides you are beginning to appreciate that the New is quite different to the Old Course and is extremely demanding in terms of accuracy.

Because the course runs in a clockwise direction there tends to be more bail out areas to the right. This is in complete contrast to the Old Course where, normally, left of the tee is the safest route.

The New Course is particularly interesting around holes eight and nine. The 8th is index 1 and heads towards the Eden Estuary. On a windy day the par 3, 9th can be a nightmare. It is 225 yards from the back (and still 206 yards off the front tee) with the Eden Estuary running all the way along the left edge of the fairway. There are no bunkers on this fairway and anything slightly right will generally feed back towards the slightly sunken green.

At the back of the 16th green you will see a rare sight for St Andrews – a clump of stunted trees. The 18th is a tight par 4 of 408 yards with the green not far from the general dining area of the visitors clubhouse so, although you may not feel as watched as on the Old Course, there is usually a number of people following your progress.

ST ANDREWS – JUBILEE COURSE

THE JUBILEE WAS BUILT IN 1897 AND WAS SO NAMED IN HONOUR OF QUEEN VICTORIA'S DIAMOND JUBILEE. THIS WAS UNTIL RELATIVELY RECENTLY A RATHER SHORT AND UNDEMANDING LAYOUT. IN THE LATE 1980'S IT WAS LENGTHENED TO AROUND 7000 YARDS AND WAS GENERALLY UPGRADED.

My own view is that the Jubilee is now the most picturesque and most fun to play of the four major courses (I have not included the Strathtyrum or Balgove courses) administered by the Links Trust. Visually, the Jubilee has the benefit of being the closest to the lovely stretch of beach along the West Sands (who can forget that scene from Chariots of Fire) and being the only course to play amongst some reasonable sized dunes.

These dunes are in play, especially around the 2nd green and the 15th hole. The need for accuracy is in constant demand. The 8th hole runs alongside the Eden Estuary and is a real birdie opportunity being a par 4 of 369 yards. This hole affords striking views across to the RAF Base at Leuchars. Whilst the green is sunken and sheltered, many airborne second shots disappear into long grass or out of bounds on the left side. The 9th is located at the far corner where the Eden Estuary meets the sea and is always exposed to the breeze. This can be a tough par 3 hitting from an elevated tee to a crowned green. If it is windy then watch your tee shot on the 10th because out of bounds is all the way along the left side.

The 15th is a strange but interesting hole at only 356 yards in length. A well hit drive should leave you with just a short approach and you are entitled to wonder how this hole can be rated fourth most difficult. All is revealed once you play your shot into the green. Just short of the green is a very deep gully and any ball landing here is pushed left or right. Both the sides and the rear of the green feature heavy gorse and if you overshoot to the back left you can finish down a bank and on the 16th tee.

Top: the Jubilee Course is in the distance nearer the dunes and the sea
Below: 1st hole Jubilee Course

Top: 2nd green and lone tree on the Jubilee
Below: 8th hole from behind the green

The Jubilee is usually less crowded than the Old or New Courses and is an ideal course for a husband and wife to enjoy together.

ST ANDREWS – EDEN COURSE

Photo David Worley

Approaching storm and the undulating 1st green

THE EDEN WAS DESIGNED BY HARRY COLT AROUND THE BEGINNING OF WORLD WAR I. SITUATED ON THE INLAND SIDE OF THE OLD COURSE, IT WAS SUBJECTED TO A NUMBER OF CHANGES IN 1993 SO AS TO MAKE WAY FOR THE NEW PRACTICE FACILITIES. THE EDEN MEASURES JUST 6195 YARDS AND IS THE ONLY COURSE ON THE LINKS AT ST ANDREWS TO FEATURE A POND AS A WATER HAZARD (14TH AND 15TH HOLES).

The original opening two holes have disappeared and the course now starts with what was the 3rd hole. The 1st green is one of the most intriguing on any of the St Andrews courses. It is divided into two by a ridge running from front to back and each half has a large swale at the front. Right at the back of the green is a stone wall behind which is the old Shepherd's Cottage which is now used as toilets.

The second is one of the five very good par 4's that are all over 400 yards in length. As is the case also for the third and fourth, out of bounds runs the whole length of the right hand side. It is important on the 4th hole to keep your tee shot left to avoid heavy rough and then the out of bounds and the Eden Estuary on the right.

The first nine holes are from the original Harry Colt layout. The 10th is a rather featureless flat par 3 with just the one bunker and a long narrow green. Index 2 is the par 4,13th. There is plenty of room for the drive and whilst there are no greenside bunkers, the left features the path of the old railway line and to the right is heavy rough and then out of bounds.

From the 14th the course has somewhat less of a links feel, especially with the large pond running along the left for the last 100 yards of the14th and all the way on the left side of the par 3, 15th. With the pond on the left and in front and four bunkers around the sides of the green then the safest strategy on the15th is to be long.

The 17th is probably the best of the newer holes. It is a challenging par 4 of 432 yards. The hole swings to the right where out of bounds runs the full length until just short of the green. If you play safe to the left then you face thick rough and six fairway bunkers.

On a windy day this course is no pushover. Whilst it has some good holes it would clearly rank in fourth place behind its more celebrated cousins, the Old, New and Jubilee Courses.

Photo David Worley

Par 3, 8th

ST ANDREWS – CASTLE (COURSE No.7)

IN EARLY 2005 WORK BEGAN ON A NEW COURSE NEAR THE EAST SANDS, ABOUT 2 MILES OUT OF ST ANDREWS AND ON THE WAY TO ST ANDREWS BAY AND KINGSBARNS GOLF COURSES.

The design by David Kidd, creator of Bandon Dunes in the USA, will be traditional links and is expected to be open for play in 2008.

This was formally farm land and is of a flat, cliff-top nature. I looked at the work to date when I was there in late June 2006. There were many well disguised man-made mounds, very much in the style employed so successfully at nearby Kingsbarns.

Some of the holes will run along the cliff edge and will have spectacular views. The 9th and 18th greens will meet in a location known as Kinkell Point and the clubhouse will be set back a little further inland from these two greens. There will be multiple tees on each hole with the course stretching to a maximum of 7200 yards.

My understanding is that there was a degree of resistance from many locals who were divided over the merits of building another course, especially one which will be in isolation from the other six administered by the St Andrews Links Trust. I can't comment on the likely financial outcome, but from a golf course perspective what I have seen so far looked quite impressive.

Photo David Worley

Castle-Course No. 7 under construction June 2006

At the time this book was nearing completion in early 2007 the name adopted for the new links is the Castle Course. This reflects the presence of Kinkell Castle on this site during the Middle Ages.

KINGSBARNS

6th green from side on

LOCATED JUST SIX MILES FROM ST ANDREWS THE 190 ACRE SITE IS A COMBINATION OF LAND ONCE USED FOR FARMING AND A PARCEL NEAR THE SEA THAT WAS THE OLD NINE HOLE KINGSBARNS LINKS WHICH EFFECTIVELY CEASED IN 1939 WHEN THE MINISTRY OF DEFENCE TOOK OVER THE LAND.

Kyle Philips and Mark Parsinen have achieved a magnificent links experience where you are always aware of the sea as you play along the one and a half miles of coastline. There is a tiered affect so that the holes furthest from the sea are raised just enough to give you views across the course and a feeling of still being close to the shoreline.

The opening hole is a lovely par 4 of 388 yards from the medal tee. It curves right and downhill and even though the sea is some hundreds of yards away you feel you are playing to a seaside green.

All the par 3's at Kingsbarns are quite different. The 2nd is my favourite. The 190 yards runs to the sea with magnificent views across the water back towards St Andrews. A slight fade aimed at the front left side will help you avoid the bunkers here.

The 3rd hole may be a short par 5 but if it is windy then the tee shot can be very demanding with seaside dunes and thick rough running all the way on the right side.

The 5th is a really high quality, shortish par 4. A precise second shot is needed if you are to avoid the bunker and grassy knoll and then stay on the green.

It is worth standing on the 6th tee for a few minutes and observing the brilliance of the course design. The tiered concept gives you the feeling of a very natural symmetry in what was the location of the original course. This is not a long par 4 but the green is at an unusual angle and there are two fairway bunkers right where you want to hit your drive. Watch out for the burn which runs behind and which separates the 6th and 16th greens.

There are no arguments that the 7th should be rated index one. It is 436 yards from the medal tee (470 from the championship tee) and has a very tricky green which is well guarded with hollows and bunkers.

The par 3, 8th is testing from the men's tee, mainly due to two very large and deep bunkers. However the ladies tee is too far forward and also provides a very easy line into the green so much so that the hole is very much a non event by comparison with the others on the course.

When I first visited Kingsbarns in 2003, my only other criticism was the 9th green which had large mounds and was almost unplayable when there was any wind. Since then they have twice reduced the height of the mounds and the problem has been largely eliminated. Nevertheless it is still a tricky shot to hold this green. It is hard to believe, but in the 2003 Dunhill Links Tournament, Lee Westwood, holed his second here for an albatross on the 558 yard par 5.

The 10th offers a little respite and is one of the easier holes. There are no bunkers on this par 4 but it is still accuracy that counts.

Picturesque opening hole at Kingsbarns

9th green and clubhouse

All four players in this group were lucky the tide was out at the par 3, 15th

Photos David Worley

The 12th to 14th holes are on a separate piece of land furthest from the clubhouse. Twelve is an attractive and challenging par 5, running right along the beach edge. The landing area for your second is very narrow with the sea on the left and bunkers and dunes on the right. This is a very long par 5 and is rated index number 2.

Thirteen is a lovely par 3, very reminiscent of 'Whinnie Brae' the 6th at Royal Dornoch. Landing on the green is not too difficult, but staying on it is another matter. Fourteen is a good example of the fun of playing a short par 4. Birdie is a chance if you drive safely but three fairway bunkers, cleverly staggered in distance from the tee, can bring you to grief.

I can't make up my mind about the par 3, 15th. You hit across the edge of the sea even if the pin is left or you have to hit a very long fade if the flag is on the right edge of the green. This is not an easy hole at 185 yards from the medal tee and on a windy day it is not uncommon to see all four players

miss the green and end up in the rocks or the sea, depending upon the tide. It is a very scenic hole but I am not so sure of its architectural merits.

All of the par 5's at Kingsbarns are very good and the 16th is no exception as you tee off from the water's edge. Be careful not to be through the green as there is a burn in play that you cannot see until after you reach the green.

The last two holes provide a very strong finish. The 17th is a very long par 4 with an uphill second shot that often runs into the greenside bunker on the right. Eighteen is another long par 4, this time with a blind tee shot. Unless you are long off the tee then you will need to lay up with your second. A burn runs about 30 yards in front of the green which sits above an almost vertical bank. This is real decision time and the wrong choice could add quite a few more to your score.

The conditioning of Kingsbarns fairways and bunkers is immaculate. The greens are also first class and very demanding. They are long, quite fast and have many large undulations so any one of them presents a three putt possibility. If you want to play five star links golf then this is it, notwithstanding the very minor shortcomings I have previously mentioned. Many new courses are launched with a fanfare of hype and often slide down the rankings after the first few years. Not so Kingsbarns. This course is every bit as good as the PR material and would have to be rated as one of the very best courses anywhere in Scotland. Traditionalists will be pleased to know that there are no motorised carts at Kingsbarns.

Photos David Worley

The long par 4, 17th, part of a strong finish at Kingsbarns

18th green with the burn running below the steep bank

Great credit must go to the owners and designers for what they have achieved.

CRAIL – BALCOMIE LINKS

Photo David Worley

15th green from the clubhouse

FORMED IN 1786, THIS IS THE 7TH OLDEST GOLF CLUB IN THE WORLD.

However the Balcomie Links dates back to 1895 when Tom Morris designed the additions to an 8 hole course already in existence on private land.

Until relatively recently it was a rather odd layout with one par 3 on the front nine but five on the homeward nine. The balance is now slightly better with two on the first nine but there is still the problem of four par 3's in the last six holes.

Don't let that deter you because the Old Course at Balcomie is a fun experience with some tricky holes due to some steep hills and the ever present wind.

All is before you on the short par 4 first hole as you hit downhill toward the coastline. With the hard summer greens it is hard to chip over the front bunker and hold the green. You will then be surprised to find a small burn right behind the green on the left side. The smart play is to drive left and come in from that angle.

The second, a par 5 from the back tee (and a par 4 from the forward tee), can be quite testing with the sea all along the right hand side. I played the par 3, 3rd hole with rather gay abandon which was very much a case of 'ignorance is bliss' as the cliff edge is much closer to the green than you realise when standing on the tee.

Four and five both necessitate driving over the edge of the North Sea, but the fifth is by far the harder and is aptly named 'Hell's Hole'. It is very difficult to know how much of the corner to take on with your tee shot. The long second shot is made more difficult by the requirement of great accuracy into a green that slopes from left to right and front to back. This means that if you play safe and push your second shot short and left so as to avoid the beach, you will have an extremely difficult pitch.

The 7th and 8th holes are both par 4's where the main danger is in hitting out of bounds into the farmland along the right hand boundary.

The 13th, like the 18th, is a par 3 where you may well need driver into the wind. Thirteen is up hill heading back to the clubhouse. If you are too long and right then you will find yourself out of bounds in the carpark. Two par 3's back to back is unusual but the two holes are very different. The 14th, 'The Cave', frequently features in photographs. The tee is high on a hill just below the first tee. Distance is hard to judge but you must carry the two greenside bunkers at the front. A strong left to right breeze could put you in the smaller third bunker which is beside the green on the right or, worse still, you may finish on the beach.

You then proceed on a pathway along the water's edge to the last four holes that are on a separate piece of land set below the clubhouse lounge for all to see.

Fifteen is a short par 4 with few problems unless you hook badly to the sea cliff on the left. The 16th is a straight out scary hole. 'Spion Kop' is a par 3 of 162 yards up a steep hill. There is gorse in front of you if you duff your tee shot. The elevated green is very wind exposed. Anything even slightly left is either in thick gorse or down a cliff. Par here is very satisfying.

The 17th is the longest par 4 at 462 yards and is rated index number 2. Downwind it can play much shorter but you must be careful not to finish on the gravel walkway which is part of the course and is only a few yards behind the green.

Eighteen is a long par 3 of 205 yards that may need driver some days. The tee shot looks more difficult than it really is due to the large bank of gorse that you must carry. There is plenty of room if you miss the green on either side but missing left on the high side will give you a more difficult chip.

Par 3, 14th 'The Cave'

Balcomie is definitely lots of fun. There are not too many bunkers for the tee shot on the longer holes, probably because wind is the principal hazard on most days. A number of tees and greens are quite close together but this is not unusual on the older links where the parcel of land available is often quite small.

CRAIL – CRAIGHEAD LINKS

Craighead Links – thick rough and plenty of wind

THE NEW COURSE AT CRAIL WAS DESIGNED BY THE AMERICAN, GIL HANSE, AND OPENED FOR PLAY IN 1998.

Situated above the old Balcomie Links, Craighead is even more exposed to the wind than its neighbour. The greens are excellent and the fairways are hard and very linksy. The bunkering is well placed but is not overdone. Whilst fairways are generally fairly wide, the primary rough was quite long and thick on the June day when I played there.

In summer be prepared to land some of your shots well short of the green if you want to be using your putter next.

There are some tough par 4's here with three of them each being in excess of 450 yards. The par 3's were a real feature with the 13th and 17th being outstanding. The 160 yard 13th plays to a green with a gully and then a steep cliff very close to the left edge. This area is also out of bounds. In the wind this is as hard an index 18 as you will ever encounter. The 197 yard 17th features the best bunkering on the links. With the breeze behind you it is almost impossible to fly the front bunkers and then hold the green.

Most of the greens on the Craighead, in complete contrast to the Balcomie Links, are very undulating. On the back nine some are also raised with mounds toward the centre. This makes it difficult to get close to the flag, even more so in the wind.

A deliberate design feature at Craighead is that there are no two consecutive holes running in the same direction. This will keep you constantly guessing if, as I did, you play Craighead in what our member friend said was a "7 out of 10 wind".

Photo David Worley

Craighead Links

In short, this is a fun course to play and, to be honest, in every aspect, it was much better than I had expected.

ST ANDREWS BAY
(NOW CALLED FAIRMONT ST ANDREWS) – TORRANCE COURSE

Photo courtesy John Cornish

The 18th is a long par 5 that dog-legs left

ST ANDREWS BAY IS LOCATED IN A QUIET COASTAL FARMING AREA BETWEEN THE TOWN OF ST ANDREWS AND KINGSBARNS. THE HOTEL, CONFERENCE CENTRE AND TWO COURSES OCCUPY A TOTAL AREA OF 520 ACRES. THE TORRANCE COURSE (DESIGNED BY SAM TORRANCE) OPENED FOR PLAY IN 2001.

'Sam's Favourite' the 448 yard par 4 17th, rated index number 1

This is a really good test of golf with fairly penal rough. There are sea views from most holes and at dusk the lights of St Andrews can be seen not far down the coast.

Although the course has the look of a links course, my only criticism would be that when I played there the fairway grass did not seem to be the usual fescue and the ball did not run as you would expect.

Holes 1-6 are around the hotel and conference centre with a burn in play, especially on the 1st and 3rd holes. These six holes are more inland and have less of a links feel.

The first really difficult hole comes at the 7th, a long par 4 of 461 yards and rated index number 2. The 9th is a good par 4 which returns close to the clubhouse, a feature that is rare on the old out and back style links.

The 12th and 14th holes are both tough par 4's of well over 400 yards. Fourteen is at the furthest point from the clubhouse and has a most attractive outlook as you head directly towards the sea. Almost right at the edge of this green is a long drop down a densely vegetated cliff running down to the beach. This is followed by a long par 3 very exposed to the wind from the sea along the left side.

The 17th, 'Sam's Favourite' is part of a strong finish. Out of bounds by way of the sea runs all the way along the right with only a three foot stone wall between the fairway and the steep seaside cliff. About 40 yards short of the green a large ravine bites into almost the centre of the fairway.

Eighteen is a long par 5 with a sharp dog-leg left for the third shot to a green that usually is subject to the ever present wind.

The back nine seems considerably harder, partly due to an extra 200 yards in length. The tees are very well presented with a choice of three for the men. Given that this course plays long, the ladies tees were thoughtfully placed a fair way forward but still provided a good test. On a windy day it can be quite spectacular watching from the hotel or clubhouse as the different coloured grasses in the rough wave in an almost mesmerising pattern from side to side. The Torrance Course should get even better as the fairways become more firm and fast running. Carts are not permitted here. You can comfortably walk the Torrance in under four hours.

ST ANDREWS BAY
(NOW CALLED FAIRMONT ST ANDREWS) – DEVLIN COURSE

Photo David Worley

The clifftop links Devlin Course is very wind exposed

DESIGNED BY AUSTRALIAN, BRUCE DEVLIN, THIS COURSE OPENED IN 2002. IT IS MORE OF A CLIFFTOP LINKS AND, ALTHOUGH IT DID NOT LOOK AS TRADITIONAL A LINKS COURSE AS THE TORRANCE, I FOUND THE FAIRWAYS MORE OF A LINKS NATURE.

17th green from left of the fairway

This course is well bunkered, at times features long rough and has first class greens, some of which are quite large. You need a cart here as there are some long distances from greens to tees, partly due to the fact that in the middle of the course there is a large area known as Kittock's Den which is unusable for golf.

As with the Torrance, the first 6 holes are more inland with ponds featuring as hazards on the 2nd and 3rd holes. The sea vistas begin from the very pretty par 5, 7th hole. The 9th and 12th share a large double green right on the edge of the clifftop. A hook on the 9th will send you over the cliff whereas a slice on the 12th will have the same result. Both fairways are very well bunkered around the approach area.

The 11th is another attractive hole with the green right on the cliff edge and out of bounds all along the right. Into the prevailing wind, the 13th is a difficult par 5 as it is also uphill.

The two finishing holes are fun and challenging with stone walls, bunkers and beautiful sea views all part of the package. Seventeen is a long par 4 requiring a blind tee shot over the crest of a hill. You then have a long downhill second to the seaside green, but watch out for the ravine (part of Kittock's Den) on your right. Although this is a testing par 4 for men (443 yards from medal tee), the ladies tee was too far forward reducing the hole to only 279 yards, mostly downhill.

The 18th is a par 3 of 182 yards running right along the cliff edge on your right. The green is well bunkered and there is a stone wall left and at the back. On a windy day, hitting the green here can be quite an achievement.

The Devlin provides for plenty of variety. Ponds on the 2nd and 3rd , Kittock's Den with an out of bounds stone wall in play on holes 7, 14, 16 and 17 and spectacular scenery from most parts of the course. Judging distances, especially to the greens along the sea, can be quite tricky in the wind.

The Devlin is perhaps not quite as difficult as the Torrance but is enjoyable to play and has some memorable holes along the coastline. A minor criticism is the placing of the ladies tees which were often a long way forward to the point of being ridiculous on the 18th which was reduced to an 87 yard par 3.

The two finishing holes are fun and challenging with stone walls, bunkers and beautiful sea views all part of the package

LUNDIN

14th tee – the furthest point from the clubhouse

Photo courtesy Ian Gust

A slight draw is ideal for the drive onto the opening hole

THE LUNDIN GOLF CLUB CAME INTO BEING IN 1868. AFTER A PERIOD OF INACTIVITY THE CLUB RE-EMERGED IN 1889, SHARING THE LINKS WITH THE MEMBERS OF LEVEN. BY 1907 THE TWO CLUBS HAD 1400 MEMBERS AND A DECISION WAS MADE TO SEPARATE THE TWO.

Two years later the members of Lundin had a new course laid out by James Braid. Essentially, this consisted of 9 holes from the original course (more or less holes 1-5 and 15-18 on the present course) and a new nine from land previously occupied by the Lundin Ladies Golf Club to the north of the railway line. When the railway line ceased running in the 1960's, the club purchased the land which was in the middle of the course, and which now forms an internal out of bounds.

The opening four holes run along the sea and are lovely old fashioned links holes. Four is by far the most difficult being a par 4 of 455 yards with a burn in front of the green. The much photographed 5th is a charming little par 3 of just 141 yards. There is a burn short and left, gorse if you are too far right and the green has bunkers all around except for front left. With the sea breeze behind you it is easy to finish in one of the bunkers at the back of the green.

Six, seven and eight are short par 4's and are real birdie opportunities. However, they are all well bunkered and a burn is in play with your second shot on the 7th and 8th holes. The 9th is a par 5 and is easily the longest hole on the course at 555 yards. The front nine does not play long and, provided you are driving straight, is the easier of the two.

Ten and eleven have a shared fairway with the shot into the 10th green being from the middle of the 11th fairway over some very oddly shaped and angled bunkers. This is a strange hole – but it works.

The 12th is a par 4 of only 149 yards but it is up a very steep hill making club selection very confusing. The green is surrounded by seven bunkers. The main trouble here is if you miss too far right.

The 13th is another unusual hole that is on a plateau above the rest of the course and near the main highway. The tee is the highest point on the course. If you drive left you are in trouble with the fairway sloping that way and if you go right then you are either in thick trees or out of bounds over the fence. Your long second on this par 5 of 499 yards is through a narrow gap in the trees to a green with lush undergrowth close by. Your second shot may well leave you only 50 yards from the green but stymied by one of the many conifers.

Fourteen is a par 3 of 177 yards down a steep hill to a green right beside the dividing fence to the Leven Links. Not far behind is the green of the par 3, 5th. This is another well bunkered green especially with many balls running through the back. The 14th tee looks straight out to sea. From here you can see every tee and green on the course and right across Largo Bay with Gullane and North Berwick in the distant outline.

The last four holes, part of the original layout, are all par 4's. The 15th and 18th are reasonably long with the 16th and 17th being very tight driving holes. Into a strong wind the burn can be in play on these two holes.

The 18th is rated index number 6 but I would rank it as the most difficult. The tee is from the area of the old railway station. It is the long second to the green that presents all the danger. The fairway is very narrow with a road, thick rough and out of bounds on the left and the first tee area on the right. The green is long and narrow and is also well bunkered. I suspect many a good score has come to ruin here.

The charming short 5th

18th green and clubhouse – the second shot into the green is full of danger

Photos courtesy Ian Gust

At just 6371 yards Lundin is probably way too short for the professionals when trying to pre-qualify here when the Open is at St Andrews. But for the average golfer this is a wonderful example of old fashioned links golf. The fairways provide plenty of run in summer and the greens are firm and true. On a windy day it might be a little disconcerting in a few places where the fairways are either partly shared or run very close together.

LEVEN LINKS

Photo David Worley

LYING AT LARGO BAY RIGHT NEXT DOOR TO ITS NEIGHBOUR LUNDIN LINKS, LEVEN BOASTS THE OLDEST OPEN AMATEUR STROKEPLAY CHAMPIONSHIP IN THE WORLD – THE STANDARD LIFE ASSURANCE COMPANY'S AMATEUR MEDAL WHICH DATES BACK TO 1870.

Clubhouse and 18th green with the wide Scoonie Burn in front

As is the case at Lundin, the first four holes run along the beach but in the opposite direction. These are all par 4's with the 1st and 4th being the most difficult. You need to be left here with your tee shot, especially on the 1st, 3rd and 4th holes.

Interestingly, the short 5th runs parallel with the short 5th at Lundin on the other side of the fence. The next is by far the longest hole at 569 yards. Out of bounds by way of Silverburn Park on the right is a popular resting place for errant second shots especially.

Holes 7–10 form a rectangle at the north end of the course. The 7th is a par 3 of 182 yards from the back tee and has no less than ten bunkers. The par 4, 8th features a wall of gorse and the Scoonie Burn on the right.

The 12th should be an easy par 5 from the championship tee (496 yards) but is a very difficult par 4 of 476 yards from the normal men's tee. If you are playing Leven for the first time then beware of the burn at the back of the green. The 13th is another par 5/4 with only 11 yards less distance making it a long 4 of 471 yards.

The 15th is the only par 3 on the homeward nine. The green can prove tricky here with one professional taking 5 putts in the 2005 Open Qualifying.

The 18th at Leven is the hole you are most likely to remember. It is a tough par 4 of 457 yards with the wide Scoonie Burn running right in front of the apron of the green. The green is on a raised area supported by wooden sleepers. If you are unlucky enough your second shot might

clear the burn, hit the sleepers and rebound back into the water. A good drive is essential if you are to have any chance of carrying the burn. With the wind blowing it can also be quite difficult to judge distance if you decide to lay up and chip over the Scoonie for your third shot.

I suspect that Lundin finished up with slightly better links land but I would still recommend you experience Leven if you appreciate links golf.

THE GOLF HOUSE CLUB – ELIE

Photo David Worley

18th green and clubhouse – the submarine periscope used by the starter is at the left

THE CHARMING TOWN OF ELIE CAN BOAST TO HAVE BEEN THE HOME OF SOME VERY FAMOUS GOLFERS, JAMES BRAID AND THE SIX SIMPSON BROTHERS TO NAME A FEW, AND HAD ITS OWN 9 HOLE COURSE AS EARLY AS 1875. BY 1895, UNDER THE GUIDANCE OF TOM MORRIS, IT WAS INCREASED TO 18 HOLES AND IN 1921 JAMES BRAID RETURNED TO MAKE FURTHER IMPROVEMENTS. EVEN TODAY, THE LADIES CARD BEARS THE ORIGINAL NAME 'ELIE AND EARLSFERRY GOLF CLUB'.

This is a short course of 6273 yards and there are one or two quirky holes but it is lots of fun in true holiday golf of the links variety. In 1971 Kel Nagle managed to go around the par 70 links in just 62 shots.

The starting hole is unique in that you hit blind over a steep hill but you cannot tee off until given the all clear by the starter who has the aid of a genuine World War II submarine periscope. This is a good opening par 4 of 420 yards. The second is a mere 280 yards but is rated index 3. It is appropriately called 'High Hole' as the green is very elevated, wind exposed and is a difficult target to hold.

From the 6th hole you are closer to the sea although there is no real duneland here at Elie. Seven is a potential birdie opportunity and eight and nine are good par 4's.

The 10th is a short par 4 of 288 yards to a hidden green near the sea and down a steeply sloping fairway. If you don't quite get your drive to the downslope then you have a very delicate pitch in order not to run through the green. This is the start of the four lovely holes at the waters edge.

'Sea Hole', the short 11th, is only 131 yards but beware if the flag is left of centre. If you are only a few feet left of this green your ball will be heading down the bank to the beach.

The longest hole at Elie is the demanding 466 yard par 4, 12th. This is a wonderful hole which dog-legs left along the seashore. There is more room than you think if you drive right of centre, provided you avoid a couple of fairway bunkers.

The 13th is an uphill par 4 of 380 yards with a much photographed green that is right beside the sea and below the high cliffs containing McDuff's Cave. The green is raised and is slightly angled so getting on here for two is not easy.

The run home is all par 4's with the 17th providing the first views again of the clubhouse. The finishing hole is a medium length par 4 with a very well bunkered fairway that contains a swale which seems to always kick the ball to the right. A straight drive that avoids these hazards will leave you with just a short iron to the green.

Although there are hills, Elie is easy walking and the rough is not too penal. The greens are excellent and quite fast by Scottish standards. There are no par 5's and only two par 3's but, despite having 16 par 4's, the golf at Elie is never boring.

The 10th green is the first of four along the waters edge

A few feet left of the green at the par 3, 11th and you will finish on the beach

SCOTSCRAIG

Photo David Worley

The engaging 4th hole with a very tricky shot into the green

SITUATED NEAR THE TOWN OF TAYPORT JUST NORTH OF ST ANDREWS, SCOTSCRAIG'S ORIGINS DATE RIGHT BACK TO 1817 WHICH MAKES IT THE 13TH OLDEST GOLF CLUB IN THE WORLD.

One of the original designers was David Robertson father of Alan, the world's first ever golf professional. Changes were made in 1923 by the ubiquitous James Braid. Today Scotscraig is largely unchanged from the 1923 layout.

Some observers may consider Scotscraig to be more of a heathland course, possibly because you have no sensation of being anywhere near the sea. In reality parts of the course are but a few hundred yards from the sea, and, although some fairways are tree lined , the sandy soiled fairways provide all the running you would expect on any true links.

Since 1984 Scotscraig has been a qualifying course for the Open at St Andrews. For events such as this, the use of tiger tees stretches the course to 6669 yards compared with 6310 from the members' tees and 6550 from normal competition tees.

The opening hole is an excellent start to the round. Whilst this is a straight par 4 of 402 yards from the competition tee, the drive is quite tight and is made more so by heather clad mounds on the left and a ridge running down the middle of the fairway which tends to kick anything hit with a fade towards the right into the heather or rough.

The 3rd is a long par 3 of 214 yards with a rather oddly shaped bunker on the left side of the green. The fourth is my pick as the best at Scotscraig. It is a par 4 of just 366 yards and yet it is rated index number one. Your drive must be accurate in order to avoid bushes and gorse on the right and a beautifully revetted bunker on the left. The green is quite small and is raised above the fairway with a large pot bunker front right. A poor second shot that is short could finish up in a heather filled gully. If you are too long then you may even finish out of bounds which is close by. Anything slightly right is in the pot bunker or may bounce into the heather and rough. This is a very attractive hole visually as well as being a fun challenge.

The 7th, 'Plateau', is another very good par 4 with a semi heathland feel about it. Accuracy is essential with the safe approach from the tee being to play the right side away from the line of conifers. The front nine finishes with a birdie opportunity on this short par 5. Be careful not to cut off too much of the left hand corner as the gorse will be waiting for you.

Photo David Worley

Approaching the green on the 402 yard par 4, 1st hole at Scotscraig

The par 5, 14th is one of the best holes on the inward nine. Positioning of each shot is important if you're going to be on this green in three. Seventeen is a par 4 with a dog-leg left. You need to be right with your tee shot so as to open up the green but beware of the fairway bunkers on this side.

The closing nine holes are rather flat and a little more open than the front nine which I feel is a far more interesting proposition with not a weak hole. From the competition tees there are three par 5's. However, from the forward men's tees both the 9th and 16th become long par 4's with a reduction of a mere 26 yards in total from the par 5 rating.

Scotscraig will test your accuracy and represents a nice change from the more traditional open and wind swept links.

NORTH BERWICK – WEST LINKS

Photo David Worley

The 14th 'Perfection' – the green is over the hill in front of the marker post at the left – stray drives from the 14th land on the 4th green on the right

Photo David Worley

THE CLUB WAS FOUNDED IN 1832 AND HAS A PROUD HISTORY OF DISTINGUISHED PAST CAPTAINS INCLUDING A FORMER BRITISH PRIME MINISTER, A G BALFOUR. NEAR THE FIRST TEE STILL STANDS BEN SAYERS' WORKSHOP. SAYERS WAS A LOCAL IDENTITY, RENOWNED CLUB MANU-FACTURER AND TEACHER, AND HAD THE DISTINCTION OF PLAYING 43 CONSECUTIVE OPEN CHAMPIONSHIPS FROM 1880 TO 1923.

4th green and Fidra Island – Robert Louis Stevenson used to row out to this island as a child – it subsequently became the inspiration for his famous book, "Treasure Island"

North Berwick itself is a lovely seaside village and coastal harbour.

So popular became North Berwick that on one day in 1903 it is recorded that on the West Links at the one time there were "the Prime Minister, the Speaker of the House of Commons, four Members of Parliament, two Bishops of the Church of England, three eminent professors and Field Marshal, two Generals and a famous Tibetan explorer".

North Berwick itself is a lovely seaside village and coastal harbour. On a still day whilst you are waiting your turn on the first tee, you cannot help but feel relaxed by the surrounding scenery. But be warned, it can also be a windy and exposed course.

Generally, the rough is not too penal but there are plenty of bunkers on the holes where the fairways are a little wider. No two holes are alike and you are bound to want to play here again as one round is not enough to take in all the unusual features.

The opening hole, 'Point Garry Out', is probably only a little difficult when you are playing it first time and have less idea of distances. Although it is a par 4, you have to hold back with your tee shot to avoid a nasty gully before playing up to the elevated green. The opening three holes all have the sea as out of bounds on your right hand side.

The tee shot on the second requires a steady nerve as you cut across the corner of the rocks and beach. You then have a long second which must carry a bunker guarding the front of the green. The burn on the third hole is only in play for a very poor drive. You have a long second shot which must clear a stone wall running across the fairway. This wall also continues across to the 16th hole and acts as a hazard for the drive.

The 4th is an appealing par 3 of 175 yards with a narrow two-tiered and sunken green. The biggest danger here is being hit by an errant ball from the 14th tee nearby. The 6th is another par 3, aptly named 'Quarry', and you will know why when you see the bunkers. Holes 6-9 all have out of bounds along the left side.

Seven is a potentially easy par 4, but be careful as you cannot see the Eil Burn which runs across the fairway just short of the green.

As the whole course is on a fairly narrow strip of coastal land, it is quite a long walk to the furthermost point around the 10th tee. The 9th is a par 5 slightly up hill and with a number of pot bunkers which should be avoided. Eleven and twelve are good holes but the four from the 13th-16th are great fun to play and possibly quite different to anything you have seen before.

Photo David Worley

At the par 4, 13th 'Pit' you have to play over the stone wall that is right at the edge of the green

The 13th, 'Pit' is a short par 4 of 365 yards but a very old stone wall about three feet high runs parallel and blocks the narrow green. You have no option but to chip over it unless you can land your long second on to this precise target. Hole number fourteen is named 'Perfection'. It is not a long par 4 but the second shot is up hill to a partly obscured green. A large bunker lies at the base of the hill. Some 50 yards over the hill is the green almost on the beach and with Craigleith and Bass Rock in the background this is a very pretty spot, particularly late in the day.

The par 3, 15th, 'Redan' hole is believed to be the most copied in golf. It is reasonably long at 192 yards with a green that is at a 45 degree angle, elevated, and guarded by several large deep bunkers. From the tee you really cannot tell much about the pin position and with different winds the club selection will vary enormously. The 16th, 'Gate', is much harder than it looks. A par 4 of 381 yards, the tee shot is over a stone wall with out of bounds running down the right side due to the adjacent children's practice course. The drive also needs a carry of about 180-200 yards to clear the burn. The shot into the green sums up North Berwick West and old fashioned links golf. The green is virtually in two sections with a deep gully of about 3 feet right across the centre. The green is also at an angle to the fairway with the approach featuring a large ridge which will kick most low running shots to the left. If the wind is from behind then a lofted shot has almost no chance of holding the front section of the green. You can watch this green for hours and I can guarantee that very few finish anywhere near the flag.

The par 4, 17th, can require a tough second shot up hill and frequently in to the wind to a green that, according to Bernard Darwin, in the early 1900's was joined to the first as a double green. The 18th is probably the weakest hole on the course. It is only 274 yards long with a plateau'd green some 50 yards from the charming clubhouse. With cars parked along the road on the right hand boundary it is rather like the last hole at St Andrews.

If you are going on a golfing holiday to Scotland then North Berwick West just has to be on your must play list. The course is always in top condition and the quirky holes all work wonderfully well here.

Photo David Worley

16th green and 17th fairway with Bass Rock in the distance

MUIRFIELD

Photo David Worley

Beautiful bunkering at the 2nd green

THE HONOURABLE COMPANY OF EDINBURGH GOLFERS CAN TRACE THEIR ORIGINS BACK TO 1744 WHEN THEY WROTE THE ORIGINAL 13 RULES OF GOLF. THE CLUB MOVED TO ITS PRESENT HOME IN 1891 WHEN THE OLD TOM MORRIS COURSE WAS READY FOR PLAY. THE LAYOUT OF TODAY HOWEVER IS MORE REFLECTIVE OF THE ALTERATIONS MADE IN 1928 BY HARRY COLT AND TOM SIMPSON.

Muirfield has the unique distinction of being the only course to have hosted the Open, the British Amateur, Ryder Cup, Walker Cup and the Curtis Cup.

Although not right on the sea, several holes are within just a few hundred yards of the beach. Muirfield has beautiful springy turf fairways, wonderful bunkers and greens that are in quality always close to the best in Scotland.

An unusual design feature is that the two nines run in concentric rings with the first nine occupying the outer edge. This ensures the wind direction constantly varies and helps create the feeling that there are few others on the course.

The 1st hole is a strong par 4 of 446 yards and is typical of the 6 par 4's at Muirfield that are all in excess of 440 yards. Five of these holes make up the five hardest holes on the stroke index.

The 2nd is one of the few short par 4's. This is a very pretty hole which runs towards the sea which is several hundred yards away. The green nestles beside a stone wall and is beautifully bunkered on the right. Birdie is a real chance here but don't let this lull you into a sense of false security, as the next seven holes are very challenging.

The second shot to the green is the key to the 3rd hole. A bunker and high grassy mound are around thirty yards short of the green on the left whilst another mound is beside the green on the right hand side.

All the par 3's are very good at Muirfield and the 182 yard 4th is one of the best of the four. Anything more than a few yards short will almost certainly be bunkered as will any ball that is not hit dead straight. You can't see many of the bunkers from the tee but they are in all the right places.

The 5th is a demanding par 5. It is only 510 yards but it plays uphill and has thick rough on both sides and a line of bunkers about 100 yards out on the left side of the fairway. Somehow Johnny Miller managed to hole out in two here in the second round of the 1972 Open Championship.

Six is a dog-leg left heading towards Archerfield Wood. If you try to cut off too much of the left corner you may be bunkered or too far right and you will be faced with a very difficult second to the green as there are a number of small bunkers and hollows protecting the right hand side. It is not unusual to see deer in the long grass near this green.

The par 3, 7th is slightly uphill to an elevated green from which there are views across the neighbouring sea – a rarity at Muirfield. The par 4, 8th is the same length (443 yards) as

This is a tough but very fair test of golf. Play Muirfield on a sunny summer's day in the late afternoon and you could not wish for more.

Photo David Worley

Par 3, 7th from behind the green. The two new courses at Archerfield are in the estate behind the trees.

the 6th but dog-legs to the right. There is a formidable cluster of bunkers on the right hand corner and a large cross bunker short of the green.

The 9th used to be a par 5 but now is a very tough par 4 of 465 yards. You are constantly aware of out of bounds which runs the full length of the left hand side. If the rough is long (especially in very early summer) you will be hard pressed to see any of the bunkers on the edge of the fairway. There is also a hidden bunker near the middle of the fairway about 40 yards from the green. The safer approach is actually to the left side near the out of bounds stone wall.

There is no respite at the 10th, a par 4 of 473 yards. The very first time I played Muirfield was after a wet spring and we teed off first from the 10th. The fairway was a narrow ribbon with three feet high grass on both sides and the hole was playing directly into a cool wind. I can't remember a more difficult introduction to a golf course.

Twelve is a lovely looking par 4 played slightly down hill. Gullane Hill is in line with the green in the far distance whilst to the right there are views to the sea. None of the greens at Muirfield are very large and most, like the 12th, are heavily protected with numerous small pot bunkers. There are five on the right side and two on the left of this green.

The par 3, 13th, features a distinctly raised green sandwiched between two small dunes. Fifteen is another wonderful par 4 with bunkers galore on the fairway and around the green. At the back of the green lies a very large boomerang shaped bunker. Into the wind the par 3, 16th (186 yards) can be a difficult proposition with thick rough on either side.

The 17th, the second of the two par 5's, is a very interesting hole. It features a big dog-leg left and two separate clusters of bunkers. The first group are all located for any tee shot pulled too far left. The second body of bunkers runs right across the fairway so as to catch the second shot.

The par 4, 18th is one of the classic finishing holes in golf. A hint of draw from the tee is ideal as the fairway proper is slightly angled from the tee. Provided you miss the two fairway bunkers on the left then, for the average golfer, you need a long second which has to avoid two bunkers at the approach near the centre of the fairway and one bunker either side. The long bunker at the right can be nasty if you finish near the face or the grass island which may stop your backswing.

I have read reviews that have described Muirfield as overrated or dull. I suspect these critics would make similar comments about Royal Troon and Carnoustie. Muirfield doesn't have towering dunes (primarily the domain of the Irish links) nor does it have holes running right alongside the sea. But it does have a brilliant layout, wonderfully disguised bunkers (about 151 in total), and fairways and greens that are second to none. It also satisfies another important criteria – there are no two holes the same.

This is a tough but very fair test of golf. Play Muirfield on a sunny summer's day in the late afternoon and you could not wish for more.

Photo David Worley

View from the 7th tee with Fidra Island in the distance

Photo courtesy Alastair Brown

18th green and clubhouse in February

GULLANE – No. 1 COURSE

Photo David Worley

Gullane No. 1 course – 1st hole

HISTORY RECORDS THAT GOLF WAS PLAYED HERE AS FAR BACK AS 1650. THE GULLANE GOLF CLUB WAS HOWEVER, NOT ESTABLISHED UNTIL 1882 WITH THE NUMBER 1 COURSE, DESIGNED BY WILLIE PARK, BEING READY FOR PLAY TWO YEARS LATER.

Apart from the town of St Andrews, nothing typifies the feel of Scottish golf better than the lovely little village of Gullane. You literally just walk a few yards from the quiet main street and there are the three courses waiting for you.

The No. 1 course is the best of the three and has hosted numerous tournaments. It is also usually used for qualifying when the Open is held nearby at Muirfield.

From the 1st tee (right beside the main road A198) you see only the first two holes heading up Gullane Hill and the 18th on your left with its green seemingly dangerously close to the passing traffic.

The 1st is a gentle par 4 but the 2nd is up a steeper hill and requires a longer second shot to the narrow sloping green.

Holes 3-6 are a slow climb to the peak at 'Queens Head', the spectacular par 4, 7th. The 3rd, 'Racecourse', is one of the best holes on these links. This par 5 of 496 yards runs along the path of what was a racecourse in the18th century. The 5th hole is a difficult severe dog-leg par 4 of 450 yards all uphill, and is appropriately rated index one. The course continues its uphill path on the short par 4, 6th where you reach the highest section and definitely one of the best views you will ever see on a golf course.

From the elevated tee of the 7th you have a magnificent view down to Aberlady Bay.

To your right is Muirfield. Straight ahead are the rippling fairways of Gullane No. 1 and No. 2 courses. Slightly left and further away lies Gullane No. 3, Luffness New, Kilspindie and Craigielaw. You won't be able to resist opening your shoulders on this tee shot but everywhere on Gullane 1 there are plenty of small pot bunkers and the rough can be quite daunting. On one occasion when I was there, the grass was nearly four feet high between the 2nd and 18th fairways.

The 8th and par 3, 9th are the holes closest to the seashore in one of the prettiest parts of the links.

Three long holes await you at the turn with ten and eleven being very tough par 4's at 466 yards and 471 yards respectively. The back nine presents a more difficult set of holes and the two par 3's, the 13th and 16th, are no exception given their length and bunkering. The 15th, 'Pumphouse,' is a challenging, heavily bunkered, dog-leg par 5 with a sloping green.

2nd green looking back to Gullane Village

Par 5, 3rd hole 'Racecourse' just before sunset

Photos David Worley

The course is beautifully maintained and is quite a stiff test, especially in the wind.

The 17th tee affords another wonderful view, this time looking back to the village of Gullane and North Berwick in the distance. This shortish par 4 is downhill all the way, but there are three bunkers in the middle of the fairway and two greenside bunkers to be avoided.

The 18th is still slightly downhill and at only 355 yards is a rather easy par 4 provided your drive avoids the four fairway bunkers and thick rough which is very penal for any errant shots.

Gullane No. 1 is hillier than most Scottish links courses but the holes are not too demanding. The course is beautifully maintained and is quite a stiff test, especially in the wind. If you can't get a game at Muirfield, then be assured, this is the next best thing.

Photo David Worley

7th green – from the elevated 7th tee you can see seven courses

GULLANE – No. 2 COURSE

Photo David Worley

The A198 is out of bounds only a few feet from the 17th green on the near side and the 1st green on the far side of the road

OPENED IN 1898, THE NO. 2 COURSE MEASURES 6244 YARDS, SOME 222 YARDS SHORTER THAN NO. 1. FROM THE PUBLIC CLUBHOUSE YOU SEE ONLY THE 1ST AND 18TH, TWO RATHER FLAT AND UNINTERESTING LOOKING HOLES ON THE EAST SIDE OF THE A198.

O nce you cross the road there is a wonderful variety of holes, some reasonably hilly. The first seven holes run alongside the No.1 course and then they head more towards Aberlady Bay.

Into the wind, the first two holes can play considerably longer than their modest yardage would suggest. The 3rd hole is uphill but is a very short par 4 of just 237 yards. Provided you drive straight then you will be close to the green with a great birdie chance.

The easy 3rd is followed by a long par 4 of 425 yards and rated index one. This is a really good hole and features no less than five bunkers in front of the green. The 5th is the only par 3 on the outward nine so you need to par this hole to keep your score respectable. The 7th is a good par 4 heading towards the water in the distance and the 9th is another well bunkered par 4.

The long par 3, 11th (215 yards) is one of the best holes on No. 2. The tee shot is downhill with thick rough on the left side to a green guarded by five small bunkers at the front and several more at the back.

The 13th is a tough uphill par 4 of 400 yards. There are two deep little pot bunkers at about 130 yards out from the green. Trouble awaits if you stray from the fairway here.

Par 3, 11th at Gullane No. 2

The 17th has the same wonderful views as its counterpart on the No. 1 course. Although 361 yards in length, down the steep hill this hole is very driveable but beware as the A198 is literally only a few yards behind this green. You cross over the road to the 18th tee to return to the public clubhouse. At only 305 yards, this par 4 presents a very real birdie prospect as you should only have a wedge for your second. Provided you drive straight then the only danger is when the flag is short right where there is a deep bunker in front of the green and a large mound at the front right.

The No. 2 course is not far behind No. 1 in terms of quality and degree of difficulty. A number of the holes are similar to those on No. 1 which is not surprising given it is essentially the same land. The greens at No. 2 are excellent and, in general, the course provided for more variety than I had expected. The bunkers here are quite small so invariably you find yourself right up against the sides or front wall with little means of escape.

It may not have the reputation of the No. 1 course, but you won't walk off disappointed after you have experienced No. 2.

GULLANE - No. 3 COURSE

Photo David Worley

THE NO. 3 COURSE OPENED IN 1910. IT MAY NOT BE DEMANDING IN LENGTH AT ONLY 5252 YARDS, BUT IT FEATURES MANY OF THE ATTRIBUTES OF THE NO. 1 AND NO. 2 COURSES.

The first and last three holes lie on the east side of the A198 and perhaps mislead you into thinking there is not much variety here. However the remaining twelve holes are all interesting and have excellent views across Aberlady Bay.

Although there is just the one par 5, the 15th, its lack of length is offset by the fact that it is uphill. The greens are excellent but are somewhat smaller that the No.1 and No. 2 so this can be a good warm up to test your accuracy.

The village of Gullane is only a few yards from the 1st tee – the area to the left of the photo is quaintly named Goose Green

KILSPINDIE

Photo David Worley

Short par 4, 18th – the green is just to the left of the wall near the Clubhouse windows

KILSPINDIE WAS PROBABLY DESIGNED BY OLD TOM MORRIS (NO-ONE SEEMS QUITE SURE) AND, DATING BACK TO 1867, IT IS THE 35TH OLDEST GOLF CLUB IN THE WORLD.

Don't let the total length of just 5480 yards mislead you. This is a wonderful course to hone your accuracy and have lots of fun. And when the wind blows (as it usually does) off Aberlady Bay you may find some of these holes play a little longer than the card would suggest.

The rough can get quite long and on most holes seems to be at its worst on the right hand side. Conversely bunkers are often more predominant on the left.

The opening hole is a par 3, well bunkered, and often plays directly into the wind. The next three are literally right along the

Photo David Worley

Kilspindie starts with a par 3 before two good holes along the edge of the sea

water's edge. The 2nd hole is the only par 5 and can require a very demanding tee shot. By the time you have completed the narrow 415 yard 3rd you will have begun to realise that Kilspindie is no pushover.

The par 4, 7th has five bunkers waiting for you on the left side. If there is a standout hole it is probably the 8th. A par 3 of 162 yards, it follows the coastline of Gosford Bay. As the hole curves right and the wind is often from offshore then you have to be brave enough to start your ball out over the water.

The first eight are possibly the best but there are some interesting holes on the back nine, especially the 16th, 17th and 18th. The 16th is a par 4 of 412 yards with eleven bunkers, mainly on your left. Downwind this hole plays quite short. The approach to the short par 4, 17th requires you play over the remnants of a stone wall.

The 18th will intrigue you. This is a very short par 4 of 252 yards and slightly downhill. Yes, the green is driveable but there are several things to consider. The clubhouse is so close to the back of the green that you are thinking about the consequences of over hitting. A low hook will hit a stone wall. A slice will be out of bounds on the adjoining course, Craigielaw. A tee shot aimed directly at the green may catch a large bunker or, worse still, finish behind another stone wall just to the front right of the green. The perfect shot is to aim for the left of the clubhouse with a very slight fade.

Kilspindie represents unpretentious, old fashioned links golf and there is much to be said in favour of that.

LUFFNESS NEW

Photo David Worley

THE FAIRWAYS AT LUFFNESS AT TIMES SEEM TO BLEND IMPERCEPTIBLY INTO THOSE OF THE THREE COURSES OF GULLANE. DESIGNED BY TOM MORRIS, LUFFNESS NEW HAS BEEN ESTABLISHED SINCE 1894 AND IS FREQUENTLY USED FOR QUALIFYING ROUNDS WHEN THE OPEN IS AT MUIRFIELD.

Five holes are on the clubhouse side of the A198 but it is the holes that follow from the 6th out to Aberlady Bay that provide a lovely peaceful stretch of enjoyable links.

The 1st hole is a par 4 of modest length but it sets the scene for what is to come. The green is hidden by a row of raised bunkers that are some 30 yards short of the green so you can be fooled as to the distance of your second shot. The 3rd can be a rather tricky index number 17. This par 3 is 196 yards uphill and features several well placed bunkers.

The only par 5 is the 4th which runs back to the clubhouse. The 5th leads us to the busy road which must be crossed for the remaining thirteen holes. The green is frighteningly close to the road which runs along the left and at the back.

The 6th is one of the best holes at Luffness. This par 3 is only 155 yards but there is plenty to think about. The rough is very thick

The par 3, 6th is one of the best holes at Luffness

both short and left to the extent that a ball here is almost certainly lost. The shot is uphill and the green is surrounded by four strategically positioned pot bunkers.

I am rather puzzled that the 7th is rated the hardest hole on the course. It is a par 4 that requires a blind drive up a steep hill but, with a total length of only 293 yards, the green is driveable in summer.

As is the case on many holes at Luffness, the bunker positioning can make distance hard to judge on the par 3, 10th. There are three bunkers here but it is the wide bunker at the front that is quite a way back from the green that may lead you to underclubbing.

The 12th hole is a good looking short par 4 with the difficulty coming from the six fairway bunkers. Fourteen can be considerably more difficult than its index 12 rating. It is a reasonably long par 4 at 435 yards and the rough here is very punitive. Conversely, the 15th is rated the second hardest and is only 346 yards. The major danger is the four bunkers around the green.

The 16th is another excellent par 3 featuring six greenside bunkers including a large one at the front. Three raised bunkers about 50 yards short of the green are the feature of the par 4, 17th.

The final hole is a good finish at 416 yards, slight dog-leg left. This green has a number of grass mounds behind to help prevent balls from going on to the nearby road.

Luffness New is not overly long but is still a very good test of your golfing skills. The rough in places is quite penal. The bunkers are neat and well defined and the relatively small greens are very true. None of the greens are raised, they are all at fairway level so you can putt from well back on the fringe.

4th green and clubhouse

Don't make the mistake of overlooking Luffness during your visit to East Lothian.

CRAIGIELAW

Photo David Worley

Par 3, 10th

CRAIGIELAW ABUTS THE COURSE AT KILSPINDIE ON THE INLAND SIDE. DESIGNED BY TOM MCKENZIE OF DONALD STEEL & CO., THE COURSE OPENED FOR PLAY IN MAY 2001. THE LAND IS SLIGHTLY HIGHER THAN THAT OF NEIGHBOURING KILSPINDIE SO THERE ARE GOOD VIEWS OF ABERLADY BAY AND ACROSS TO GULLANE FROM MOST PARTS OF THE LINKS.

The fairways can get very hard and fast – a deliberate policy as there are no sprinklers other than on tees and greens. The bunkers are all quite deep and are very well placed. When I was there in late June, the course was very dry and it was difficult to lob any ball over the bunkers and then hold the green.

There are also a number of stone walls across parts of the fairways and the rough so that an errant drive is punished accordingly. None of the holes play long when the fairways get hard but it can be quite tricky to leave your ball in the right position for a short iron into the green.

The first hole plays tougher than its modest length of 327 yards from the back tee would

1st hole with Kilspindie Clubhouse and Aberlady Bay in the distance

Photo David Worley

suggest. There are two fairway bunkers just left of centre of the fairway and to the right is fairly thick rough. The green is crowned and gives you almost no option (because of the greenside bunkers) other than the aerial route.

The 4th, a par 5 of 583 yards is rated the most difficult. Several fairway bunkers are waiting and there is an angled stone wall as you get closer to the raised inverted saucer green. The par 3, 6th definitely favours the exponents of the draw. You hit over a stone wall to a green with deep bunkers at left front. As the wind is usually left to right then you will need to hit a draw or be very straight. There is danger at the par 4, 7th for any sliced tee shot in the form of a pond you can't see behind a stone wall and out of bounds on the right (by way of the neighbouring 18th fairway at Kilspindie) further along towards the green.

The 10th is a good par 3 of 174 yards with some stately houses in the background. It is very difficult to get up and down if you miss the green on the left. Whilst the 11th is a reasonably long par 5 of 540 yards, it is downhill and, in summer especially, may be reachable in two. However, due to the presence of a small burn in front of the green then you may be best to lay up with your second.

The course architect, Tom McKenzie names the 14th 'Gullane Hill' as his favourite. He comments: "Playing downhill and in an easterly direction, a central hump in the drive landing area must be carefully negotiated: downwind it can give a friendly kick on towards the green, but slightly weaker shots will be kicked left towards a line of drive bunkers and right towards the rough and a wall. The green is a tumultuous affair and the player who holds the ball on the left of the fairway will gain maximum benefit by playing down the length of the green".

The only distance markers at Craigielaw are posts indicating 150 yards to the centre of the green – a move I whole heartedly applaud. Whilst links golf should be natural, these fairways can get almost too hard and fast, especially given the nature of the greens and the bunkering. One other criticism I would make is in respect of the condition of the greens which were rather bumpy due to little clumps of foreign grasses.

I suspect Craigielaw would be just a little easier and more enjoyable when the fairways are slightly softer and greener.

ARCHERFIELD – FIDRA LINKS

Par 5, 11th

IN THE MID 19TH CENTURY THERE WAS A 13 HOLE COURSE AT ARCHERFIELD, LOCATED MORE OR LESS BETWEEN THE 8TH HOLE AT MUIRFIELD AND THE 9TH AT NORTH BERWICK. THIS AREA IS STEEPED IN HISTORY WITH THE NAME DERIVED FROM THE ARCHERS OF KING EDWARD I WHO PITCHED THEIR TENTS HERE DURING THE ENGLISH INVASION OF 1298. WITH THE HELP OF NORTH BERWICK PROFESSIONAL, BEN SAYERS, THE COURSE WAS EXTENDED TO 18 HOLES AROUND 1910.

Shortly after the outbreak of World War II, the estate was taken over by the British Army and in the following decades fell into complete disrepair.

Fortunately there are now two new magnificent courses designed by David Russell and the marvellous 17th century Archerfield House has been painstakingly restored.

There are 4 sets of tees on the Fidra course and from the very back it measures a healthy 6948 yards. The first 11 holes of this links course wind through lovely tree lined fairways whilst the final seven are more in the open and provide views of Bass Rock and Fidra Island. It is believed that Robert Louis Stevenson used Fidra for his inspiration when he wrote 'Treasure Island'.

Since the Fidra links originally opened in 2004, a further 20 new bunkers have been added.

The first hole gives you a good idea what to expect, for the next 10 holes at least. The fairways are excellent, fast running, and are lined with magnificent stands of trees. The fact that

This area is steeped in history with the name derived from the archers of King Edward I who pitched their tents here during the English invasion of 1298.

Photo courtesy Archerfield Links

Archerfield House

this has been a forest for so long meant that man's agricultural habits have not spoilt the sandy nature of the soil. Bunkers on this course are more of the pot bunker style and, if anything, are slightly understated.

The course emerges from the trees after the 11th, a lovely par 5 which also features a number of revetted bunkers along the fairway.

The standout hole is probably the 12th, a par 4 of 384 yards that flows beautifully through mounds and grass plantations and then dog-legs right about 50 yards before the slightly raised green.

Out of bounds appears not far behind the green on the 13th, a par 3 of 161 yards. It also features all along the left side of fourteen and fifteen, two tough par 4's rated index 1 and 3 respectively.

A number of these latter holes are heavily mounded with grass and wild flower plantations on either side so as to create a greater sense of privacy on each fairway.

Fidra ends with a long par 5 and a fairway that narrows considerably and has a number of bunkers starting at the 222 yard mark. The green is protected by three bunkers and tends to run to the sides and back so holding a long third shot here will be quite difficult.

This is a well presented course with two distinct feels as you go from treed to more open fairways. In parts of the back nine you are actually only a few hundred yards from the sea.

I imagine the new course being built next door ('The Renaissance') and designed by Tom Doak will have a similar hybrid feel to the Fidra. A partly tree lined links course is not a unique phenomenon or a contradiction in terms as anyone who has played Formby will know.

Photo courtesy Archerfield Links

The par 4th, 12th will be breathtaking when all the plantings have matured

The standout hole is probably the 12th, a par 4 of 384 yards that flows beautifully through mounds and grass plantations and then dog-legs right about 50 yards before the slightly raised green.

ARCHERFIELD – DIRLETON LINKS

Photo courtesy Archerfield Links

1st hole Dirleton Links

THE DIRLETON LINKS WAS READY FOR PLAY IN 2006. IT HAS A MORE TRADITIONAL LINKS APPEARANCE THAN THE FIDRA, WITH SOME HOLES LOOKING A LITTLE LIKE THOSE AT NEARBY MUIRFIELD.

As with Fidra, there are four choices of tees and the back tee distance is almost the same at 6946 yards. Dirleton features rather more menacing revetted bunkers and has some very colourful native wild flowers in abundance along the mounds and dunes bordering many of the fairways.

Amongst other outlooks, the course offers scenic views of Dirleton Castle and the Isle of May.

The opening hole can be a tough introduction. This is a long par 4 of 418 yards with bunkers and the fairway narrowing from around the 260 to 300 yard position from the tee. The green will deflect any ball not hit toward the centre and there is a deep little pot bunker with almost vertical sides at the front right.

The par 3, 7th may be rated the easiest on the course but you need to exercise care here. The green falls away at the back and on the right. The left is heavily bunkered and if you pull your tee shot too far left there is then a ditch and out of bounds. At 191 yards from the back tee or 167 yards from the blue, this is no pushover.

The 9th is a very demanding par 4 at 454 yards in length. The fairway can get a little narrow in parts and there are grassed mounds all the way along on both sides.

The short par 5, 10th is one of the best. There is a slight dog-leg right where a number of bunkers occupy just right of the perfect line. The third shot area is downhill with two bunkers in the fairway and further bunkers set into the side of mounds at the fairway's edge. A ditch that is difficult to see runs across the front of the green.

Index 1 is the 16th, a long par 4 of 463 yards. The hole dog-legs to the right and features four fairway bunkers along the right side. There is also heavy rough and then thick vegetation for any ball sliced. Beyond the mounds is out of bounds. There is also a drainage ditch along the right which forms a Y and then runs both sides of the green from about 130 yards out.

The par 3, 17th will give you some respite. The drainage ditch is only in play for a very poor tee shot, otherwise your main obstacle is one large bunker at the front right of the green.

The 18th is your third very long par 4 in the last four holes. The bunkers along this fairway are as good as I have ever seen. Although penal, they are a reasonable size so you should at least be able to play forward. The walls are a perfect example of revetting and the sand is a good texture. A number of these bunkers have only the one entrance or exit area by way of small steps at the back. This is both practical and is an attractive look. Whilst you are admiring these bunkers on the 18th you need to be very aware that a thick bank of gorse runs along the left and if you hook your drive you will probably be out of bounds.

The Dirleton was not long open for play when I was there in 2006, so I'm sure it will look even better when the grasses and native plantations have matured a little. I was also unfortunate to visit (in mid summer) on a very damp and misty day. In late spring with the gorse and all the wild flowers in bloom the Dirleton would be quite a picture.

DUNBAR

DUNBAR IS THE SOUTHERN MOST TRADITIONAL LINKS ON THE EAST COAST OF SCOTLAND AND IS MORE OR LESS MIDWAY BETWEEN EDINBURGH AND BERWICK-UPON-TWEED OVER THE BORDER. EYEMOUTH IS A LITTLE FURTHER SOUTH BUT IT IS MORE OF A CLIFFTOP LINKS NATURE.

Par 3, 3rd hole with the haar (mist) coming in off the sea

Tom Morris deserves a fair amount of credit for squeezing 18 holes into the land occupied by the now 150 year old (in 2006) Dunbar Golf Club. You can't get much closer to the sea than this unusual design.

The course is in two sections with a narrow slither of land in the centre bordered by the old deer park stone wall on one side and the sea on the other. This strip is just wide enough for two fairways and contains the 6th, 7th and 15th to 17th holes.

The other unusual feature is that the opening two holes are both par 5's and all three of the par 5's are on the front nine.

Despite the fact that the first two holes are short par 5's of less than 500 yards they have an index rating of 9 and 3 respectively. The fairways are quite narrow and they are punctuated with plenty of bunkers. If it is not blowing a gale and you keep the ball straight then birdie is a prospect.

The third is a delightful par 3 from a high tee heading straight to the sea. This is not a good place for a bad shot as the green has the clubhouse on the left and professional shop on the right. You will often be into the wind so the 173 yards can be somewhat of an illusion. There is one large bunker well short of the green and a further six surrounding all but the very front entrance.

The fourth runs along the seashore but from then onwards you play the inland side of the course until the eleventh.

The 6th hole is a par 4 of 347 yards but manages a rating of index one. I can only imagine it plays more difficult on a very windy day. The wall is on your right and when playing your second shot you have to avoid the sea on the left and a burn 25 yards short of the green. Neither of these hazards should be a problem as a reasonable drive will mean you ought to be playing only a short iron into the green.

Photo David Worley

1st and 2nd holes in the foreground – beyond the wall is the 18th and then the narrow strip just wide enough for two fairways

The other unusual feature is that the opening two holes are both par 5's and all three of the par 5's are on the front nine.

Seven has a quaint feel as you dog-leg right to a green with a stone wall on the right and the old boat house to the left. Whilst Dunbar is essentially flat, the par 5, 9th provides for a blind tee shot up a hill from where the views are superb. The drive is made a little more intimidating by the stone wall along the right. Generally speaking, it is safe to say that Dunbar would not be a happy place for a chronic slicer.

The 11th and 12th are both tricky par 4's with the sea and long rough all along the right. The biggest danger on the 13th is the presence of two fearsome fairway bunkers about 40 yards short of the green.

The sea is very much in play for the second shot on the 14th and both shots on the par 4, 15th. Each of these holes is also well bunkered. The par 3, 163 yard 16th will certainly test your nerve. You can run the ball onto the green if you are straight but you cannot help but think about the sea which is very nearby the right edge of the green. The temptation will be to pull your shot left which may then leave you near the stone wall.

The two finishing holes are each good par 4's. Seventeen is not long at 338 yards, but you must hit over a burn with both your drive and your approach and the sea runs close by along the right. The 18th runs parallel with the 4th but the two fairways are separated by an internal stone wall which becomes out of bounds if you stray from the 18th to the 4th. If you play safe and hit too far left then there are three fairway bunkers that will trap you.

Provided you don't get the heavy mist known as the haar that can come in here very quickly, then you will enjoy this wonderful links experience and the constant sea views. The greens are first class and the fairways are everything a true links should be.

Photos David Worley

Above: 7th green and the old boathouse behind – playing the hole from the left of the photo the stonewall is the boundary line all the way down the right side

Right: par 3, 16th

EYEMOUTH

Photo David Worley

EYEMOUTH IS A CLIFFTOP LINKS WITH SOME SPECTACULAR HOLES. ALTHOUGH THE CLUB WAS FOUNDED IN 1894 THE COURSE WAS LARGELY REBUILT, ALONG WITH A NEW CLUB-HOUSE, IN 1997. IF YOU ARE HEADING SOUTH DOWN THE EAST COAST THEN THIS IS THE LAST COURSE YOU WILL PLAY BEFORE CROSSING THE BORDER INTO ENGLAND.

The first four and last two holes are on the inland side of the road that dissects the course. These are less of a links nature. As these holes are on higher ground, you will be surprised when you reach the 155 yard par 3, 3rd hole. This hole could ruin a stroke round rather early as there is a large pond immediately in front of the green. Over club for safety and you will find that at the back the ground falls sharply downhill.

You cross the road to the 5th, a par 4 which runs down towards the cliff edge to the North Sea. From the 5th green you walk around the edge of an inlet to the 6th tee and then you begin to wonder 'where is the fairway?'. From a small teeing area you hit straight across the inlet several hundred feet

The daunting par 3, 6th 'A-still-no-ken'

below. It is carry all the way, and uphill, to the green 170 yards in the distance on the other side of the cliff. When this hole formed part of the original 9 hole course it was called 'A-no-ken' (I don't know) because wind variations made club selection so difficult. Now, as part of the 18 hole course, it has been cleverly renamed 'A-still-no-ken' (I still don't know). Based on my experience I can understand exactly what they mean. If you over club and hit a big fade you may finish up against a stone wall. They can't be serious in rating this as the third easiest hole.

The 7th hole is almost as daunting. 'Gullies' is a par 4 of 331 yards with a very dangerous second shot over a deep precipice beside the cliff and just short of the green.

The back nine heads to higher ground with the first few holes not far from the cliff edge. The views across the sea and along the coastline are superb, but this can also be very wind exposed. Apart from being a big dog-leg right, the par 5, 10th has a ditch and a pond in front of the green. The 15th is rated index number 1 and is certainly quite demanding. A long par 4 of 457 yards, there are ditches at both the left and the approach to the green. The 16th is over 600 yards in length and with the 18th being another par 5 it is not surprising that this nine is 412 yards longer than the outward nine.

Photo David Worley

This is where you will be heading if you hook your tee shot at the 6th

Clifftop links provide for spectacular views and often spectacular holes. Eyemouth is no exception and is probably worth playing just for the 6th which, some years ago, was voted the most extraordinary golf hole in the British Isles.

SOUTHERNESS

The aerial photograph reveals the extent of the gorse and heather

Par 3, 10th hole Southerness

The 12th green is right beside the beach on the Solway Firth

SOUTHERNESS WAS THE CREATION OF MAJOR RICHARD OSWALD WHO DECIDED IN 1946 THAT THIS WAS A GOOD LOCATION WITH SANDY SOIL. MACKENZIE ROSS DID THE DESIGN AT THE SAME TIME AS HE WAS INVOLVED IN THE POST WAR REVIVAL OF TURNBERRY.

Progress of the club was slow until around the late 1980's when Southerness held a number of important events which led to it being given more recognition. The Scottish Ladies Championship in 1988 was followed a year later by the British Ladies and then in the following year the British Youths Championship was held.

Southerness is the most southerly of Scottish links courses on the west coast. Situated on the Solway Firth, not far north of Silloth, there are lovely views of both the sea and the nearby Galloway Hills.

There are no towering dunes but if you miss the fairway the one common feature is the large expanses of thick heather. The 1st is a good opener, a par 4 which bends right with the road and out of bounds along the right hand side. The 2nd is a long par 4 of 450 yards which turns left but still with out of bounds along the right. Whilst heather will catch the wayward drive on the 1st, it is gorse that you must avoid on the 2nd.

By the time you have reached the 3rd hole you will feel like the whole course is yours. Farmland and cattle on the right and nothing but fairways and greens elsewhere – hardly a building in sight.

The par 3, 7th is a good test at 215 yards but the best part of Southerness is undoubtedly the three par 4's from the 12th to the 14th. The 12th is 421 yards and any drive either left or right of centre will finish bunkered. The shot into the green can depend entirely upon the wind as you are hitting right to the edge of the sandy beach on the Solway Firth. The 13th is a par 4 of 467 yards. There are a number of nasty bunkers and the lighthouse and town form a backdrop behind the green.

The 13th and 14th are about the only holes where you are aware of anything other than the course itself.

Pretty much all of the holes are of similar terrain so the opening and closing holes are a good cross-section of the rest. The holes all run in a variety of directions. As a result, there is never any feeling of sameness and I have no doubt that if Southerness was located closer to the Open courses, it would certainly be used for qualifying rounds.

With five par 3's, you might think it is a little on the short side. Surprisingly, it measures 6566 yards even though the two par 5's are just under 500 yards. The length comes from some testing par 4's of which eight of the eleven are over 400 yards.

Southerness is not as tough as nearby Silloth but it is still a very good test that is enjoyable for golfers of all standards. Most of the time you will feel very much alone on the course in this quiet stretch of countryside. That is a very rare and precious commodity in the world of today so don't miss out on experiencing Southerness.

TURNBERRY – AILSA COURSE

Photo David Worley

The long par 4, 8th hole with the hotel in the distance

WITHIN A FEW YEARS OF ITS COMPLETION IN THE EARLY TWENTIETH CENTURY, TURNBERRY'S AILSA COURSE HAD HOSTED THE LADIES BRITISH AMATEUR. SECONDMENT BY THE RAF CAUSED SUBSTANTIAL DAMAGE TO THE LINKS BUT FORTUNATELY THE FLATTENING OF FAIRWAYS FOR THE RUNWAYS WAS AWAY FROM THE LOVELY COASTAL STRETCH THAT NOW CONTAINS THE 4TH TO THE 11TH HOLES.

Mackenzie Ross did a magnificent rebuild in the years immediately following the Second World War. The Walker Cup was held there in 1963 but the final seal of approval was the 1977 Open when the now famous duel took place between Tom Watson and Jack Nicklaus.

I have never seen Turnberry in anything other than near perfect condition although admittedly, each of my three visits was just prior to either the British Amateur or the Senior British Open. Perhaps I am being a bit hard to please but it is almost in danger of now being too manicured and is losing some of the real links feel on the fairways.

The starter told me that the first nine was the more difficult mainly because of the long par 4's. That may be so from the championship tees, but from the medal tees I found the back nine slightly harder. There is certainly more potential trouble from a bad drive on the back nine but overall I don't think it is as difficult as Carnoustie or Royal Troon.

The round starts with three par 4's, the 462 yard (409 yards from the medal tee) 3rd being the most demanding. The par 3, 4th is the start of the glorious seaside holes. There is just the one bunker, at the front right, but anywhere left may finish down the cliff and on to the beach.

The 5th is another difficult par 4 at 442 yards (medal 416). The fairway runs through an attractive valley that bends left to an angled green that is very well guarded by four bunkers.

Six is a very long par 3 of 231 yards (medal 221). The green is on higher ground with a dune on either side of the green in addition to four bunkers. Short but straight is ok but getting on the green in one is not an easy task.

The 7th is a par 5 of 529 yards from the championship tee but is a harder par 4 of 475 yards from the medal tee. A burn can be in play at about 230 yards after which the fairway dog-legs left and is uphill all the way to the green.

Another long par 4 greets you at the 8th. The rough is thickest on the left beside the low seaside dunes but the right hand side of the fairway is well bunkered. The green is raised and provides beautiful views out to sea or back to the hotel. The green is tiered and has some deep pot bunkers at the sides just at the apron.

There are many memorable holes on the Ailsa but the par 4, 9th is probably the stand out. The tee is on a little rocky outcrop from where you hit blind and slightly uphill to a hog-back fairway. To your left is the lighthouse and the

Photo David Worley

Par 3, 11th with the lighthouse and Ailsa Craig in the mist

craggy outline of Robert the Bruce in the rocks. As long as you hit a straight drive then this hole is not as hard as it looks as your next shot is downhill to a bunkerless green.

The 10th can be a tricky long par 4 with the lower level green not far from the seashore on the left. Be wary of the large island bunker in the middle of the fairway 60 yards out from the green.

The par 3, 11th heads away from the sea and then from the 12th the holes head back to the clubhouse with the old runway on the left. The 12th is a good par 4 where a solid drive is the key. Anything slightly left is in a bunker but if you hook then you will be in the long grass. To the right of the green is a large dune with a tall monument to the lost airmen who were stationed at Turnberry during the two world wars.

The 14th is another long par 4 that proved to be the most difficult hole in the 1986 Open. Errant shots here will be in the rough or the gorse which is the thickest around this part of the Ailsa.

Fifteen is a super par 3 of 209 yards (177 medal). It can play long into the wind and anything short or right can be in heavy rough and heather. Left side of the green near the bunkers, is the best line of attack.

Provided you miss the one fairway bunker at the left on the 16th, you will then have the tantalising decision to contemplate with Wilson's Burn set deep in front of the green. It may be safer to lay up with your second if you are into the breeze but this can be a hard shot to judge since the burn is hidden from view. Anything just short of the green will roll down the bank and into the burn.

Seventeen is a short par 5 and I am surprised it is rated index number 4. The fairway is quite narrow about 100 yards out but otherwise it is straightforward. Eighteen dog-legs left with three bunkers at the corner. Stay down the right to the green which has only one bunker about 20 yards forward at the left side.

The Ailsa is a most enjoyable golfing experience with a wonderful variety of holes. On a still day it would be at the mercy of the top professionals, especially with its well watered fairways helping with ball control. However, in a strong wind and with thick rough in spring then it can really show its teeth.

TURNBERRY – KINTYRE COURSE

Photo David Worley

The memorable 8th green – one of Donald Steel's new holes

THE ORIGINAL ARRAN COURSE WAS LAID OUT IN 1909. AT THE BACK OF THE 11TH ON THE AILSA WAS BAIN'S HILL WHICH HAD BEEN USED FOR CATTLE GRAZING. THE ACQUISITION OF THIS LAND ENABLED NEW HOLES TO BE BUILT NEAR THE SHORE LINE. THE COURSE WAS REWORKED BEAUTIFULLY BY DONALD STEEL AND IN 2001 IT WAS REOPENED AS THE KINTYRE.

Photos David Worley

The 11th is aptly named 'Doon'n Roon'

Holes 1-5 and 13-15 are inside the triangle formed by the old runways. The 16th to 18th are alongside the Ailsa but it is the new holes, mainly higher up from 6-12 that really lift the Kintyre.

The 7th is unusual in that it is framed by thick trees. All the trouble is with the second shot on this par 4. Stay to the left and use the camber of the fairway.

The 8th is certainly one of the memorable new holes. This par 4 of 306 yards is more or less straight and it is downhill all the way, but you cannot see the green from the tee. The fairway narrows about 70 yards out where you get a good glimpse of the green in a little cove right on the edge of the low cliff beside the sea. Everything runs toward the sea so chip your approach short and run your ball in between the two bunkers. If you try to drive the green there is heavy rough and gorse along the banks on the right so you could easily lose your ball.

The par 5, 9th runs high up along the cliff top to an undulating green with the lighthouse and Ailsa Craig in the background. The 10th runs back in the opposite direction to the 9th. Straight hitting is needed up the hill on a fairway that slopes heavily to the left.

The 11th is a picturesque par 4 running downhill to a green partly hidden from view by a thicket of scrub and gorse on the side of Bain's Hill.

The next four holes necessitate some straight driving if you want to stay away from the prolific clumps of gorse. At the dog-leg on seventeen you need to stay left, away from the burn. The long second shot to the green then needs to avoid the two bunkers at the front left.

The final hole is very heavily bunkered and is probably rather more of a challenge than its counterpart on the Ailsa.

The Kintyre is an excellent course in its own right and compliments the Ailsa beautifully.

KINTYRE
DOON N'ROON
11 PAR 4
YDS 392
S.I. 12

PRESTWICK – OLD COURSE

Photo David Worley

17th green and the large Sahara bunker at the right

PRESTWICK BEGAN IN 1851 AS A 12 HOLE COURSE WITH OLD TOM MORRIS APPOINTED AS THE KEEPER OF THE GREEN. THE FIRST OPEN CHAMPIONSHIP WAS HELD AT PRESTWICK IN 1860 AND WAS WON BY WILLIE PARK. IN 1883 SIX MORE HOLES WERE ADDED TO THE LAYOUT. THE OPEN HAS BEEN HELD TWENTY FOUR TIMES HERE, THE LAST OCCASION BEING IN 1925. PRESTWICK BECAME A VICTIM OF ITS CONFINED SPACE WITH INADEQUATE ROOM FOR CROWDS, CAR PARKING, AND PERHAPS THE SHORTNESS OF THE COURSE ITSELF ALSO CONTRIBUTED TO ITS DEMISE AS AN OPEN VENUE.

There aren't many better opening holes than the 1st at Prestwick. A par 4 of just 346 yards that is almost dead straight – what could be more simple? Well, firstly, the railway line runs along the right and by the time you reach the green the stone boundary wall is only a few feet away. There is a clump of gorse on the right also but to the left there is heather followed by very thick gorse.

The par 3, 2nd hole can be a difficult green to hold especially with a following breeze. The 3rd, 'Cardinal', is a short par 5 but is rated index one. The Cardinal bunker dominates the hole with its huge size and sleepered supports. The 4th hole brings in to play another famous hazard – the Pow Burn. Between the burn and the middle of the fairway lies a

The 1st hole at Prestwick – one of the best opening holes in golf

The railway line runs along the right and by the time you reach the green the stone boundary wall is only a few feet away.

bunker that was the work of James Braid. When J H Taylor met his peril there in the Open one year he said that the man who put that bunker there should be buried in it "with a niblick through his heart".

There is no more famous blind par 3 than the 5th 'Himalayas'. The tee shot is over a huge dune to a flat area containing the green with bunkers at the sides. It can often play shorter than its stated length of 206 yards.

Having two par 3's early in the round is not good for speed of play so don't be surprised if it has taken you quite a while to play the first five holes.

Holes 7-10 are all par 4's of 430 yards or more. Avoiding the deep bunkers is necessary if you are going to par this stretch. The 13th is another very demanding par 4 of 460 yards. There is thick rough along the boundary side at the right and the green is a real challenge with contours in varying directions. Fourteen feels more like it should be the 18th as you drive from an elevated tee over scrub towards the green near the clubhouse. The 14th green is heavily bunkered whereas the 18th is rather more open and something of an anti-climax.

The 15th and 16th are real fun short par 4's. The drive on each must be accurate, especially on the 16th. The 15th is the most difficult of the greens with its undulations and pot bunkers very close by.

After driving through a gorse lined valley, seventeen requires a blind second shot to a green with the enormous 'Sahara' bunker to be avoided. The 18th, a par 4 of 284 yards is probably one of the weakest at Prestwick. The bunkers at the edge of the fairway are not too difficult and the green is fairly open. It is a pity that the end is so tame but this should not detract from the many unique delights of Prestwick. It is a wonderful insight into how golf was played in the very early days but, be warned, you could be in for a long day if the links are busy with four ball groups and their caddies.

Huge undulations on the 13th green

18th hole at Prestwick from behind the forward tee

PRESTWICK – ST NICHOLAS

Photo David Worley

Gorse, bunkers and a two-tiered green at the par 3, 2nd

THE ST NICHOLAS CLUB WAS FORMED SIMULTANEOUSLY WITH THE PRESTWICK GOLF CLUB AND THE TWO SHARED THE ORIGINAL 12 HOLES UNTIL 1877. THE ST NICHOLAS CLUB MOVED TO THE SOUTH EAST BUT BY 1892 THEY MOVED AGAIN, THIS TIME TO THE PRESENT LOCATION ON THE SHORE BETWEEN PRESTWICK AND NEWTON-ON-AYR.

Henry Cotton was right on the money when he described Prestwick St Nicholas as "a miniature championship course".

Although it measures just 5952 yards, there are some tight drives through gorse and there is almost always the wind to contend with. The first three and last three holes are on the clubhouse side of Marlborough Road and feature some very undulating fairways.

All the par 3's right from the 2nd hole are testing. The 2nd hole has a steeply sloping split-level green. Anything short will invariably be in a difficult lie and several little pot bunkers are located on both sides of the green.

The land is somewhat more level on the other side of the road. The 6th is a good par 4 with a blind tee shot over low sandhills. A wall and out of bounds is close by on the right. The 7th and 8th play around a lake that was once a quarry. The 7th is a good hole – a long par 4 and rated index one. The tee is right beside the adjacent beach and is very exposed to the elements. Accuracy is needed for the second shot on the 8th as your line is over the edge of the water. If you over club you might finish on the 6th green directly behind but on a higher level.

The back nine opens with a par 3, a par 5 and then another par 3. The par 5, 11th has out of bounds along the right but if you play safe down the left then you need to avoid four bunkers.

This is not the course to play if you tend to slice your tee shots. Sixteen and seventeen have gorse and then out of

bounds along the right and the 18th, a long par 3 of 227 yards, has out of bounds by way of the car park on the right.

There is gorse, water and out of bounds but not too much in the way of long grass. Prestwick St Nicholas is a lovely course to play and, despite its lack of length, is a good test of your golfing skills. As testimony to its qualities, until relatively recent times it was used as a qualifying course for the Open Championship.

Photo David Worley

6th green Prestwick St. Nicholas

IRVINE

Photo David Worley

Irvine in late spring

The second shot into the 18th green needs to allow for bunkers and the nearby carpark

Photo David Worley

AFTER A MEETING AT THE KINGS ARMS HOTEL IN MARCH 1887 THE IRVINE GOLF CLUB AT BOGSIDE WAS BORN. THE COURSE OF TODAY IS VERY MUCH THE LEGACY OF JAMES BRAID AND THE WORK HE COMPLETED IN 1926.

You will be punished for any errant shots at Irvine as most fairways are flanked by heather, gorse and broom.

The heather is very thick along the long par 4, 1st hole of 418 yards. The second shot is blind to an upturned saucer green with bunkers on the right.

The 2nd is the only par 5 on the course. The 4th is a par 4 of only 289 yards but it is rated index 11. Your drive must negotiate thick gorse on the right and a railway on the left. The temptation is to play slightly right but then you play from a hollow to an elevated green which has a stone wall at its edge and right behind is the railway line. Speaking from experience, it is easy to hit straight over the wall and send your ball on the next train to Prestwick.

Irvine mainly has a real links feel but in several areas the holes are more those of an inland course. The 6th requires a very straight drive up a narrow fairway which then looks down upon lusher flat ground with the green against the boundary fence beside the River Irvine. Large fairway bunkers and a ditch add to the difficulty of the second shot.

The par 4, 7th is not long but it is up a steep hill to an angled green. The tee shot on the par 3, 8th must carry thick rough and avoid deep bunkers which surround the green. The 9th, index 3, is a long (456 yards) par 4 that dog-legs right. The site of the old racecourse is out of bounds along the left and there are bunkers at the right side of the fairway and at the front of the green.

Around the 12th and 13th, the holes are more like reclaimed farmland but the run home resumes the links feel. The 17th features large bunkers about 100 yards from the tee in an upward sloping fairway. They would be very much in play for many lady golfers. The 18th is a delightful par 4, not long, but with an extremely difficult second shot. Cross bunkers, greenside bunkers and mounds and hollows will catch any shot not hit to perfection. As a word of caution, don't park your car in the spots that are often left vacant because they are dangerously close to the side of the green.

An interesting design aspect of Irvine is that there are only two par 3's and one par 5. The remaining fifteen par 4's are all different but at no time is there any sense of repetition. Irvine is somewhat underrated even though it is used for Final Qualifying when the Open is at Turnberry or Royal Troon.

GLASGOW GOLF CLUB – GAILES LINKS

Photo David Worley

The tee shot at the 3rd is over gorse to an angled fairway

FOUNDED IN 1787, THE GLASGOW GOLF CLUB IS THE 9TH OLDEST IN THE WORLD. THE COURSE IN GLASGOW (WHICH MOVED SEVERAL TIMES IN THE 1870'S) IS LOCATED AT KILLERMONT, FIVE MILES FROM THE CITY CENTRE ON THE NORTH BANK OF THE RIVER KELVIN.

In 1924 the club purchased Gailes golf links from the Duke of Portland, 12 years after the course had been revised by Willie Park Jnr. The original layout was by Willie Park of Musselburgh and opened for play as long ago as 1892. Glasgow Gailes is in that marvellous stretch of land between Troon and Irvine that yields lovely springy turf fairways.

The 1st and 3rd holes are particularly tight driving holes and each is well bunkered in front of the green. The drive on the 3rd is over gorse and then heather to a fairway that angles right. You need a strong fade but anything sliced will be lost in a forest of gorse. The par 5, 5th is rated index one. This hole was lengthened by way of a new tiger tee so it now measures 593 yards from the back. From the normal white tee it is only 536 yards and does not seem to justify its high degree of difficulty rating. This is a good looking hole with a very narrow fairway for the last 60 yards. There is plenty of trouble by way of thick scrub if you are too strong with your shot into the green.

The par 3, 6th is an excellent short hole. Although only 152 yards, the green is a difficult target with three bunkers at the front and two along the left edge.

Into the wind, the par 4, 8th is a daunting driving hole. Out of bounds runs the entire length on the left. On the right there is thick heather for the drive and a bank of gorse that may claim the second shot.

The inward nine opens with two solid par 4's, each well in excess of 400 yards. The par 3, 12th is a real tester. It is 220 yards from the back (182 yards white) to a green that is hard to see because of a thick patch of gorse about half way from the tee. Serious trouble by way of gorse and long grass is uncomfortably close to the green.

Thirteen is a short par 4 that is a real birdie chance provided you drive straight and avoid all the heather down the left. The two par 5's, the 5th and 14th, are rated the two hardest holes. Both need accurate drives and both have a very narrow fairway near the entrance to the green.

Fifteen is an attractive short hole with an elevated green guarded by three bunkers at the approach area and two on the right hand side.

Sixteen is a long par 4 of 438 yards (413 yards white) with rough and then the railway line on the right. Three cross bunkers may catch the second shot. The round closes with two straight forward par 4's, the 17th being the easier of the two.

The greens at Glasgow Gailes are as good as any in the area. I first played here in 1998 in a howling gale that turned into sleet that was so severe we walked off the course at the 9th – the furthest distance from the clubhouse. I returned in 2003 and experienced a lovely warm but breezy day. When the wind blows across the links from the side, the fairways suddenly become much narrower targets and you will pay the price in most cases if you miss the short grass. This is a tougher test than first appearances might suggest. There are no really memorable holes but there aren't any weak ones either. Glasgow Gailes is an Open Qualifier and would be probably rated much higher if it was on the other side of the railway and able to provide the same sea views as Western Gailes.

Photo David Worley

The long par 3, 12th hole – 220 yards

WESTERN GAILES

18th green from side on and clubhouse

The par 3, 7th green in a lovely dell setting

WESTERN GAILES DATES BACK TO 1897 AND WILLIE PARK. NOT MUCH CHANGED UNTIL THE REVISION BY FRED HAWTREE IN THE 1970'S. NOW MEASURING 6899 YARDS FROM THE BACK TEES, IT HAS HOSTED MANY MAJOR TOURNAMENTS THE FIRST OF WHICH WAS WON BY HARRY VARDON IN 1903, AND IS ALWAYS ONE OF THE FINAL QUALIFYING COURSES FOR THE OPEN WHEN HELD AT TURNBERRY OR ROYAL TROON.

Western Gailes is laid out on a narrow stretch of land between the railway line and the sea. Except for the short 13th, all holes run north or south with never enough room for more than two fairways side by side. With the lovely clubhouse more or less centered, the first four holes run north followed by a brilliant stretch from the 5th to the 12th that run south along the shore line. These holes turn at the 13th so that the last five run north beside the railway line and back to the clubhouse.

On the other side of the railway line at the north end lies Glasgow Gailes and at the southern end is the newcomer, Dundonald.

The 1st is a good short par 4 with a drive over the edge of heavy gorse. This is not as difficult a hole as it appears when you are standing on the tee. The par 4, 2nd is index 3. It is testing at 434 yards with the railway line along the right. The hole dog-legs left where there is plenty of heather if you pull your drive. Two bunkers 30 yards short of the right side of the green are very much in play.

The 4th is an excellent par 4 of 416 yards with four fairway bunkers and another three in front of the raised green. The 5th is the first of the seaside holes. Index 1, it is 499 yards from the back tee and 453 from the white. As it is a par 4 you don't want to be into the wind. The fairway bottlenecks 110 yards out from the well bunkered green.

An accurate drive is needed at the par 4, 8th

Six is virtually the same length from the back tee but is a par 5. The green is in a delightful setting amongst dunes.

The par 3, 7th green is similarly surrounded by dunes but with the additional hazard of six bunkers. The drive at the par 4, 8th needs to avoid the dunes and rough along the shoreline and one large bunker at 200 yards on the left. A narrow burn runs across the fairway only ten yards short of the two-tiered green.

Nine and ten are relatively short par 4's. You need to keep away from the heavier rough along the right. A burn runs in front of the 10th in a similar fashion to the 8th green burn. The 11th and 12th are somewhat longer par 4's, each bending slightly to the right.

The par 3, 13th runs sideways across the southern end of the course. This lovely short hole (153 yards) has the last of the three burns running on an angle along the front of the green. The rest of the green is protected by a horseshoe of seven bunkers.

Fourteen is by far the longest hole at 562 yards. The drive is over gorse to a fairway with plenty of rough and bunkers on both sides. Out of bounds and the railway line is in play on the right on all the holes from the 14th with the exception of the par 3, 15th. There is almost no fairway on the 194 yard 15th. There are two bunkers at the start of the apron about 20 yards out and a further five bunkers are at the sides of the green.

The remaining three holes are par 4's of reasonable length. At the 16th the second of the three burns is 31 yards out but the fairway slopes down to the burn about 15 yards earlier. Seventeen bends left along a fairway split in two by a heathery ridge about 90 yards from the green.

The shape of the 18th might tempt you to fade the drive but there is a cluster of four bunkers along the right at approximately 210 to 225 yards from the tee. A very large bunker lies in wait short of the left side of the green in addition to four smaller greenside bunkers.

Westers Gailes is such a joy to play that you will be very sorry to see the round come to an end. On a fine sunny day there can be few better vistas than to stand on the 7th tee looking down the course through the dunes. In the distance to the left is the fine clubhouse and to the right is the sea and the peaks of the Isle of Arran and the outline of Ailsa Craig further south.

DUNDONALD

Par 3, 6th at Dundonald

DUNDONALD WAS ORIGINALLY BUILT UNDER THE NAME OF SOUTHERN GAILES. IT IS LOCATED ON THE INLAND SIDE OF THE RAILWAY LINE, THE OTHER SIDE OF WHICH IS WESTERN GAILES. THE COURSE WAS ACQUIRED IN EARLY 2003 BY LYLE ANDERSON AND OPERATES UNDER THE BANNER OF THE LOCH LOMOND GOLF CLUB.

The links was designed by Kyle Phillips as a championship course of 7300 yards from the back tees. Interestingly, in the early 1900's there was an old golf course named Dundonald on the site of the new course. It was converted to military use in World War II, at which time it was known as Dundonald Camp.

The course is predominantly for the use of Loch Lomond members and their guests, but there are tee times available for visitors.

From the championship tees Dundonald is a serious test of golf. For example, the opening hole is a par 4 of 465 yards and is 435 yards from the medal tee.

The first par 3 is the 4th hole which is a very testing 220 yards (200 medal). Thankfully the only bunkers are at the sides of the green so you can land short and run your ball on to the green. The 5th is a long par 5 that dog-legs left. There is a hidden bunker in the middle of the fairway about 150 yards short of the very undulating green.

The 6th is one of the best holes at Dundonald. This lovely par 3 of 170 yards (155 medal) has a wet ditch running down the left side. Anything pulled left of the ditch will be in long grass. The green is elevated with dunes at the back where there is also a small pot bunker you can not see from the tee. Any wayward shot will be severely punished here.

Seven, eight and nine are par 4's in excess of 400 yards. You need to avoid the small pot bunkers on the fairways and at the 9th green there is a ditch and two nasty bunkers in front.

The par 3, 11th is just 125 yards but selecting the right club can be difficult. There is a marshy area with long grass and then an elevated green that is wind exposed and has three deep pot bunkers set into the side of the hill. Anything left can finish in trouble so your preferred line is straight over the right hand bunker.

Thirteen is a very good par 4 flanked by the railway line along the left side. Your long second shot has to clear a dangerous small pot bunker at the right.

The run home from the 15th features four very demanding holes. Fifteen is a par 3 of 215 (205 medal) yards with a gully and then a raised green with several penal bunkers at the front left. There is room to chip in from the right edge so this is the safer approach.

Index 1 is the 16th, a long par 4 of 485 (460 medal) yards. There are four fairway bunkers including one 30 yards out that you can't see when playing your second. The green is on two levels and has a bunker on each side. Don't be too disappointed if you write down 5 on your card on this hole. Seventeen dog-legs to the left so although you need a draw with your drive, you need to be careful of the bunkers at the inside of the corner.

The 18th is the longest hole at 585 (555 medal) yards. There are a number of pot bunkers at the sides to catch your drive and three cross bunkers are in place for the second shot. The third shot is even more difficult. A burn runs in front and then along the right edge of the green which is also protected at the front right by a large, thickly

grassed mound. Pot bunkers lie at the back. During a professional tournament here in 2006 when the flag was at the right near the burn, several of the competitors deliberately played into the bunker pin high on the left side of the green.

Although Dundonald is a par 72, the CCR can get up to 78. Many of the greens are elevated and have swales that kick the ball away from the centre so your approach shots must be perfectly placed. The bunkers are penal as they are generally small and quite deep. The ever present wind and the number of dog-leg holes makes it difficult to stay out of the rough.

The Loch Lomond members now have an excellent linksland alternative. In 2006 Dundonald was one of the three courses used as a qualifier for the Senior British Open. Based on the way the course is set up you can expect to see more tournaments at Dundonald in the near future.

Photo courtesy Iain Lowe

The par 4, 9th green and across the course

From the Championship tees Dundonald is a serious test of golf.

Photo courtesy John Cornish

The 15th is a very difficult par 3 of 215 yards

KILMARNOCK – BARASSIE LINKS

Kilmarnock Barassie

FOUNDED IN 1887, THE KILMARNOCK (BARASSIE) GOLF CLUB NOW BOASTS A TWENTY SEVEN HOLE COMPLEX. THE BARASSIE LINKS CONSISTS OF NINE OF THE ORIGINAL HOLES AND NINE NEWER HOLES INLAND THAT IS CLOSER TO THE NEARBY DUNDONALD LINKS. THERE IS ALSO AN EXCELLENT ALTHOUGH RATHER SHORT NINE HOLE COURSE KNOWN AS THE HILLHOUSE.

The Barassie Links is nearly 7000 yards from the back tees and has been used for final qualifying for the Open, Senior British Open and the British Amateur.

The opening hole should be an easy par 5 with its length being just 509 yards. You need to keep away from the right which is a wall of trees bordering out of bounds and the bunkers on both sides of the fairway at driving distance.

A burn angles across the fairway starting at 270 yards on the par 4, 2nd hole. The green is a difficult target with two bunkers on each side and a steep fall away if you take too much club.

The 3rd is the first of several testing par 4's over 400 yards. Unless you hit a good drive you may need to play up short of the burn with your second. If you are coming into the green from the left you will have a very tricky shot as it slopes to the right where there are also two bunkers.

I felt that one of the weaknesses at Kilmarnock Barassie is that there are no standout par 3's. The 155 yard 4th is the best of them. The green is slightly raised and has just one bunker which is front right, whilst the left is edged with sleepers. All along the left is a burn which is very much in play. On the day of my visit the wind was coming into you from the left so you had to start your shot over the burn and trust that it would drift back.

Index 1 is the 439 yard par 4, 7th hole. A very accurate drive is essential as the fairway dog-legs right at around 230 yards. If you cut the right hand corner you hit a mound with heavy rough but if you are a little too far left then you can run through the fairway.

Photo courtesy Kilmarnock Barassie GC

Kilmarnock Barassie Clubhouse

The par 5, 8th is a double dog-leg whilst the par 4, 9th bends sharply to the left where there are wide expanses of heather and rough. The 10th and 11th are also par 4's that bend left so you have three consecutive holes with a similar shape.

The 12th is a very difficult par 4 of 437 yards. There is heavy rough, a ditch and then out of bounds on the left. The fairway bottlenecks at 270 yards and remains narrow from there all the way to the two tiered green. If you pull the second shot left you will be lost ball amongst the gorse.

The par 4, 13th is an attractive hole, particularly when the gorse is in full bloom. A burn runs in front of the tee and then along the right of the fairway. If you play safe by being too far left then you might find a large bunker at the 227 yard mark.

Fairway bunkers are the biggest danger at the par 4, 15th. The 16th is a short par 5 that may yield a birdie but you need to watch for the three bunkers that narrow the fairway substantially about 30 yards from the green.

Anywhere off the fairway on the 17th will put you in rough or gorse. The home hole dog-legs right and requires a semi-blind drive. You need to keep a little right but if you stray too far right there are three bunkers. The green is large and has three tiers and just the one bunker on each side at the front.

Photo David Worley

4th hole – the best of the par 3's

Kilmarnock Barassie has its own character and is an enjoyable easy walking course. As with all the links courses is this area, you cannot score well unless you stay on the fairway.

ROYAL TROON

8th hole 'Postage Stamp' has a tiny green and five well disguised bunkers

TROON GOLF CLUB OFFICIALLY BEGAN IN 1878 AND BY 1888 THE LINKS HAD BEEN EXTENDED TO 18 HOLES LARGELY UNDER THE GUIDANCE OF GEORGE STRATH, THE CLUB'S FIRST PROFESSIONAL. HIS SUCCESSOR, WILLIE FERNIE, IMPLEMENTED FURTHER CHANGES AND IN 1895 THE SECOND COURSE, THE PORTLAND, WAS OPENED. TROON RECEIVED ITS ROYAL ACCOLADE IN ITS CENTENARY YEAR.

From the championship tees Troon is considerably longer than from the normal visitors' tees with a number of tiger tees pushing the length out to 7150 yards. A feature of Troon is the number of small, often hidden, bunkers. In some areas, such as the right of the 11th, the gorse is extremely thick, and the back nine boasts some very demanding par 4's.

The first six holes run along the coastline in a southerly direction. After a gentle opening par 4, the 2nd is somewhat more difficult because of the presence of seven fairway and four greenside bunkers. The 3rd is a similar length but has a burn crossing the fairway at about 285 yards from the tee.

The 4th is a par 5 that dog-legs right. You need to avoid the deep bunker at the corner 252 yards out and then accuracy is required to keep to the narrow fairway. The par 3, 5th is very close to the shore line so any lofted tee shot is likely to be wind affected. This is a testing length at 210 yards (194 from the medal tees) and there are four bunkers, mainly around the front section of the green.

The 6th is the longest par 5 (599 yards) on any of the Open Championship courses. Three bunkers are in place for the drive. Along the right as you get closer to the green are seaside dunes with thick rough. The green is in a lovely setting with dunes on both sides and out of bounds at the back.

The next six holes are probably in the most interesting terrain with dunes more prevalent. The elevated 7th tee provides a wonderful outlook over this hole which bends to the right around the 'Postage Stamp' 8th. Heavy rough and gorse is along the left and there are six fairway bunkers. The green is set between sand hills and is well bunkered.

Photo courtesy Kenneth Ferguson www.photoscot.com

The small pot bunkers around the 1st green are typical of the bunkers at Royal Troon

The 8th runs across the course, so usually the wind is side on to the green and this is its narrowest part, being only about 25 feet wide. On the left is a large grass covered dune with two bunkers in front of it and below the level of the green. Anything hit right or long will fall down a nasty bank and may end up in one of the three bunkers guarding that side. Only the first of these five bunkers is visible from the tee. There are many famous stories involving the 8th. In 1973, at 71 years of age, Gene Sarazen holed out during the Open, won that year by Tom Weiskopf. Sarazen was the winner of the first Open played at Troon 50 years earlier in 1923. In the Open of 1950, a German amateur by the name of Herman Tissies took five strokes in one of the 'Postage Stamp' hole bunkers, finally got on the green for twelve and, I am sure with a sigh of relief, holed out for fifteen. Many linksmen will tell you that on the windy courses the short par 3's are the hardest because you have to use a more lofted club.

Nine and ten are both long par 4's with plenty of trouble if you are inaccurate. The green at the 10th is on a plateau with gorse close by on the left and a sharp drop at the right.

The 11th is rated index 1 and proved to be the most difficult hole during the 1997 Open when the weather was extremely benign. This brute of a par 4 measures 488 yards (421 from the medal) with the railway line and gorse along the right. Anything hooked will also be in thick gorse. As the hole gets nearer the green the railway line is even closer at the right. During the 1962 Open, Arnold Palmer took the bold line from the tee and in his five rounds (including the qualifying) he had an eagle, three birdies and a par. In the final round that year Nicklaus took ten on this hole.

The 12th is a par 4 of 431 yards and is almost as difficult as the preceeding hole. The fairway bends to the right with thick clumps of gorse on both sides. The two-tiered green is raised and falls away on the left. There is one bunker short of the green on the left and another at the right edge.

From the 13th all holes run in a northerly direction back to the clubhouse. After two par 4's and a medium length par 3, the 15th is the start of four very tough finishing holes. Fifteen is a par 4 of 481 (445 medal) yards with three bunkers waiting for the drive and a further three closer to the green.

On the par 5, 16th, the same burn that crossed the 3rd hole now runs across at 283 yards out from the tee. This hole is very heavily bunkered with four on the fairway edges and five around the sides of the green.

The 17th is the most difficult of the short holes. At 222 (210 medal) yards it can be a very long par 3 into the wind. There are five bunkers, four of which are at the front of the green. The par 4, 18th is rated index 17 – presumably based on the medal tee length of 374 yards. However it is 453 yards from the championship tee which makes it a long par 4. The start of the fairway proper is narrow and has four bunkers starting at 262 yards. There are two bunkers thirty yards in front of the green with another three at its side. If you run through the green and finish on the path near the clubhouse then you will be out of bounds.

There is probably no course used regularly for the Open where the championship tee distance is so much longer than the normal back tees. Royal Troon is indeed a very exacting test of golf but I have to be honest and say that it is not a layout that endears itself to me.

Photo courtesy Kenneth Ferguson www.photoscot.com

Par 4, 12th hole from behind the slightly raised green

WEST KILBRIDE

Photo David Worley

Par 4, 13th at West Kilbride

FOUNDED IN 1893, WEST KILBRIDE IS THE NORTHERN MOST OF AYRSHIRE LINKS COURSES. THIS DELIGHTFUL SEASIDE LINKS IS LOCATED IN THE VILLAGE OF SEAMILL BETWEEN ANDROSSAN AND LARGS WHICH IS AROUND 30-40 MINUTES DRIVE FROM PRESTWICK.

The James Braid design follows an anti-clockwise route along a narrow strip of land beside the sea. The opener is a short par 4 of 335 yards and is tame if you hit the ball straight. However out of bounds and heavy rough runs all along the right and there are four bunkers on the left edge of the fairway. A narrow burn dissects the fairway some fifteen yards in front of the green. This should be a very easy hole but you need to take care.

The par 4, 2nd is a difficult hole when you are playing the course for the first time. Thereafter I suspect it is much easier. The hole bends right around a high ridge with thick rough – the difficulty lies in knowing how much of the corner you can take on with your drive. A solid fade is the safe tee shot as the fairway slopes away to the left side.

The 3rd is a shortish par 5 with out of bounds along the right. You need to watch out for the two sets of bunkers in the middle of the fairway 133 yards from the green and then at about 50 yards out. Out of bounds is still running along the right at the 4th, a par 3 of 178 yards. This is a lovely little hole with four bunkers in front of a green that falls away at the back.

Five and six are both straightforward medium length par 4's. Seven is a good looking par 5 with a number of small bunkers along the edge of the fairway. Eight is a solid par 4 followed by a par 3 of 191 yards. Out of bounds is well to the left but is very close to the back of the green. For the front nine, the out of bounds has been mainly along the right. From the 10th to the 12th it runs on the left side. On the par 4, 10th out of bounds is particularly close to the left and the back of the green. The par 4, 11th is just 256 yards and is driveable. Provided you miss the fairway bunkers then be careful of being too strong with your approach as the green runs away at the back and there is an impenetrable bush hedge only fifteen feet from the back of the green.

The 12th is another attractive par 3. Accuracy is a must as there are six bunkers surrounding the green. The 13th is a very good par 4 of 444 yards. The hole dog-legs slightly right where out of bounds again lurks. It remains on the right for the next three holes. The final six holes are all par 4's.

The 17th has a water ditch on the left of the fairway at around 200 yards and on the right at 245 yards. The green is a double green which is shared with the 6th. The closing hole features a narrow fairway with bunkers mainly on the left. Do not over club with your second shot as out of bounds is only a few yards behind the green.

West Kilbride is a really enjoyable course to play. Beside the opening holes there are attractive houses beyond the out of bounds fence and on the run home there are lovely sea vistas including the majestic Isle of Arran. This is not a long course so big hitters can leave their driver at home. Apart from a general lack of length, the layout could do with one long par 3.

The course was in wonderful condition when I played there in early June. I found it to be not too difficult but there was hardly a breath of wind and any links course will play much easier on the rare days when all is still.

This is one of the most pleasant and peaceful settings for golf that you will ever experience, my only regret is that I did not discover this little gem until my fourth trip to Scotland.

MACHRIHANISH

The wonderful landscape at Machrihanish that inspired Old Tom Morris

THE KINTYRE GOLF CLUB AS MACHRI-HANISH WAS INITIALLY KNOWN, BEGAN IN 1876. THREE YEARS LATER OLD TOM MORRIS WAS ENGAGED TO EXTEND THE LINKS FROM 12 TO 18 HOLES AFTER NEW LAND HAD BEEN PURCHASED. THIS INCLUDED THE WONDERFUL PIECE OF LAND WHERE THE FIRST HOLE WAS PLACED. OLD TOM IS FOREVER REMEMBERED WITH HIS DESCRIPTION OF THE LAND AT MACHRIHANISH AS BEING "SPECIFICALLY DESIGNED BY THE ALMIGHTY FOR PLAYING GOLF". FURTHER ALTERATIONS TOOK PLACE IN 1914 UNDER THE HAND OF J H TAYLOR AND FINALLY, 30 YEARS LATER THE LAST CHANGES WERE MADE BY SIR GUY CAMPBELL.

Photo David Worley

Looking back to the 1st tee in the heavy mist

Photo courtesy John Cornish

The highly regarded opening hole, 'Battery'

By car it is at least a three hour drive from Glasgow down the Mull of Kintyre to nearby Campbelltown. Nothing much has changed here so be prepared to stop for sheep and cattle wandering across the road.

Campbelltown is a pretty seaport. Machrihanish I suspect would not exist without the golf course which supports the small number of private hotels.

My wife and I arrived in late afternoon. The nearby farmland was partly under water and huge pools lay on the 1st and 18th fairways. The weather was not forecast to improve so I felt very let down about the prospect of playing a wet, soggy windswept course. Rain or no rain, we booked our round for mid-morning the next day. Heavy mist lay along the foothills. The sea was clear, so it was eerie looking back from the course to see the inland mist. The first lines of Paul McCartney's song came unmistakably to mind.

The 1st hole is claimed by many to be the best opening hole anywhere. I would not dispute that. 'Battery' is a par 4 of 428 yards. The tee shot is literally a carry of about 150 yards across the Atlantic Ocean. The problem is really in knowing how much of the corner you can bite off, especially when the wind is blowing. The safe shot is towards the 18th fairway but you might catch the bunkers or else you have a long shot to the green. If the tide is out, then you might experience my fate which meant playing my second shot from the beach sand. This is quite permissible as the beach beside the 1st is treated as a lateral water hazard.

We found that the wind was assisting us on many of the holes on the front nine so scoring was easier especially if you hit a reasonable length accurate drive. From the 3rd to the 16th you are on the other side of the Machrihanish burn and this is beautiful links terrain. I call this country 'spot the fairway' because with the native grass and bumps and hillocks, you often only see tees and greens and seemingly no fairways exist.

The well bunkered 3rd hole is the start of some holes that feel quite unique. You are so far removed from the hustle and bustle of everyday life that you are drawn in to admiring the harsh beauty and the pattern of the wispy grasses that form the not too difficult rough. The 4th is a rather short par 3 in amongst the low dunes and wild grasses with the shoreline along the left. With the exception of the 7th, the 5 par 4's that make up the rest of the front nine are not long so good drives can set up birdie chances.

On the inward nine, we saw the distant lights of the airbase which seemed more like something from a science fiction movie with the mist and dark skies highlighting the lights even at early afternoon. The 11th and 16th are two long par 3's and were both demanding tee shots into the firm breeze. The 13th and 14th are excellent par 4's with very tricky greens and approach areas.

The only weak parts of the course for me were the 17th and 18th holes which are rather flat and uninteresting. Even so, you must negotiate the burn on the 17th and the 9 hole course, used mainly by children, is out of bounds on the left of both holes. I might add that the day we played, the Machrihanish burn was a raging torrent that looked more like a mountain river.

The fairways and bunkers were in excellent condition and the greens were nothing short of superb. Considering the enormous amount of rain that had fallen, this was quite remarkable.

Photo David Worley

17th green – the greens and bunkers were in superb condition considering the nearby farmland was under water

The next evening I ventured out again determined to master the shot off the magical 1st tee. I am still convinced it is a harder shot than it first appears. But, if you get a good drive away down the middle with a slight draw, then you will wonder what all the fuss is about and why the 1st is rated index 3.

I can't guarantee the weather but I can guarantee you will fall in love with the links at Machrihanish.

MACHRIE

7th green and three sheep

THE MACHRIE ON THE ISLE OF ISLAY FIFTEEN MILES OFF THE WEST COAST OF SCOTLAND HAS TO BE THE ULTIMATE IF, LIKE ME, YOU ENJOY THE EXPERIENCE OF GOLF THAT IS ON COMPLETELY NATURAL SURROUNDS.

Machrie was laid out by Willie Fernie in 1891. No mechanical equipment was used so the tees are about the only leveled areas. This is a teaser of a course. At 6292 yards it is about the same length as Machrihanish. There are a number of short par 4's, for example the 1st, 3rd, 8th, 15th and 17th, where the blind shot is not from the tee but rather to the green which may be tucked behind a large dune. In fact almost every hole has some sort of blind shot except for the 2nd, the 9th and the three par 3's.

Often the green is on a downslope behind a dune so your ball will tend to run through the back. If you try to play short and run your ball on then there are holes like the 17th where natural bunkers and rough are on the blind side of the dune you are hitting over.

The nature of the undulating fairways and hidden greens has negated the need for bunkers and as a result there are only ten on the whole course. The light rough at the edge of the fairways is actually quite thick so you will get very little run if you are just slightly off line. Beyond the first cut, the rough is very dense and is lost ball territory.

The extremely undulating 8th fairway with the green hidden in a hollow in front of the dune

Photo David Worley

The first three holes are all potential birdie opportunities. The 2nd is a short par 5 which dog-legs left around a burn and farmland that is out of bounds. You have to take on some of the dog-leg otherwise you will run out of fairway. The 3rd is just a drive and a wedge but it is very hard to get near the flag because the prevailing wind is from behind and you are pitching blind to a steep downslope. The 4th typifies Machrie with the natural bumps and swales of the fairway blending almost imperceptibly into the green.

Seven, eight and nine run alongside Laggan Bay on the left and are bordered by lovely dunes along the right. The 7th, index 2, requires a blind drive over a dune and then a long second shot to a hidden green. The rough is so thick that even missing the green by just ten yards could mean lost ball. The green at the par 4, 9th is shaped so as to kick your ball away from the centre so getting up and down is very tricky here.

The par 3, 10th has the Machrie Burn in play on the left. Like the 5th, the wind tends to be from behind so staying on the green is the trick even though you may only be hitting an eight iron. Not so the par 3, 12th ,'New Mount Zion', which is 174 yards uphill and usually into the wind. Don't miss this green on the left side as this could spell disaster – there is plenty of room on the right.

Photo David Worley

17th green from behind

There are some good par 4's on the back nine but none better than the 17th. The shot into the sunken and hidden green is a real test of skill. It is far better to be a little long, rather than short, on this hole otherwise you may have a virtually unplayable lie in the little craters that form natural bunkers. The par 4, 18th finishes with a blind second over a very high dune in the centre of the fairway and only about 35 yards short of the green.

In June 1901 the world's richest ever professional tournament was played at The Machrie. The 31 players competing for the total prize money of 170 Pounds included James Braid, Harry Vardon, J H Taylor, Andrew Kirkaldy, Willie Fernie and Ben Sayers. The Glasgow Herald reported the Machrie links "provides a splendid test of golf. Of great expanse, and blessed with the best turf, the links form a golfer's paradise". The third round of the matchplay event was in gale force winds. Taylor defeated Vardon on the 24th whilst the other winners were Braid, Herd and Kirkaldy. It was considered fitting that the final was played between Braid, the current Open champion, and Taylor, the former champion. Taylor won a splendid match on the 36th hole and in doing so collected 100 Pounds.

You cannot come to Islay just to play Machrie once as it is only after two or three rounds that you can enjoy the nuances of the blind shots. You might also want to allocate time to experience some of the very highly regarded whisky distilleries on the Island which gives a unique taste to its product because of the peat affected water.

The weather here can be wild but if you are lucky with the conditions then this is a truly wonderful place to enjoy the fun of genuine old fashioned links golf. The course is in very good condition, especially considering the ground staff numbers just four. The highlight for me was the 7th green where we took a little longer than usual to putt out due to the intrusion of a hedgehog and several sheep.

In June 1901 the world's richest ever professional tournament was played at The Machrie.

ENGLAND *3rd green at Royal Cinque Ports*

ENGLAND

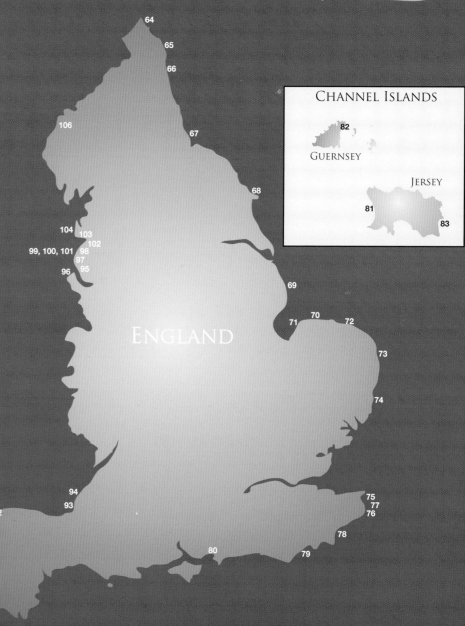

CHANNEL ISLANDS

GUERNSEY

JERSEY

ENGLAND

155

BERWICK-UPON-TWEED
GOSWICK LINKS

Photo David Worley

6th green from side on with out of bounds only a few yards away

BERWICK-UPON-TWEED'S GOSWICK LINKS LIE A FEW MILES SOUTH OF THE TOWN. ALTHOUGH THE COURSE WAS BUILT A NUMBER OF YEARS EARLIER, THE CLUB WAS FOUNDED IN 1890. JAMES BRAID HAD A HAND IN THE ORIGINAL NINE BEING EXTENDED TO EIGHTEEN IN 1894 AND NOTHING MUCH CHANGED UNTIL 1964 WHEN THE FRONT NINE HOLES WERE MODIFIED BY FRANK PENNINK.

There is no easy start to get your confidence up at Goswick. The opening hole is a real tester. A par 4 of 392 yards, there is a big dog-leg right where out of bounds runs the full length. The green is further away than it looks and is both elevated and tilted from the back.

The par 3, 2nd is aptly named 'Crater'. If you land short you may finish in a deep depression but anything too firm will be hard pressed to hold this fast green. The par 4, 3rd and par 5, 4th are both testing and are also dog-legs to the right. Balance is restored with a dog-leg left at the 5th, a long uphill par 4.

The par 5, 6th will also give you plenty to think about. Out of bounds is on the right where there is a line of dunes. Closer to the green are fairway bunkers on the left side. There is a very big hollow in front of the green which is set in the side of a hill.

The 7th runs along side the railway line on the right where there is also very thick rough. Like the previous hole, the two-tiered green is well protected by bunkers on the 'play safe' left hand side.

Your drive needs to take the brave line along the right on the 8th so that your shot into the green can avoid the tricky mound on the left. The 9th is a par 3 back to the clubhouse. It does not play as long as the 199 yards might suggest it should. There is plenty of room if you are short but out of bounds is all along the right.

This is not a course you will enjoy if you are prone to slice. Very thick rough again features on the right on the par 4, 10th. Some tough holes lie ahead. The par 5, 11th can be diabolical if you don't hit straight. Out of bounds runs along the right and there is a wet marshy area all down the left side. The shot to the green can be a blind one over a dune. The front of the green is raised with everything sloping quickly from right to left.

The 12th is a dog-leg right with a marshy area in play along the right. The second shot to the green is obscured by a dune but, thankfully, there are no bunkers here, only grassy hollows. Eleven and twelve are rated 4 and 8 on the index but, into the wind, they can lay claim to being the two most difficult holes.

Thirteen is the pick of the four par 3's. Although the tee is elevated you are hitting uphill to a green with three bunkers in front and one either side.

The 14th is a most attractive par 4 of 393 yards but I am puzzled as to how it could be rated as the second hardest given that my second shot to the green was only an 8 iron. The green is almost in an elevated dell. Anything a little right should feed back to the putting surface.

Fifteen is another good par 3 hitting from high up down to a green with water and marsh land at the rear. There are plenty of greenside bunkers but the front is open. The green is angled to suit a slight fade so the ideal landing area is the front left hand side.

The 17th is a short par 5 that offers a birdie opportunity as does the short par 4, 18th. From the elevated tee on the closing hole you have every chance of driving the green as it is a mere 269 yards in length. To achieve this you need to avoid the cross bunker that is about 40 yards short of the green and also keep clear of the ridge running parallel with the left side of the fairway. Anywhere over the cross bunker and short of the green will give you an easy pitch to the flag.

The Goswick Links is for straight hitters. The greens are excellent but can be tricky as a number are tiered or tilted. Not surprisingly, this is a venue for regional qualifying for the 2008 Open.

The well bunkered par 5, 17th

Photo David Worley

SEAHOUSES

SEAHOUSES IS A DELIGHTFUL LITTLE SEASIDE COURSE (5542 YARDS) IN NORTHUMBERLAND JUST SOUTH OF SEAHOUSES VILLAGE ON THE B1340. IT IS PART LINKS AND PART CLIFF-TOP LINKS.

Founded in 1913 as a nine hole course, it was upgraded to 18 holes in 1976. It features two of the best par 3's (the 10th and 15th) in the north of England.

Holes 3-8 are on the inland side of the coastal road. The 5th is the most difficult at just over 400 yards with out of bounds all along the right side and quite close to the fairway. The small pond in front of the tee should only catch a very poor drive.

A burn acts as a boundary and is in play along the right side of the 3rd and behind the 2nd and 17th greens. The layout can get a little confusing with some holes not adjacent to the next. From the 8th green you have to walk past the 18th tee to get to the 9th tee and from the 9th green you must bypass the 1st hole to reach the 10th tee.

The back nine has the stand out holes. The 10th, 'Logan's Loch', is a par 3 of 165 yards almost all of which is carry over the water.

Photo David Worley

Par 3, 10th hole 'Logan's Loch' – the tee is 165 yards to the left

Fifteen, 'The Cove', is just 124 yards in length but must be one of the most difficult short holes you will ever encounter, especially if the wind is blowing. The first part of the tee shot is carry over the cliff edge and then you have to land on a small green only a few feet from a drop of over 100 feet to the rocks and sea below. To make it even more difficult, the green slopes away from you and towards the cliff. Depending on conditions, you may need anything between a wedge and a three iron.

The 16th is a short but tricky par 4 of 322 yards. If you pull your drive left you can be in the sea inlet. If your second shot is too far left, you can finish on the 10th green or even in 'Logan's Loch'.

You turn back to be almost on the beach at the 17th tee which is on lower ground not much above sea level. This is an excellent tight par 4 of 388 yards with out of bounds and the beach all the way along the left. To further confuse the visitor, you reach the 18th tee by walking past the 2nd green and the 9th tee with the last hole being parallel and almost identical to the 9th hole. Fortunately the plan of the course is easy to follow on the scorecard.

Whilst Seahouses is not long, the wind is almost always a factor that will add to the difficulty. When I visited Seahouses the greens were good but rather slow, possibly due to a hot dry spell at that time creating concerns for green-keepers.

Photo David Worley

Par 3, 15th 'The Cove' from behind the green

You will be hard pressed not to enjoy the holiday golf and friendly atmosphere here.

NEWBIGGIN

Photo David Worley

Double green and the power station

NEWBIGGIN GOLF CLUB WAS FOUNDED IN 1884 WHEN THE MEMBERS WERE GRANTED VIRTUAL PERMANENT TENANCY OVER THE FREEHOLD LAND. SADLY, ALL THE ORIGINAL CLUB RECORDS WERE DESTROYED WHEN THE CLUB HOUSE WAS BURNT DOWN IN 1921. HISTORY REPEATED ITSELF IN 1971. SEVERAL YEARS LATER A NEW BUILDING WAS ERECTED AND THIS IS THE BASIS OF THE PRESENT DAY CLUB HOUSE.

The course is laid out over moorland at the northern end of the village. This is a genuine seaside links but the course is generally very flat and visually suffers from the presence of an ugly power station on the inland side of holes 5-7.

The most attractive holes are those along the seashore where the ground is slightly more elevated, namely the 3rd, 4th and 15th.

The course is surprisingly long at 6723 yards from the back tees. This is primarily achieved by having only two par 3's, the 12th and 17th.

Due to houses encroaching onto the course, there is quite a walk from the 18th green back to the club house. Most of the greens are flat and are at the same level as the fairway which tended to make the whole layout less interesting.

This is strictly holiday golf but to be honest, there is not much to recommend Newbiggin.

SEATON CAREW

Photo David Worley

From green to tee on the long par 3, 16th 'Cosy Corner'

FORMED IN 1874, SEATON CAREW WAS INITIALLY KNOWN AS THE DURHAM AND YORK-SHIRE GOLF CLUB. BY 1887, AS THERE WERE NOW OTHER CLUBS IN THE AREA, THE NAME WAS CHANGED TO SEATON CAREW, A CLUBHOUSE WAS BUILT AND BY 1891 FOUR HOLES WERE ADDED TO PROVIDE AN 18 HOLE LINKS.

Hartlepool is a few miles to the north and, unfortunately a power station and petro chemical plant is just to the south. This certainly taints the views but this course is so good you soon become oblivious to the industrial eyesore nearby. Bernard Darwin described Seaton Carew as 'grand golfing country but there was not quite enough of it'.

Perhaps this persuaded the committee in 1925 to engage the good Dr. Alister MacKenzie to lengthen the course to 6500 yards and some holes were moved easterly closer to the seaside and sandy soil. The prevailing sea breeze was considered such a problem that over 1000 buckthorn bushes were planted as a wind break.

They now form as impenetrable spiky wall along the right hand side of 'Chapel Open', 'Dog Leg', 'Snag' and 'Home'.

In 1974 the club agreed to an oil pipeline under part of the course. The proceeds from this concession enabled them to build four excellent new holes on the eastern side where the land was once covered by the sea. This gave them 22 holes which are played in four slightly varied 9 hole sequences. For this reason I shall state the hole name as well as the hole number. The day I played at Seaton Carew the holes that are always the 1st (Rocket) and the 18th (Home) on all four sequences were out of play as the greens had been recently returfed. The card provided identified this layout as 'Summer Course No. 1'.

'Long Trail' (1st) is quite a tricky long par 5 of 565 yards and rated index number 3. Out of bounds by way of the practice fairway runs along the right. The approach to the green is rather narrow and features bunkers on either side of the fairway about 40 yards out.

'Doctor' (2nd) is a wonderful par 3, un-changed from 1874 except the sleepers in the bunkers have been removed. The green is elevated and has four bunkers at the front, two on the left and three bunkers plus grassy dunes on the right.

Not much fairway at the par 3, 11th 'Mashie'

'Dunes' (3rd), 'Pond' (4th) and 'Bents' (5th) all require very accurate driving with the latter two featuring out of bounds on the right. 'Road' (6th) is a good short par 4 of 354 yards. This hole dog-legs right at around 200 yards giving you a straight shot into a narrow fronted green with plenty of bunkers and mounds on both sides.

'Lagoon' (9th) exemplifies the precision shot making needed at Seaton Carew. The hole is a straight ahead par 4 of 371 yards but there are two large bunkers right in the centre of the fairway at the 193 and 225 yard mark from the tee. All along the right is a large swampy area that runs to within about 80 yards short of the green. The last 65 yards of the fairway are very narrow with thick grassy mounds along the left and back of the raised green.

'Mashie' (11th) appears a rather fearsome par 3 from the tee but there is a small landing area, not visible from the tee, in front of the green. 'Gare' (13th) is one of the new holes and runs east-west whereas all other holes run more or less north-south. 'Gare' does not feature on the first two combinations known as The Old Course and The Brabazon Course. More's the pity because I would rate it as one of the very best in this wonderful complex. This hole heads straight to a green that is right beside the beach. Lovely dunes feature all along the right of the fairway and behind the green. The narrow entrance to the green is made more so by a bunker on the left and large grassy mound at the right.

'Chapel Open' (14th) and 'Beach' (15th) are also newer holes and rate amongst the most difficult. Both have buckthorn all the length of the right side but 'Chapel Open' is a more daunting prospect from the tee as you need to hit a long fade around the buckthorn at the 90 degree corner dog-leg to the right. 'Beach' is so named as it literally runs right along the seaside.

'Cosy Corner' (16th) is a testing par 3 of 205 yards from the back tee. There are two bunkers well short of the green and one at either side at the entrance.

The two final holes 'Dog Leg' and 'Snag' provide for a very difficult finish with accurate drives being essential. Buckthorn features on the right for the second shot on 'Dog Leg' and primarily the tee shot on 'Snag'. Normally the 17th on all four combinations, 'Snag' is one of the best holes. As you near the green the fairway continually narrows. The green is raised with two bunkers on each side at the front. There is a nasty, almost hidden, bunker at the foot of the large mounds on the left edge of the fairway about 25 yards short of the green. Anywhere in here may mean at least one stroke lost.

The buckthorn was planted to provide protection from the prevailing sea easterly. The day I played the wind was blowing strongly from the west which pushed all my shots towards the buckthorn so the last four or five holes were rather scary.

This is a seriously good test of golf and a first class course. The fairways are excellent, the bunkers are deep and penal and the rough can be quite thick. A few of the remaining old greens were a little bumpy but most of the holes now have the new grass in play.

GANTON

Photo David Worley

The 17th, 251 yards across the road – is it a long par 3 or a short par 4?

THE FIRST PERSON I MET AT GANTON WAS FRED, THE DELIGHTFUL STARTER AND CADDIE MASTER. HE UN-ASHAMEDLY STATED THAT GANTON "IS THE BEST COURSE IN THE UNITED KINGDOM".

He may not be far wrong. The fairways are fast and firm, greens are excellent, bunkers are beautifully presented and very punishing, gorse and broom abounds and the wind is always a factor. I guess the only thing lacking is the sea views. Fred has been at Ganton long enough to remember when the train would arrive at the nearby station. A bell would ring which was the signal for the caddies to meet their player on the platform. Ah, those were the days.

You may be surprised that I have included Ganton in a book reviewing only links courses. Thousands of years ago this site was actually an inlet from the North Sea and as a result the sandy subsoil is the equal of any seaside links. I am categorising Ganton with

Thousands of years ago this site was actually an inlet from the North Sea and as a result the sandy subsoil is the equal of any seaside links.

the unique description of an 'inland links'. Ganton Golf Club is located eleven miles inland from Scarborough.

Since golf was first played here in 1891, many people have had a hand in the course of today. The original work was by Tom Chisolm of St. Andrews. In 1896 the great Harry Vardon became the club's professional and the winning of his first Open at Muirfield in the same year helped put Ganton on the golfing map. A major redesign took place in 1905 with input from the four most illustrious men in golf at the time – Vardon, Ray, Braid and Taylor. Subsequent changes have come from Colt, Alister MacKenzie, C K Cotton and Pennink.

There are many wonderful holes at Ganton, none better that the par 4, 405 yard 4th. The second shot is across a gully to an undulating and raised green with a very well placed bunker on the right side. Gorse awaits any ball finishing through the back of the green. The elevated 5th tee provides a splendid view of the first of only two par 3's. Three bunkers are greenside and a pond awaits anything pulled long and left.

Index 1 at Ganton is the very tricky 7th. This is a par 4 of 434 yards that dog-legs right with a nest of four bunkers right where you need to aim at the corner of the dog-leg. The 9th is not a long par 5 but the green is quite small. There is gorse aplenty, two bunkers about where you might land your second shot and another two on either side of the green.

Photo David Worley

16th hole from behind the green

The final four holes are a great finish. Fifteen and sixteen are very long par 4's and you will do very well to be on these greens in regulation. The 17th can be looked at as a very long par 3 or short par 4 (251 yards from the back tee). The tee shot is over the road to a green heavily protected by bunkers. A wayward shot could also find thick rough which is why this short par 4 gets an index rating of ten.

Along with the 4th and 17th, the final hole is one of the best. The drive to the dog-leg left must be perfectly placed so as to provide a shot to the sloping and well bunkered green. Any second shot pulled left could well be a lost ball in the gorse.

Ganton has held many major events including the Ryder Cup, Curtis Cup, and Walker Cup. Tournaments there have been won by some great golfing names including Joyce Wethered, Max Faulkner, Guy Wolstenholme, Michael Bonallock and Nick Faldo.

You will need all your golfing skills here. From the back tees the course measures 6752 yards. Any stray shots will be severely penalised in the deep bunkers or abundant gorse. And did I mention the wind? During an amateur tournament in 2006 (all low markers) the wind was so prevalent that nearly everyone was going out of bounds on to the practice fairway when playing the short par 4, third hole.

Be assured, Ganton is a not to be missed golfing experience.

Wonderful bunker 100 yards from the 1st green

Photos David Worley

Clubhouse from thick gorse beside the 18th green

SEACROFT

2nd green

SEACROFT WAS FOUNDED IN 1895 AND WAS ORIGINALLY A RATHER SHORT 9 HOLE COURSE. LIKE SO MANY OF THE EARLY LINKS COURSES, ITS VERY EXISTENCE IS PROBABLY DUE TO THE ARRIVAL OF THE RAILWAY IN 1873 AND THE SUBSEQUENT INCREASE IN POPULATION. THE CLUB WAS UNABLE TO OBTAIN A CONTINUING LEASE OF THE LAND SO IN 1900 THEY RESOLVED TO ENGAGE WILLIE FERNIE TO DESIGN A NEW 18 HOLE LINKS NEARBY ON WHAT IS NOW THE PRESENT SITE. THE NEW COURSE WOULD BE KNOWN AS 'THE SEACROFT LINKS NEAR SKEGNESS'. TO CELEBRATE THE OPENING, IN 1907 A 36 HOLE MATCH WAS ARRANGED BETWEEN J H TAYLOR AND ARNAUD MASSEY WHO HAD JUST WON THE OPEN AT HOYLAKE IN THAT SAME YEAR.

Seacroft is a traditional out and back layout on the Norfolk coastline a few miles south of Skegness. The far end of the course is near the nature reserve at Gibraltar Point and it is here you will find a lovely sense of isolation from the modern world.

The opening hole is a good par 4 featuring a large cross-bunker and a magnificent sycamore tree behind the green. When the wind is blowing you certainly don't want to be a slicer as the 1st, 2nd, 5th and 8th all have out of bounds nearby along the right hand side.

The best position from where to play into the green on the 2nd hole (as with the first) is on the right towards out of bounds or thick rough. The 3rd hole requires a blind tee shot and then you play to an elevated green. Anything right will be in a nasty swampy area. The 4th can be a difficult par 3 with the green situated on top of a high mound.

From the elevated 6th tee you get a good look at the long ridges running like spines along various parts of the course. Although this hole measures 343 yards, in summer you can reach the greenside bunkers with a good drive. The bunkers are the only real danger on this hole.

Index 1 is the 7th, a par 4 of 422 yards with a green hidden by a low dune. The slope of the fairway suggests your second should be a long fade but then it becomes difficult to avoid the two greenside bunkers.

The par 8th is one of my favourite holes. You drive over the corner of the road (probably best you wait 'till there are no cars – see photo) and need to be near the out of bounds fence on the right for the best angle into the green which is slightly raised behind a large bunker. Birdie is a chance here …but so too is double bogey.

The 9th is a short par 5 and 10 is a short par 3; they are probably your best chance for a birdie. You are then faced with two of the toughest holes. Twelve is a very long uphill par 3 of 210 yards which plays longer than it looks. The ladies' tee is 10 yards further back but, for them, the par is four. Thirteen is a short par 5 of 499 yards but the last half of the hole presents all the trouble. If you go straight for the green with your second and you are short you will find there is no safe area. The green is on a ridge and a marshy area is nearby.

The 14th is the most attractive of the four par 3's. The principal danger here is the pot bunker to the left.

The last four holes are all par 4's which can play short if you have a following wind. The 15th requires a semi-blind tee shot down a split level fairway towards a partly hidden green. The key to each of these holes is to avoid the fairway bunkers with your drive. The 18th tee is near the boundary fence but there is plenty of room if you aim for the left side of the green.

Seacroft has a deliberate policy of minimising the use of water on the fairways so as to preserve the natural links feel. This is to be applauded but, unfortunately, I was there during the hottest and driest July on record. The front nine was a good test but with the wind behind some of the longish par 4's on the home nine were reduced to a drive and a lofted approach.

In normal conditions Seacroft is an interesting old style links course. Some of the holes are similar to those at Hunstanton, its neighbour on the south side of the The Wash. Everything here is very natural and has its own distinctive feel. This lesser known links should definitely be added to your list of courses to experience.

You need to take a very brave line with your drive at the par 4, 8th hole

Par 4, 15th with its split level fairway

ROYAL WEST NORFOLK

Low tide beside the 9th green

IF YOU REALLY WANT TO KNOW WHAT IT WAS LIKE TO PLAY GOLF 'BETWEEN THE WARS' THEN I HEARTILY IMPLORE YOU TO VISIT ROYAL WEST NORFOLK AT BRANCASTER. DUST OFF YOUR OLD PERSIMMON WOODS AND DUNLOP 65'S AND THE EXPERIENCE WILL BE ENHANCED ALL THE MORE. TIME HAS STOOD WONDERFULLY STILL HERE BOTH IN THE CLUBHOUSE AND OUT ON THE LINKS. EVEN THE SCORE CARD IS REFLECTIVE OF DAYS SINCE PASSED.

Not only are parts of the course subject to daily tidal flooding, but so too is the entrance road, so be sure to check the notice board showing the tide times. To reach the first tee you must walk across the sandy approach to the beach and then you enter through a large old wrought iron gate.

Even though you may have the wind behind you for most of the outward nine, the first three holes are quite demanding each being a par 4 in excess of 400 yards. On a windy day the drive on the 1st is not without a number of perils. The tee box is angled towards the edge of the 18th green and fairway. A slight draw is needed but any thing resembling a hook will finish in long grass in the sand dunes or even out of bounds on the beach. The fairway is shared with the 18th, a fact you can easily forget when playing the final hole and thinking about avoiding the huge greenside bunker.

The 2nd and 3rd have rough and then farmland on the right and consequently are heavily bunkered down the left side. The right side of the 3rd also has a large marshy area.

The par 3, 4th is only 129 yards but it tends to play longer as it is uphill and often into the sea breeze. The green has a large bunker in front and then is raised as if on an island with the perimeter reinforced by a wall of vertical sleepers. This is a common sight both around the greens and in the bunkers at Brancaster.

A huge bunker runs in front of the 18th green – the sea is just a few yards to the right of the grand old clubhouse

Photo David Worley

Bathing boxes beside the 16th tee – a uniquely English setting

The greens are excellent, the fairways are lovely crisp turf, the wind is always a factor and there are some brilliant if somewhat quirky holes. I loved every minute of it.

The 6th is another par 3, but somewhat longer at 184 yards. Both the 6th and 7th have out of bounds only about 20 feet from the edge of the green. The par 5, 7th also features a marsh and out of bounds cattle fence almost the whole length of the right side.

Your most lasting memory of Royal West Norfolk is probably going to be the area at the far end of the course featuring the 8th and 9th holes. Eight is rated the hardest on the course even though it is a par 5 of only 494 yards. Darwin described the hole with the analogy…'of a man crossing a stream by somewhat imperfect stepping stones, so that he has to make a perilous leap from one to the other'.[1] There is a large tidal marsh area in front of the tee, then a strip of land followed by another tidal wetland with fairway recommencing about 60 yards short of the green. Depending upon the wind and where your drive lands, you may have to employ some creative thinking on this hole. I recall driving a little too far left, then hitting a 9 iron sideways and finally playing a 5 iron over the wetland on to the green.

The 9th hole features the frequently photographed green raised up on land supported by sleepers and nearby the sea inlet and numerous yachts moored or just lying on the sand. This is my favourite hole. Tidal marsh land runs along the first part of the fairway on the right. If you are game, the ideal tee shot is a fade towards the hazard. This must be followed up by a well struck mid-iron over another tidal area to the raised green. You are better to aim for the left side of the green but long grass awaits anything too far off line or too long.

In true classic links style, at the par 3, 10th the course turns back towards the clubhouse. Many of the following holes are alongside the sand dunes and the low lying grazing land that is partly subject to tidal flooding. A bad slice on the 10th will put you out of bounds. The green is raised and features some very deep bunkers front and right.

The 11th is a par 5 of merely 476 yards but is rated index 4. Your drive is over the corner of the out of bounds fence on the right where there is also very long grass all the way to the green. The middle of the fairway features an area of rough and a cluster of bunkers.

Twelve and thirteen are par 4's with unusual green positions, the 12th green resembling a raised dell. Fourteen is a very difficult and unusual par 4 of 430 yards. The green is uphill but is hidden behind a dry wasteland containing some nasty bunkers. Unless you have hit a very long drive you may have to consider laying up short of this area with your second.

The par 3, 15th features one of the biggest bunkers you will ever see on a short hole. Fortunately it is about 50 yards before the green so anything straight has a large landing area once over the bunker.

On a sunny day you will most likely be able to chat to the beachgoers as you stand on the 16th tee. There is a line of bathing boxes beside the tee behind which there are lovely dunes and the beach. The 16th has six fairway and one greenside bunker. The green is on a high sandy area close to

out of bounds and the beach. You need to keep your second toward the right side of the green otherwise your ball with run down a steep slope into a bunker.

The 17th runs diagonally across the 2nd fairway away from the sea. Eighteen is a straightforward par 4 except for the huge bunker that lies in a semi-circle in front of the green. If you can't carry the bunker with your second, there is room to play left of the green and chip from the side.

Royal West Norfolk has history written all over it. The first Captain was none other than Horace Hutchinson who also had a hand in the design along with Halcombe Ingleby. The Prince of Wales was Captain in 1929.

The greens are excellent, the fairways are lovely crisp turf, the wind is always a factor and there are some brilliant if somewhat quirky holes. I loved every minute of it.

1. *Golf Courses of the British Isles* – Bernard Darwin

HUNSTANTON

Photo David Worley

The superb par 3, 7th with a fearsome bunker at the front

This is certainly one of the premier links on the east coast of England.

HUNSTANTON, AND ITS NEIGHBOUR AT BRANCASTER 7 MILES DOWN THE COAST, HAD ITS BEGINNINGS IN 1891. THE ORIGINAL DESIGN HAS BEEN CONTINUALLY STRENGTHENED STARTING WITH THE ADDITION OF 40 NEW BUNKERS IN 1907 UNDER ADVICE FROM THE UBIQUITOUS JAMES BRAID.

The card shows a maximum length of 6759 yards, but for championship events the course is stretched to 6911 yards. Coupled with heavy bunkering, thick rough and constant sea breezes, this is a very solid test of your golfing ability.

Hunstanton has two most unusual aspects. With the exception of a recently introduced concession for Tuesdays, only two ball games are permitted. The course also features 'traffic lights'. The 14th is a long blind par 3. Green light on the tee will tell you it is safe to hit. There is also a public access walkway to the popular beach that runs across the 18th fairway. If the walkway is being used then sensors will activate a red light.

A feature of the course is the long spine of dunes that runs along or beside many of the fairways.

Photo David Worley

The raised and angled 18th green can be a difficult target

The first few holes can play much easier when the wind is behind. As with many of these courses, the key is to avoid the fairway bunkers with your drive. There is a huge bunker on the opening hole but it should not be in play as it dates to when the tee was located on the site of the present 18th green. A hidden danger on the par 5, 2nd hole is the burn that is only about ten feet from the back left of the green. Whilst the 3rd is a par 4 of 443 yards from the white tees and is rated index 1, with a breeze behind it was only a drive and a mid iron. The 5th and 6th can both be birdie opportunities if you keep on the fairway.

The 7th is a striking par 3 that certainly has the 'wow' factor when you see it for the first time. The fairway of 173 yards runs through a valley with large dunes on either side. One enormous deep bunker lies in front of the green. The face is made up of vertical railway sleepers so I would not fancy playing from right up against them. If the wind is behind then it is quite difficult to carry the bunker and then hold the green. Fortunately, on my visit, whilst the course was drying out, the greens were well watered.

Eight and nine are short but tricky par 5's. The 8th is a dog-leg left to right with lush grass and then out of bounds on the right. A narrow but deep burn runs across and may catch a long drive.

The 10th is an attractive uphill par 4 with a green on a high sandy area not far from the beach. Most of the bunkering is on the right, the direction to which the ball tends to feed.

The tee shot on the par 4, 13th requires accuracy over a high plateau and then a traditional links shot downhill through numerous bumps and mounds to a green tilted from front to back.

You will be surprised that the par 3, 14th is rated the easiest on the course. Playing there first time all you see is a hill in front of you. Once you clear the hill your ball may run to the green 222 yards away but anything a little to the right will be in long grass.

Fifteen is a slight bend left first through a valley and then uphill to a well bunkered fairway. The par 3, 16th is one of the best holes at Hunstanton. The elevated tee gives sea views and looks down to a split level green encircled by bunkers. There is no fairway, only long grass, so this is not the time to duff your tee shot. Somehow or other in 1974 Bob Taylor holed in one here on three consecutive days. The distance is 191 yards from the white but a little more comfortable at 158 yards from the visitors' tees.

Now comes a very tough finish. Seventeen is a long par 4 (447 yards) with a tight drive and then a narrow green with anything poorly executed running off to the right. The 18th runs through a slight valley with very heavy rough on either side. A row of bathing boxes runs along the right just over the boundary fence. The green is on a sharp rise and is at an angle making the target smaller. Anything right will kick down to a hollow leaving you with a delicate chip in front of the members' gaze.

This is a really enjoyable and testing course. The fairway bunkers are penal but if you can stay out of them then some holes play relatively short. It may have just been the wind on the day, but I found the back nine holes to be considerably more difficult than the outward nine. This is certainly one of the premier links on the east coast of England.

Photos David Worley

Top: par 4, 10th hole
Above: delightful par 3, 16th – there is no fairway and the green is encircled by bunkers
Below left: "traffic lights" at the 14th tee

SHERINGHAM

SHERINGHAM GOLF CLUB CAME INTO EXISTENCE IN 1891 DURING A PERIOD OF FRENETIC GOLF COURSE CONSTRUCTION PARTICULARLY ON ENGLAND'S EAST COAST. THE ORIGINAL COURSE DESIGNER WAS TOM DUNN AND BY 1898 THE NINE HOLES HAD BEEN EXTENDED TO EIGHTEEN.

Above: the long par 4, 5th hole
Below: 11th green from the 12th tee

The course is a picturesque clifftop links laid out between the North Norfolk Railway line on one side and the North Sea on the other. It is very wind exposed and has seven par 4's in excess of 400 yards. Sheringham has been the venue for three English Ladies Championships, the most famous being when Joyce Wethered won her first championship at just 18 years of age.

The opening hole is a good start, an uphill but short par 4 with a tricky, tilted green. The 2nd is a long par 5 downhill from an elevated tee. The 3rd and 4th greens are very wind exposed.

The 5th hole and view from the tee is nothing short of spectacular. This par 4 is 456 yards in length and is index 1. Fortunately it is downhill but you have more than just length to contend with. There are bunkers on both sides of the fairway for the drive and then the fairway narrows with many second shots bouncing left down the bank. From the tee the hole follows the clifftop and the green appears to have nothing to prevent anything other than a perfect long second shot from tumbling down steep banks on the left side and at the back. There is room to miss on the right but this may leave you with a difficult chip.

The 11th is a lovely uphill par 3 of 159 yards. The green is set at the foot of large grassy hills and all access to the green, other than in the air, is blocked by way of five greenside

bunkers. The view from the par 4, 12th tee is nearly as good as the wonderful aspect from the 5th.

The 17th is the furthest from the sea cliffs and has the railway line and out of bounds all along the right. A steam train still uses the line, bringing back memories recounted in the club's official handbook. "It was on the 17th green, set close to the railway fence, that Miss Wethered laid a long putt dead to make certain of her first championship, studying the line with such concentration as to be completely oblivious of the 4.20pm train out of Sheringham rattling past behind her". The green is in a lovely setting on the side of a hill with a little woodland behind and above it.

Eighteen is an excellent finishing hole of 420 yards. The approach to the green is downhill but there are several large and deep bunkers for any shot misdirected.

As clifftop links courses go, Sheringham is pretty good. The greens are excellent and the fairways are firm and fast. (In contrast, its neighbour Royal Cromer a few miles south is clifftop but the soil is much heavier and the fairways certainly do not have a links feel. It is also treed in places so for these reasons it was not included in this book.) Sheringham is quite hilly in parts, but on the day I was there most of the golfers were middle-aged or older and it did not seem to worry them.

GREAT YARMOUTH & CAISTER

GREAT YARMOUTH & CAISTER IS SEASIDE DUE EAST OF THE CITY OF NORWICH. FORMED IN 1882, WITH A RATHER INAUSPICIOUS BEGINNING WITH PRAC- TICALLY NO MEMBERS, IT IS THE OLDEST CLUB IN NORFOLK. IT IS ALSO PROBABLY THE MOST EASTERLY LINKS COURSE IN THE UNITED KINGDOM.

The distinctive bunkering is exemplified at the 10th green

Par 3, 14th with the racetrack rails in the distance

Photos David Worley

This is certainly links land but I have to say that I found the whole aspect of this course as being quite weird. A racecourse runs right through the middle of the course and is undoubtedly the predominant feature. On the occasion of my visit the presence of the racecourse was amplified as the links were brown and extremely dry whilst the racetrack was very lush and green.

There is plenty of gorse and rough but the terrain is of necessity one of low mounds rather than high dunes so as not to spoil the view for the racing fraternity.

Whilst the 1st hole is a fairly short par 4, it cuts across the racetrack at the turn so you have to negotiate it twice.

The 4th is the first of the more difficult holes. A par 4 of 452 yards, the fairway narrows about 120 yards from the green. A line of bunkers runs across the fairway and gorse is on either side.

The 7th is the only par 3 on the front nine and it is 191 yards in length with a two-tiered green that falls away on both sides for any shot that is not accurate. Eight is quite rightly index one. It is a par 4 of 468 yards with fairway bunkers along the left and two bunkers and plenty of gorse on the right near the green.

Index 2, the 10th is a good looking par 4 of 419 yards. The hole is on marginally higher ground with the green back near the clubhouse. Two sleepered bunkers lie on the left of the green which slopes in their direction. The 11th needs no bunkers. This long par 4 is in a slightly valleyed fairway and thick rough runs the length of the fairway on both sides.

Fourteen is a lovely short hole of 161 yards. There are several clumps of gorse for a really poor tee shot, but the view of the green is dominated by two large bunkers with vertical sleepers.

The par 4, 18th requires an extremely accurate drive. There are wet ditches and then trees close by on both sides forward of the tee. The drive must also clear the racetrack, the rails of which are classified as an immovable obstruction but with special rules applying for the 1st, 15th, 16th and 18th holes.

Maybe it takes a bit of getting used to, but for me the ever present racecourse spoils the golf and the two are not compatible.

FELIXSTOWE FERRY

Photo David Worley

*"With one consuming roar along the shingle
the long wave claws and rakes the pebbles down
to where its backwash and the next wave mingle,
a mounting arch of water weedy-brown
against the tide the off-shore breezes blow.
Oh wind and water, this is Felixstowe."*

John Betjeman

Sea defences alongside the 15th fairway – the original 15th was washed away overnight during a storm in January 1963

FELIXSTOWE WAS FORMED IN 1880 AND THIS MAKES IT THE FIFTH OLDEST CLUB TO HAVE BEEN FORMED IN ENGLAND. TRAVELLING DOWN THE EAST COAST OF ENGLAND, THIS IS THE LAST LINKS COURSE BEFORE HEADING SOUTH OF LONDON TO DEAL AND SANDWICH. THE BOOM IN GOLF COURSE DEVELOPMENT WAS QUITE AMAZING AS BY 1886 THE NUMBER OF CLUBS IN ENGLAND HAD GROWN FROM FIVE IN 1880 TO FORTY, AND BY 1906 THERE WERE FIVE HUNDRED.

The original 9 hole course was designed by Tom Dunn. In the opening year, Willie Fernie was appointed as both green keeper and professional. It was at Felixstowe as early as 1884 that a young Bernard Darwin first took an interest in golf.

Two years after the First World War the links were reconstructed under the supervision of James Braid and a further 9 holes was added.

Substantial damage was done during World War II as the course was part of the coastal defence system. The task to resurrect the course after the war was allotted to Henry Cotton and Sir Guy Campbell.

More recent threats have come from sea storms and king tides. In 1953 almost the whole course was flooded and in January 1963 the then par 3,15th hole was completely washed away overnight. The new 15th now runs slightly away from the coastline and a large concrete retaining wall has been built along the beach perimeter of the course. Various rock gabion walls have also been used to protect the beach but the downside of this has been that the sea water is churned up and is a permanently a rather brown colour.

The course is pretty much divided in two by a public road. Holes 1–3 and 13–18 are on the sea side of the road and have the more natural true links feel. These seaside holes are also rather more exposed to the wind which can get pretty strong here at times.

The first hole is a reasonably difficult start being a par 4 of 428 yards. Whilst a draw is the ideal tee shot you need to be careful to avoid the road on your left. Thick rough is on either side as is the case with the par 5, 2nd hole. The 3rd and 4th are shorter par 4's but the dog-leg 4th gets quite narrow from about 80 yards short of the green.

The par 3, 5th marks the beginning of 7 holes where a burn is in play. The burn is on both sides of the fairway on 7th, 8th and 10th holes. Whilst the 11th has the burn on the right hand side, there is also the road and out of bounds along the left. On a windy day these rather flat and tame looking holes can be deceptively difficult.

The 12th is a par 3 of 144 yards and has the unusual feature in that you hit across the main roadway to an elevated green set below the club house. There is a high wire mesh fence to protect local traffic from low tee shots.

This is followed by a long walk from the 12th green, past the 18th green, to the 13th tee which is right beside the seaside and coastal storm wall. Your line for the drive is the left side of the Martello Tower. Thirteen and the next two holes all run alongside the sea wall. The greens on the first eleven holes are basically flat but from the 12th onwards they have more slope and undulations.

The 14th and 15th are two of the newer holes (following previous coastal erosion) and can play longer into the wind than their yardage would suggest. These holes have a different architectural feel as a result of being the work of Martin Hawtree.

A long par 3 of 204 yards awaits you at the 16th. The bunker at the front is well short of the green so there is really only the right hand bunker and a green that runs away left and back that you need to watch for. The 17th is a long par 4 dominated by the presence of the famous Martello tower which dates back to the Napoleonic Wars.

The 18th is 321 yards and uphill but with summer fairways and a following breeze it is almost drivable. A ridge across the fairway and three greenside bunkers are the main obstacles but a straight drive should leave you with just a short approach.

The greens at Felixstowe are very good. The bunkers are not overly difficult or numerous in quantity. However, you will have to contend with the ever present strong wind, thick rough and several burns that are bound to get your unwanted attention.

1st fairway – the public roadway runs close by on the left

The 13th green and historic Martello Tower

Despite what some may think, links courses are definitely not all the same as exemplified by Felixstowe Ferry which has an ambience all of its own.

PRINCES

Photo courtesy Richard Kimber/Princes GC

9th hole, Shore Nine

THE COURSE AT PRINCES FIRST OPENED IN 1906 AFTER THE FOUNDER SIR HARRY MALLABY-DEELEY DECIDED TO ESTABLISH A NEW LINKS AT SANDWICH. PRINCES HAS ALWAYS BEEN A PRIVATELY OWNED CLUB.

The original course was designed and built by Mallaby-Deeley in conjunction with his friend Percy Lucas and the 1902 Amateur Champion, Charles Hutchins. The first Captain of the new club was A J Balfour who had been Prime Minister until 1905.

Princes quickly gained a fine reputation. In 1922 it staged the Ladies Open won by the marvellous Joyce Wethered. In 1930 the Prince of Wales became its President and just two years later the Open was held at Princes. Gene Sarazen won the event and in doing so he broke numerous records. This was also the first time a sand wedge (designed by Sarazen) was ever used in a tournament.

Due to its location, Princes was requisitioned during World War II and it quickly became an overgrown battlefield. Fortunately, Royal St Georges next door was spared. According to the club's history, "by the end of the war the course had been practically obliterated and the Royal Marines were considering it as a permanent rifle range. The coastguard cottages were destroyed and the clubhouse was a roofless wreck". [1]

The restoration took place under the guidance of Aynsley Bridgland, an ex-pat Australian engineer who had also been involved in the building of the Sydney Harbour Bridge. Guy Campbell and John Morrison were appointed to construct the new course which would consist of 27 holes. This was all completed in 1952.

This is largely the course of today which consists of the Shore, Dunes and Himalayas nines. When major events are played it is the combination of the Shore and Dunes that is used.

The Shore follows a clockwise loop initially south along the coastline down to the old clubhouse. The first hole is a long par 4 and whilst the 2nd is a short par 5 it can be very difficult to stop the ball on the aprons and greens in summer.

The par 3, 3rd hole features a very deep pot bunker with a vertical face at the front left of the green. The next three holes are all par 4's of around 400 yards. There is plenty of run on the fairways but the rough, by way of long grass, is very thick if you are inaccurate. The 7th is a long par 5 with a narrow fairway and then a slightly raised green.

The par 3, 8th has just one greenside bunker at the front but falls away steeply if you miss the green on the left.

The Dunes runs anti-clockwise with five holes heading to the boundary of Royal St George's and the last four back to the clubhouse. The 1st is one of the most difficult on this nine. The hole dog-legs left where all the trouble lies. You can run out of fairway on the right. The green is narrow and raised with a ridge along the approach that may kick your ball away from the target.

The 2nd is a par 3 of 172 yards from the back tees. The power plant chimneys dominate the skyline in the view behind the green and there are three pot bunkers at the front. The 3rd is an excellent par 5 that is some 66 yards longer from the very back tee compared to the next tee position. A ditch and out of bounds runs the full length of the hole along the right side.

The 4th, a par 4 of 430 yards, is rated index 1. The hole dog-legs left and has five very penal fairway bunkers plus another two green-side. The 5th is a similarly shaped hole. Anything pulled left will be in very long grass. Beware of the large railway sleepered bunker about 90 yards short of the green.

The 6th is a short par 5 that presents one of the few birdie opportunities. Apart from a cluster of bunkers 130 yards from the green, the main risk is a burn on the left which is more

The dry summer of 2006 – par 3, 3rd hole, Shore Nine with a deep pot bunker at the front left

in play as you approach the green. Seven is a short par 4 but the prevailing wind seems to push your second shot toward the four bunkers at the front left of the green.

The par 3, 8th may only have one bunker but the hole measures 217 yards from the back tee and 207 from the white. The 9th is a strong par 4 with a ditch along the left. Thick rough abounds so this is not a place to spray your shots.

Princes is a very good test of golf. Whilst they have adequate water supplies and sprinklers in place on the fairways, they tend to use the bare minimum in summer so as to retain the true links playing surface. There are no distance markers of any description. The course is also designed so there are no blind shots, quite a contrast with Royal St George's next door. The greens are good but can be very firm and quite difficult to hold. A feature of the fairways are long ridges and undulations that often run parallel and can kick a good drive off line and into the rough of which there is plenty.

You will do very well to beat your handicap at Princes.

1. *Princes Golf Club, A Celebration of 100 Years*

ROYAL CINQUE PORTS

The rolling fairway of the par 5, 3rd

A NINE HOLE COURSE WAS LAID OUT HASTILY IN 1892 AT DEAL. A SECOND NINE WAS FINISHED FOUR YEARS LATER AND THEN IN 1919 JAMES BRAID RE-ORGANISED THE ROUTING AND MADE A NUMBER OF OTHER CHANGES INCLUDING VIRTUALLY NEW HOLES AT THE 10TH AND 11TH. FOLLOWING WORLD WARD II, SIR GUY CAMPBELL AND HENRY COTTON WERE GIVEN THE TASK OF RESTORING THE COURSE TO ITS PRE-WAR CONDITION.

Deal is a qualifying course for an Open at Royal St George's. The Open was actually played at Deal in 1909 (won by J H Taylor) and 1920 (won by George Duncan). It was scheduled there again in 1938 and in 1949 and on both occasions a high tide and strong winds swept the sea over the course rendering it unplayable and as a result the Championship was moved nearby to Royal St George's.

The opening hole is a relatively easy par 4 with a generous fairway. The greenside burn although fairly wide, is hard to see from the distance so better to be long than under club with your second.

The short par 5, 3rd hole is one of the best and most interesting at Deal. The fairway is a series of rolling mounds, rather like waves, with the green virtually hidden behind the last of the mounds.

The 4th is a lovely bunkerless par 3 of 152 yards. The white cliffs of Dover are predominant in the distance. This hole looks a little longer than it is so you need to be careful with club selection. The 6th is an old fashioned short par 4 with a deep gully in front of the green. If you over club you could finish on the beach. The 7th provides for a very heavily bunkered par 4, especially on the left side. Be careful to avoid the hollow at the front left of the green as this will generally run your ball into the bunker nearby.

The par 3, 8th heads easterly towards the beach whereas the majority of holes run north/south. The front and sides of the 8th green are surrounded by nine bunkers.

The 9th, 10th and 11th holes are each a dog-leg left where a good drive with a slight draw is needed. All of these par 4's are well bunkered. The 13th is a dog-leg slightly right and contains two bunkers at the 200 yard distance in the right hand corner which is exactly the line you would prefer to choose. The shot into the green must keep right to avoid the three bunkers at front left.

1st green and clubhouse – the burn in front of the green is hard to see if you are not familiar with the course

Gary Player has described these last four holes as
"the finest four consecutive holes on any course in the world".

Photo David Worley

3rd green from side on

Take one more club than you think on the long par 3, 14th which is uphill and feeds balls left of the green where the rough can be especially heavy.

The next few holes have extremely bumpy fairways so keeping your ball out of the rough is a difficult achievement, especially if you are into the wind. Gary Player has described these last four holes as "the finest four consecutive holes on any course in the world".

The short par 5, 16th is, like the 3rd , one of the best at Deal. This can be a birdie chance but you will have to contend with a narrowing fairway and a large mound and bunker just short of the green. Fairway mounds stop you from seeing your second shot land and anything a little strong will be in very long grass close to the green.

Keep your drive to the right at the 17th but this is also where the rough is at its worst if you are not accurate. The 18th fairway is a flatter affair but this hard running fairway contains a burn that can catch a long drive. Play your drive to position then there are no bunkers to worry about with your second to the slightly raised green.

Royal Cinque Ports is a wonderful links course with some really good holes. It was unfortunate that when I was there it was the hottest July ever recorded in England and this area had been on water restrictions for over a year. The main rough is not cut here – a deliberate policy because of the large number of birds that nest in these grasses.

ROYAL ST GEORGE'S

The famous 'Maiden' bunker at the 4th

ROYAL ST GEORGE'S COURSE WAS OPEN FOR PLAY IN 1887 WITH DR LAIDLAW PURVES BEING LARGELY RESPONSIBLE FOR CHOOSING THE LOCATION AND DESIGNING THE HOLES. PURVES WAS A SCOTTISH OPHTHALMOLOGIST WHO WAS BASED IN LONDON AT THE TIME. REMARKABLY, WITHIN FIVE YEARS THE CLUB HAD HOSTED THE AMATEUR CHAMPIONSHIP AND THEN IN 1894 BECAME THE FIRST ENGLISH CLUB TO BE THE VENUE FOR THE OPEN (WON IN THAT YEAR BY J H TAYLOR).

To date, twelve Open Championships have been held at Royal St George's and each has had its fair share of drama. An unlucky loser must surely have been Harry Bradshaw in 1949. On the 5th hole his ball lay half in a broken bottle in the rough. Rather than wait for a ruling he played his ball where it lay and effectively dropped two shots. He eventually tied with Bobby Locke but lost the 36 hole play-off. Other great names to have won at Sandwich include Vardon, Hagen, Cotton, Lyle and Norman.

In the 1993 Open, heavy rain prior to the tournament had softened the course and as a result Els and Norman became the first to ever complete The Open with all four rounds under 70. Norman's record low score for an Open final round of 64 included a missed putt of not much more than a foot on the 17th. Langer is purported to have told

Starters hut and clubhouse at dusk

Photo David Worley

The 5th is a dramatic par 4 with a line of bunkers along the left

The 5th green is almost hidden by the two dunes

Norman, as they walked down the 18th, that this was the finest round of golf he had ever witnessed.

The 1st hole has all the features that make you remember Royal St George's. Two very accurate and long shots are needed to avoid the deep hollows and three green side bunkers.

Out of bounds is close beside you on the right of the 2nd tee. Two fairway bunkers occupy the left corner of the dog-leg. There is a very deep swale at the right hand edge of the green.

The par 3, 3rd hole is 198 yards (210 from the championship tee) and has no bunkers. It doesn't need the extra hazards as there is thick rough for quite a distance in front of the tee and the green has a severe slope from back to front.

The 4th is one of the best and certainly most famous holes in British golf. From the white tees it is a par 4 of 417 yards but from the back it is a par 5 of 497 yards. Your drive needs to be a slight draw over the Maiden bunker or a slight fade left of the bunker. The fairway then dog-legs left to an elevated green protected by a mound on the left side and out of bounds immediately behind.

The par 4, 5th is also one of the best, and most dramatic, of the layout. The drive must be very accurate to avoid a line of bunkers on the left side which is the position you need to be near for the tricky second through or over a narrow gap between two large dunes. A ridge running along the centre of the fairway can either kick your tee shot left into the bunkers or right into the thick rough. Out of bounds and the beach is not far from the right hand side of the green.

Six is an attractive par 3 with an angled green and four bunkers. A slight fade might be your best option here into the dell green. The 9th is a good looking golf hole when surveyed from the tee. The view to the green is dominated by two very penal bunkers set into a mound just left of the green. In the distance is the unmistakable outline of the one tall and narrow and three wide chimneys of the power station.

The 10th is a straight par 4 with the difficulty being the shot into a raised green which slopes towards the two bunkers at the left. Eleven is a very long par 3 of 216 yards from the white and 242 yards from the back tee. There is also a sloping green and five bunkers to contend with. Twelve dog-legs right through a very bumpy fairway and five bunkers just short of the green.

Index 2 is the long par 5, 14th hole. There are three dangers here. Out of bounds runs close by the fairway for the whole length of the right side. There is a burn running across the fairway 330 yards from the tee. There are also two small bunkers in the centre of the fairway about 60 yards before the green. If you are playing a long shot into the green you will be very aware of how close the out of bounds boundary lies from the right side of the green but there are also another two bunkers front left for the 'involuntary draw'. This hole is often remembered as where Bernhard Langer lost the 1993 Open. Only a shot or so behind Norman, Langer played safe on the tee for each of the first three rounds and made par. Inexplicably, in the final round he used his driver and promptly dispatched his ball over the fence.

The 15th is a very long par 4 with five bunkers waiting for your drive and three more running across the fairway in front of the green. All of the par 3's at Royal St George's are excellent and the 16th is no exception. Land on the green you must as there are four bunkers at the front and two on either side of the green.

Both the 17th and 18th are good long par 4's where strong driving is the key. The large open spaces on the right of the last hole make it an ideal area for grandstands virtually from tee to green. The 18th green falls away on either side, with

the hollow on the right affectionately known as Duncan's Hollow after George Duncan took three to get down from there when a par of 4 on the last would have put him in a playoff with Hagen in the 1922 Open.

Royal St George's stands out as being quite different to any other links. As you would expect, the greens and fairways are first class. Your education is not complete until you have experienced the delights and chicaneries of Royal St George's. Each hole is varied, some are very memorable. The blind shots and bumpy fairways add to the fun for most, but probably this aspect is not endearing to many of the professionals.

Perhaps Darwin should have the last word: "Sandwich has a charm that belongs to itself, and I frankly own myself under the spell. The long strip of turf on the way to the seventh hole, that stretches between the sandhills and the sea; a fine spring day, with the larks singing as they seem to sing nowhere else; the sun shining on the waters of Pegwell Bay and lighting up the white cliffs in the distance; this is as nearly my idea of Heaven as is to be attained on any earthly links." [1]

1. *Golf Courses of the British Isles* – Bernard Darwin

Photo: David Worley

Par 3, 6th green

LITTLESTONE

Photo David Worley

18th hole with clubhouse at the right of the green

LITTLESTONE IS LOCATED ON THE COAST, MORE OR LESS MIDWAY BETWEEN FOLKSTONE (ENTRANCE TO THE CHANNEL TUNNEL) AND RYE.

The club was founded in 1888 and the clubhouse, still used today, was built in 1901. The present layout dates from the 1920's, when Dr. Alister MacKenzie modernised the course and made significant changes to the 6th, 8th, 14th, 16th and 17th holes. In 2000, five new back tees were added to give a length of 6676 yards from the blue tees.

Littlestone has an interesting historical claim in that at the same time, the club had the Prime Minister of the day (Asquith) as Captain and the Leader of the Opposition (Balfour) as President.

The opening is a rather gentle affair. This is a drivable par 4 of 300 yards with little by way of hazards if you hit it straight. The 2nd hole provides some intrigue as to what lies ahead with the approach to the green played through a gap in two dunes that are large by Littlestone standards. A narrow burn runs across just in front of the dunes. The 3rd requires a rather frightening blind tee shot into the unknown beyond heavily grassed dunes that will stop anything not well struck. The par 4, 4th hole has bunkers to be avoided at the corner of the slight dog-leg and then bunkers at the front right of the green. Do not hit your second long as anything through the green will run down the bank to long grass close by.

The 6th is the first of the par 3's. Although only 159 yards in length it is rated index number 4. There is a pot bunker set into a mound on the left some twenty yards back. The less obvious bunker at front right will gather any ball with a slice. The green contains many undulations and is raised at the back. Short but straight is the only place to be if you are not on the green.

Seven is a shortish par 5 that needs to be treated with caution. Thick rough lines the fairway and a deep ditch, thick with plants and grasses, runs across about where your second shot is likely to finish. The slightly elevated green is in an attractive setting with bunkers either side at the front and trees in the near distance.

The 8th and 9th form the boundary far from the clubhouse with houses as the backdrop on the left side. Eight requires a very accurate drive slightly right but not behind the dune.

A number of bunkers must be avoided with your second especially the small pot bunker very close to the right edge of the green. Nine is a long par 3 from the blue tees (212 yards) with plenty of long grass and bunkers if you are not on the green.

Your drive at the par 4, 10th should be left of centre. There is a pond on the right that you cannot see and further along on the same side towards the green there is a large bunker with a vertical face cut into the side of a large mound.

9th green

The 11th poses the classic question asking you to decide how much of the corner can you take on. This par 4 of 408 yards is shortened considerably if you aim right of the green with a draw. Anything too far left will be in trouble in the deep wet ditch or long grass. Hit a prefect drive and you will think it is an easy hole.

The 12th features a large cross bunker with a marker post above to help you with your blind tee shot. The green here can be quite tricky. The 13th runs towards the sea with both a blind first and second shot. The bunkers that appear to be greenside are actually 50 yards short so don't be fooled.

It is unusual to find par 3's with a low index rating. Not only is the 6th index 4, but the 187 yard 14th is rated number 5. The green is undulating and is encircled by bunkers at the front and sides. A draw that avoids the bunkers can provide you with a birdie chance on the 15th.

The last three holes are a good finish. Sixteen is a long par 4 of 469 yards running along the sea wall. The fairway is wide but if you try to over hit and go left you will be in very long grass along the side of the bank. The second half of the fairway runs uphill with bunkers at the beginning of this area. Anything right of the green is in serious trouble. Your target is to aim just left of the tall church tower.

The 17th is a very good par 3 and is one of the best holes at Littlestone. The tee is from the seaside boundary to a green partly blocked on the left by a low dune and a bunker. There are three bunkers on the right including two short of the green. The desired shot to the green is a slight draw but anything too far left will be in heavy rough. Similarly, if you run through the green then you will fall away into a rough area. On a windy day this can be the toughest par 3 on the course.

The 18th is a straight ahead, relatively short, par 5 on flat terrain. The dangers lie with the five fairway bunkers and the steep faced bunker at the right edge of the green.

Photo David Worley

17th green from side on – note the sea wall in the background

On the negative side, visually the course is fairly flat and the views from the seaside holes are now somewhat spoilt by the concrete sea wall that runs not far from the 9th, 11th, 13th, 15th and 16th greens.

There are no fairway sprinklers and no distance markers which will please the purists. The greens are firm and quite fast as are the fairways in mid summer.

This is a good test of links golf even if there aren't any spectacular holes.

RYE

Photo David Worley

15th green looking from near the 13th

THE BIRTH OF RYE GOLF CLUB IN 1894 LED TO THE ELECTION OF HARRY COLT AS THE FIRST CAPTAIN. HIS DESIGN AT RYE IN 1895 WAS HIS FIRST AND MARKED THE NEW CAREER FOR THE FORMER SOLICITOR. THE CLUB SOON FLOURISHED, HELPED BY THE OPENING OF THE 1 MILE RAILWAY LINE FROM RYE TO THE GOLF LINKS STATION AT CAMBER.

Bernard Darwin became captain in 1906 and was re-elected again 50 years later in 1956. He said, with much affection, that 'to arrive at the Dormy House at Rye is to gain some impression of what Eternity will be like'.[1] Darwin moved into the Dormy House in 1954, after the death of his wife, and it was there he died in 1961 at the age of 85.

By the 1930's it was considered too dangerous to have holes on the other side of the road so changes were made, first by Tom Simpson and then by Sir Guy Campbell and the green keeper, Frank Arnold. By 2006 Rye had employed only three green keepers in nearly 100 years.

The only par 5 at Rye is the 1st hole. A straight drive is needed into a fairway which is somewhat wider than it first appears from the tee. The 2nd is a good par 3 of 180 yards. The green has five bunkers at the sides and a bumpy ridge across the front.

The 3rd is the first of nine par 4's that are in excess of 400 yards in length. Heavy rough runs along the left but a cluster of bunkers are on the right so you need a long and straight drive. The green is on higher ground in front of the old coast-guards' cottages. Judging distances and then not running through the green can be quite tricky.

The 4th is difficult enough at any time but even more so in summer when the fairway is hard and fast. The fairway runs

Par 3, 7th from green to tee

along a high ridge. Your ball is likely to run off on either side from the drive but near the green there is a steep slope along the right so you may finish down near the 2nd green.

Any of the five par 3's at Rye can ruin your score. The 5th is a wonderful par 3. You hit over a valley to a green on top of a flattened dune. Anything short or left will run back down a steep bank. However, the green slopes from left to right so your correct line is to play to the left side perhaps with a slight fade.

The 6th, index 1, is a very difficult par 4 of 468 yards. The drive is blind over a marker post on top of a high ridge. Unless you are very long, a draw on this dog-leg will finish in the rough. Four bunkers are at the sides of the narrow entrance to the green so you might want to consider playing short of them and then you will have a fairly simple pitch.

The 7th is a wonderfully wild looking par 3 at the far end of the course abutting the 9 hole Jubilee course built in the 1970's. Sand dunes run along the left and behind the green.

Unfriendly rough lies in the hollow between tee and green and a clump of low trees is to the right. There are three bunkers but the larger one right at the front edge of the green is the danger.

Eight and nine are short par 4's running back to near the clubhouse. Just short of the green the 9th is punctuated by a very bumpy fairway.

The par 4, 10th, dog-legs right with very thick gorse on both sides of parts of the fairway. With so much gorse to worry about, bunkers are deemed unnecessary here. The 11th is the last of the short par 4's. The hole is only 324 yards and bends right following the edge of the lake – a flooded gravel pit. If you don't hit a fade from the tee then you are likely to run through the left side of the fairway. Both the 10th and 11th are rather out of character with the other holes at Rye.

The 12th tee is right beside the wetlands with the Rye docks on your right. Once you have driven over the rough the hole is fairly straight forward. Thirteen is anything but straight forward. This is a long par 4 with a ridge of high dunes blocking any view of the green. The dunes start at 290 yards from the tee so for the average golfer you need to play short and then position your second shot onto the next section of fairway and accept your bogey 5. When playing your second you need to be aware that the green is more to the left than you may have imagined.

Photo David Worley

A blind second shot is required to the 13th green

The same ridge of dunes runs along the left side of the par 3, 14th. Three bunkers are on the left and anything right will tend to kick on to slightly lower ground.

Fifteen is a demanding par 4 with plenty of rough and bumps and hollows. There is also a ditch all along the right hand side. The 16th entails a blind tee shot over a ridge. If you don't hit a good drive or you are a little left then you may still be playing a blind shot for your second. Be careful as the green is more left than the line off the tee would suggest.

Seventeen is the longest par 3 at 222 yards but it is the least attractive. The hole is flat with light rough for much of the distance. The only bunkers are at the left of the green.

The 18th is a great finishing hole and, for me, it is tougher than its rating of index number 8. The fairway bends to the right but there are so many undulations it can be hard to define. The clubhouse clock is your line for the drive. Severe trouble awaits any ball off line, especially down the right when playing your second into a difficult sloping green.

Rye has some really wonderful golf holes and their greens are close to the best in Britain, but be prepared for dry fairways in summer as there are no fairway sprinklers on the course. On the other hand, Rye is playable all year round with the famous President's Putter event having been played there in early January since 1920.

1. *Green Memories* – Bernard Darwin.

HAYLING

Photo David Worley

12th green from the 13th tee

FOR SOME STRANGE REASON THERE IS PRACTICALLY NO GOOD LINKS LAND ON THE SOUTH EAST COAST OF ENGLAND ONCE YOU TRAVEL WEST OF RYE. THE ONE NOTICEABLE EXCEPTION IS HAYLING GOLF CLUB LOCATED AT THE FAR END OF HAYLING ISLAND, JUST NORTH OF THE ISLE OF WIGHT. THE 'ISLAND' IS NOT REALLY AN ISLAND AND IS JOINED TO THE MAINLAND BY A BRIDGE.

A few of the undulations on the course are courtesy of German air raids as during the Second World War the course was lit up at night so as to make it appear to German pilots that they were bombing nearby Portsmouth. The clubhouse escaped damage, but all the outhouses were destroyed including the professional's shop along with its stock.

Hayling predates many of the more famous links having started in 1883. In 1897 alterations were made by J H Taylor and when the club finally gained the land as freehold in 1924 they instructed J Simpson who made further changes three years later.

The first four holes are on fairly flat and uninteresting land but from the 5th the course becomes far more varied and challenging. This is a great short hole of 163 yards. There is hardly any fairway before a raised green that is long, but very narrow being only twelve yards wide. One steep faced bunker is at the front left edge of the green.

The par 4, 6th, is index 1 for good reason. The tee shot is semi blind, there is gorse and trees if you are off line and there is a water hazard on the edge of both the left and right side of the fairway at about 100 yards from the green. This hole of 434 yards can play very long into the wind.

The 7th is a short par 5. The line for the drive is quite tight between the gorse plantations and the green has a steep tier at the front. Eight requires a fairly long carry before the drive reaches the fairway. There is a pot bunker at 214 yards on the right. The second shot is through a gap between two dunes with an area of no fairway, only rough, about 90 yards from the green.

By the time you assess the situation at the 9th tee you begin to appreciate that this is definitely a course for very accurate driving and it is a little disconcerting having so many blind drives on a course you do not know. The marker post stands on top of a heavily grassed ridge. Anything slightly left may catch a bunker which cannot be seen from the tee. The hole dog-legs to the left where the ridge is at its highest so a well controlled draw just right of the marker post is ideal.

The 10th is a very cleverly designed short par 4. The hole is 270 yards slightly uphill with one large bunker at about 210 yards on the left. The shape of the hole dictates a slight draw but this is not a hole for a wayward drive as there is thick rough left of the bunker and gorse at the right hand side of the fairway. The hole is named Pan-Ko-Chai which is Malaysian for Hell.

The short 11th runs right to the seaside boundary. Rough abounds and the tilted green has five bunkers mainly for anything short. Left has less trouble by way of sand hazards but here the rough is more unforgiving. Twelve is the longest par 4 (444 yards) and presents yet another rather scary drive with no fairway in sight for the first 180 yards. Out of bounds and gorse is to your left but this is the preferred angle of approach to a pretty green nestled into a hill.

One of the most memorable holes is the 13th, 'Widow'. The tee shot is blind and there is no fairway in sight. The beach is to your immediate left and is out of bounds. A straight drive into the centre of the fairway over the hill is the key. You then have an approach down a steep hill to the green. It is very easy to run through the green but be

Top: par 3, 11th hole
Above: 18th green and the distinctive Art Deco clubhouse
Far right: blind tee shot at the 13th 'Widow'

careful as out of bounds is only a few yards away. Originally there was a huge bunker to catch the drive at the top of the hill. Purportedly, a male golfer was playing a shot from the bunker when it collapsed, burying and killing him. This led to the bunker being filled in and the hole gaining the name 'Widow'.

Fourteen is a dog-leg left par 5 that is lined with gorse and has the sea inlet on the left. Fifteen requires an intimidating tee shot over gorse and a water hazard in front of the tee. The fairway is heavily bunkered especially at around 130 yards short of the green.

The 16th is a tricky par 3 of 183 yards. There is only one bunker (on the right) but there is virtually no fairway and the green is angled and has a ridge just in front of the apron. The drive on the par 4, 17th is through a narrow opening with very thick gorse on either side. All along the far left is the lake which reaches almost to the lovely old art deco clubhouse. The temptation on seventeen is to cut the corner but your best line is right of centre. The cross bunkers 98 yards out should not be in play but they tend to make the second shot look shorter than it really is. The name of the hole, 'Sailors Grave', is believed to be due to a body being washed ashore nearby. Another legend from the early days is that an old horse named Sailor lies buried under the first bunker.

The 18th features a wall of gorse on the left and clumps of gorse and heavy rough to the right. The green is 43 yards long so the pin position may require you take one more club.

The cleverly designed short par 4, 10th

Photo David Worley

On a windy day this can be a seriously difficult golf course, especially if you are playing Hayling for the first time. Accurate driving is absolutely essential otherwise you will be reaching into your bag for a new ball more often than normal. I will leave the final word to an entry in the club minutes of 1895 – 'The Honourary Secretary is authorised to procure shelter so that old and valued members may not risk their lives in wet and stormy weather'.

ROYAL JERSEY

IN 1877 PERMISSION WAS GRANTED FOR A GOLF COURSE TO BE CREATED ON COMMON LAND ALONG THE EASTERN SEASHORE AT GROUVILLE BAY ON JERSEY IN THE CHANNEL ISLANDS. THE FOLLOWING YEAR THE JERSEY GOLF CLUB WAS ESTABLISHED AND ONE YEAR LATER QUEEN VICTORIA GRANTED APPROVAL FOR THE 'ROYAL' AFFIXATION.

The great Harry Vardon was born here in 1870, not far from the 12th fairway. Another local was Ted Ray, seven years the junior of Vardon, who had the distinction of being the only British golfer to win both the US and British Open in the same year until Tony Jacklin (a Jersey resident) repeated the feat in 1970. Harry's medals are on display at the Jersey museum in St Helier.

Whilst Royal Jersey measures just 6110 yards, there are three par 5's on the front nine. The first four holes follow the coastline with the castle of Mont Orgueil in the distance.

The par 5, 1st requires a drive over the left edge of the 18th green. Any hint of a fade with your tee shot and you may finish in the sea. The short 2nd is slightly away from the shore so as to make way for the 3rd tee. The shortage of land here dictates that a number of tees and greens are close by.

The 3rd is a lovely par 5 of 554 yards through a slightly valleyed fairway full of undulations. The par 3, 4th has only one bunker but the green can be hard to hold as it slopes away to the back.

Holes five, six and seven run back and forth at the far end of the links. Each of these par 4's is around the same length at just under 400 yards but the 7th (index number 2) poses the greatest threat with gorse and a raised green.

The 8th is only 129 yards and is made even shorter by the tee which is some 40 feet above a well guarded green. You almost feel like you are in someone's back yard in this little wooded area. This hole was only opened in 1984.

The par 5, 9th and par 4, 10th and 11th holes all run in different directions. The 10th is an interesting dog-leg left with plenty of bunkers waiting for your second shot. The par 4, 12th is rated the hardest hole. There are three bunkers across the fairway about 90 yards from a green that has gorse and low bushy trees not far away.

Three of the next four holes feature split level greens. The par 3, 16th also requires that you hit over the entrance road. As is the case with many greens at Royal Jersey, the 17th is an elevated target which is built on an old German bunker. The 18th is a short par 4 where the green is slightly sunken.

If you are lucky enough to get a calm sunny day then this is wonderful holiday golf with views to match.

ROYAL GUERNSEY

THE LINKS ARE LOCATED AT L'ANCRESSE, A POPULAR HOLIDAY SPOT ON THE NORTH OF THE ISLAND.

Royal Guernsey has more to look at than just the usual features of a golf course. There are clusters of large stones which indicate ancient burial grounds – you will be pleased to know that you can take relief without penalty. Martello Towers are there from the Napoleonic Wars whilst more recent confrontations have left a smattering of World War II pill boxes.

You will also need to watch for the cars and beach goers as you hit across a public road on at least three occasions. Be polite to the walkers as the course is laid out on common land for all to enjoy. I just wish the non-golfing walkers knew how dangerous an errant golf ball can be.

Founded in 1890, Royal Guernsey, as with the other seaside courses of the Channel Islands, required substantial restoration after the German war time occupation. This was supervised by Mackenzie Ross who, at around the same time, was involved at Turnberry and Southerness. Further alterations were completed twenty years later by Fred Hawtree.

After a gentle short par 4 opening hole, the 2nd is a solid par 4 of 401 yards along the first of 2 coastlines abutting the course. Clumps of gorse are about the only thing that will stop you admiring the adjacent bay of Grand Havre. The par 3, 3rd hole continues along the shore. There are two bunkers short of the green and three around the front and right side.

There are very few fairway bunkers, but the gorse is a major hazard that will punish inaccuracy, especially on the front nine which concludes with a demanding par 4 of 461 yards.

With the exception of the par 3, 7th, most of the outward nine holes run north-south. By way of complete contrast, all of the inward nine up to the 17th hole run in an east-west direction. The greens are also rather more varied on this nine with the 10th being sunken and the 13th and 14th raised and at an angle to the fairway.

The 15th and 16th are the last of the holes alongside the beach with a Martello Tower standing out from the flat terrain.

Seventeen is a dog-leg right and uphill. From the short walk to the 18th tee there is a wonderful view across the course with the clubhouse to the left of the 18th green and L'Ancresse Bay behind it. This unusual finishing hole is a short par 3 with the green well below the high tee. I'm not sure that I am fond of starting or finishing with a par 3, but you certainly can't beat the view as you prepare to complete your round.

Royal Guernsey in the spring haze

Photo courtesy Royal Guernsey GC

LA MOYE

Photo Ian Stanley

Par 3, 14th 188 yards uphill

LA MOYE GOLF CLUB IS ON THE SOUTH WEST SIDE OF JERSEY AT ST BRELADE OVERLOOKING ST OUEN'S BAY.

La Moye is deeply indebted to George Boomer, a village schoolmaster who was denied access to Royal Jersey so he set about making his own course. He taught Vardon and Ray and his own son, Aubrey, was runner up to Bobby Jones in the Open.

La Moye's reputation was enhanced dramatically when it engaged James Braid to redesign the course. The finished product was officially opened by Harry Vardon in 1935. Sadly, under German occupation a few years later, the fairways were ruined and the clubhouse was destroyed to improve the sight lines for the German artillery. By the early 1960's a new clubhouse was built, course alterations by Henry Cotton were completed and La Moye's star was in the ascendancy. Subsequently, a much more lavish club house was then built in 1987.

The outward nine is the longer of the two but has the unusual feature of two par 3's in the first three holes. The 1st is slightly uphill to a plateau green. It might be index number 17, but you don't want to be short left or long and right with your first shot of the day.

The 2nd is the longest hole at 514 yards. It is a big dog-leg right with a wall of gorse and trees, especially along the left. The par 3, 3rd is a Henry Cotton addition to the layout. It is reasonably long at 181 yards and needs just one bunker as anything not perfectly struck will run off the plateau green.

The par 4, 4th hole is the hardest on the course and is one of six par 4's that exceed 400 yards. The fairway bends right then slightly left. Out of bounds is along the right for your tee shot and on the left right up to the green for your second shot. The 6th heads out towards the cliff tops with a narrow area

in front of the tee and a rocky outcrop on the left starting at 52 yards before the green.

The 7th has out of bounds along the left and, at one point, has no fairway proper for 50 yards commencing from about 100 yards short of the green. There is also plenty of rough on both sides of the fairway. You are faced with another tight tee shot as well as gorse and then out of bounds on the right on the par 4, 8th. The par 4, 9th demands a very precise second shot to a raised green. The shot is made more difficult by the fact that the fairway twists to the left for the last 60 yards.

The narrow par 5, 11th bends uphill between sand dunes and trees to a green with a very narrow entrance. Not surprisingly it is rated the second hardest. Thirteen is a lovely hole through dunes and stunted pines. Unless your drive is over the hill then you will have a difficult blind second shot to the green.

The 14th can be a difficult par 3. You are hitting 188 yards uphill to a green with a bunker on both sides at the front and a steep fall away at the back. Holding the green will not be achieved by anything other than the perfect shot.

The 15th leads back out to the cliff tops with simply wonderful panoramic views. This is not the time to be nervous on the tee as your drive needs to carry across a valley of gorse and sandy scrub before the fairway commences at 178 yards. Everything runs to the right as you approach the green and this is where there is a row of gorse for the last 100 yards. There are two bunkers at the front left of the green but at least you will find your ball there.

The short par 5, 16th offers a little respite before two very good finishing holes. Seventeen runs parallel with the 15th back towards the stunning view out across the Atlantic Ocean. Out of bounds and the cliff edge is at the back of the green.

14th green from side on

The final hole dog-legs left but a straight drive is your best option as a draw may find one of the three bunkers on the left at the bend. The second shot is uphill to a green that slopes from back to front and right to left. There are two bunkers on the right and three on the left eagerly awaiting your failed attempt to hit and hold this wind exposed green.

Some exciting holes and superb views make La Moye a memorable experience. With a length of 6664 yards it also represents somewhat more of a challenge than either Royal Jersey or Royal Guernsey. Pray for a calm day otherwise you will also remember the bunkers, gorse, trees and, as Bernard Darwin would put it, 'wonderfully tenacious rough'.

MULLION

Photo courtesy Mullion GC

Mullion is the most southerly course in England

MULLION IS LOCATED ON THE CLIFFS OF THE LIZARD PENINSULA IN SOUTH WEST CORNWALL AND IS THE MOST SOUTHERLY COURSE IN BRITAIN.

The club dates its beginning back to a meeting in June 1895 and over the years has been a favourite golf location for Conan Doyle, A P Herbert and AA Milne. It was from these cliffs that Marconi sent the first trans-Atlantic radio signal.

The course is situated between two coves and offers magnificent views across Mounts Bay to Lands End. There are some really memorable holes at Mullion. The 4th hole provides a clifftop tee and is also the longest hole at 489 yards.

The short par 4, 6th slopes steeply downhill and to the right. Unless you aim left you face the prospect of a lost ball. The long par 4, 7th leads to Gunwalloe Cove, the final resting place of many sunken ships. The old church bell-tower is your correct line.

The 8th is a par 3 of 156 yards where any hint of a fade or slice will result in you playing your next from the beach. The 9th is a par 5 of just 482 yards. However you will realise that this is no pushover when you see the steep uphill climb. The par 4, 10th descends to the beach but it is the second shot that poses all the problems as a ravine lies between the beach and the elevated green. The 11th tee returns to the cliff edge.

The 17th, described as 'the warmest spot in England' is another very scenic part of the course. Out of bounds runs all along the right hand side.

Mullion is rather short at only 6083 yards but on most days the wind will make up for the lack of length. You will be disappointed if you forget to bring your camera.

WEST CORNWALL

West Cornwall with railway line and the sands of St Ives

WEST CORNWALL IS THE OLDEST IN THE COUNTY, STARTING OUT AS A NINE HOLE COURSE IN 1889. IN 1921 THEY MOVED TO A NEW LOCATION AT LELANT, OVERLOOKING ST IVES, WHERE THE PRESENT 18 HOLE LINKS WAS DEVELOPED.

It was here that Jim Barnes was born and honed his golfing skills. After four years as assistant professional at West Cornwall, Barnes left for the United States and in 1916 was the inaugural winner of the USPGA Championship. He is one of the only eight players to have won three of the majors and it should be noted that he never competed in the Masters.

Photo David Worley

West Cornwall is not long at only 5884 yards, but some of the holes are very tightly situated, particularly with greens up against boundary fences and cliff edges. The first two holes especially can be very tough if you have not played the course before. The opening hole is a par 3 slightly downhill and 229 yards in length. The green is well guarded with bunkers and mounds and, for the first-timer, it is very difficult to judge the actual length of the shot. Anything hit right or through the green can be in deep trouble in terms of the rough, and especially to the right the terrain and camber of the fairway can cause the ball to kick almost out of bounds to the roadway.

The second hole is index 3 on the card and takes on the appearance more of the typical sort of blind shot to the green that one expects on Irish courses. Two large sand dunes guard the green with only a portion of it being open to view for the second shot. Anything slightly left or right of the target will almost certainly remain wedged in some of the furrows along the steep banks of the dunes. More of a problem, if you aren't familiar with the course, is the fact that directly behind the rock-hard green is a large drop, so that any ball through the green can go well down the hill and lead to a very difficult chip back.

2nd shot to the green on the 2nd hole at West Cornwall

The 4th hole also has an interesting aspect in that any shot pushed out to the right can finish up being in the grounds of a nearby church, and there is also an additional hazard of the sunken pathway which acts as a right-of-way walking path for those wishing to get to the nearby beach. A number of holes then follow that run right along the coast with only a single gauge railway line between the golf course and the edge of the seaside dunes and clifftops.

The par 4, 11th is a very good hole with the tee right beside the railway line. The second shot is over a ridge to a green in front of a gorse-clad hill. The 12th and 16th are the only par 5's and run more or less parallel, but in opposite directions, on higher ground. Sandwiched between them amongst the dunes is the difficult 14th, a par 4 of 446 yards.

The 17th is a par 3 of 194 yards uphill. Three of the five par 3's are over 190 yards so you won't achieve a good score at West Cornwall unless you play the short holes well.

The greens are good but some of them are not very large and in summer they can get rock hard. Keep the ball straight and you should not have a problem in matching your handicap and you will have more opportunity to admire the views across the cliffs and the white sands of the beach at St Ives.

My wife Irene and I enjoyed West Cornwall so much that we played it twice on the day of our visit.

PERRANPORTH

Photo courtesy Perranporth GC

4th green

IF YOU ARE TRAVELLING THROUGH CORNWALL ON THE A30/A39 THEN YOU WILL NOT EVEN GET A GLIMPSE OF WEST CORNWALL, PERRANPORTH, TREVOSE, ST ENODOC OR BUDE AS THEY ARE ALL HIDDEN AWAY ON QUAINT LITTLE COASTAL ROADS.

12th green

Perranporth overlooks Perran Bay and is about midway between West Cornwall and Trevose. This is another James Braid design and dates back to 1927. You can bet that very little earth was moved except for tees and greens. You will encounter plenty of hills and consequential blind shots so it is much more difficult playing here on your first occasion.

A yardage of 6272 is quite respectable for a hilly course with the longest hole, the 561 yard 11th, appropriately named 'Formidable'. You won't have played any course with names as good as Perranporth's first two holes – 'Yn Nans' (Downhill) and 'Whym Wham' (This Way and That).

Spectacular views out to sea and across the sandy inlet abound from all parts of the course and a number of greens are alarmingly close to the cliffs and dunes running along the shore line. It is hard to concentrate on your putting when you look up from the 4th and 12th green in particular.

Index number 1 is the 14th ('Braid's Finest') which is a super par 4 reminiscent of holes at Ballybunion or Lahinch. A dune protects the left of the green and anywhere right is straight down the cliff.

The greens are excellent and many are raised and are undulating. When Perranporth dries out in the summer season your ball control abilities and short game will be fully tested. I can't understand why no one mentioned Perranporth to me on my first two trips to Cornwall. This is a lovely hilly links course, but don't judge it too harshly if you lose the odd ball or two.

14th green

Trevose with Booby's Bay in the distance

TREVOSE

THE LINKS AT TREVOSE WERE DESIGNED BY HARRY COLT AND OPENED FOR PLAY IN 1925. TREVOSE GOLF AND COUNTRY CLUB HAS ALWAYS BEEN PRIVATELY OWNED AND THE CURRENT OWNERS, THE GAMMON FAMILY, HAVE HAD CONNECTIONS WITH THE CLUB SINCE 1936 AND FULL OWNER-SHIP SINCE 1955.

Situated on the north Cornish coastline, Trevose is just south of Padstow beside Booby's Bay and Constantine Bay.

There are four sets of tees, and from the back (blue) tees, it now measures a very healthy 6863 yards. The white tees also provide a good test at 6415 yards.

From the very first hole I was impressed with the lovely springy turf of the fairways and high quality of the greens. Although the par 5's are all relatively short, there are a number of par 4's that are well over 400 yards. The holes run in every possible direction so judging the constant wind can be difficult.

Playing from the blue tees the first two holes are long straight par 4's. If the wind is howling in off Booby's Bay then you are in danger of being out of bounds left all along the second.

The 3rd and 4th are the only holes that actually run along side the shoreline. Three is a good one-shotter of 173 yards over a thickly grassed valley and with one bunker on the right edge of the green. The par 5, 4th dog-legs left following the coast and runs between low dunes. The fairway runs down to a green near the water's edge overlooking Booby's Bay with the unusual shark fin like rock formation jutting out of the water.

The 5th, index number 2, is a very difficult par 4 of 466 yards. The hole runs away from the sea and dog-legs left around the boundary. The par 3, 8th where you play over a burn is only 156 yards, but for some reason, choosing the right club is extremely difficult and anything hit even slightly right of the green will finish down a steep bank.

When I last played Trevose the 10th was an excellent par 4 of 467 yards with the added hazard of a burn meandering along the edge of the fairway. It is now 472 yards from the white, and still a par 4, but it becomes a par 5 of 510 yards from the blue tees.

The par 5, 13th runs along another boundary so anything hooked is likely to finish out of bounds. Two short par 4's are then followed by the demanding last three holes.

Sixteen is a very long par 3 of 229 yards. The par 4, 17th has a cluster of three bunkers on the right for the drive and then there is a burn not far short of the green. The 18th will also test your ability to reach the green in two as it is 432 yards and is uphill all the way.

The outward nine is the more interesting of the two. With the possible exception of the three short par 4's (the 6th, 14th and 15th) every hole at Trevose will require very good golf to achieve par. The fairways and greens are well conditioned but so too is the rough.

There is also a 9 hole course, the Headland, which opened in 1992 and a small 9 holer known as the Short Course which was built in the 1970's.

Whilst you are wandering through the rough near the Short Course you may come across a well which is believed to date around 400 AD, and there are also the remains of the original Church of St Constantine.

ST ENODOC

The delightful par 4, 9th hole

ST ENODOC IS ALMOST HIDDEN AWAY AT THE LITTLE VILLAGE OF ROCK BESIDE THE CAMEL ESTUARY AND OVERLOOKING THE PRETTY HARBOUR OF PADSTOW. THERE ARE TWO COURSES, BUT IT IS THE CHURCH LINKS YOU WILL WANT TO PLAY.

There are no two holes alike at St Enodoc and some of the unusual features will keep you wondering what is coming next. The 2nd and 3rd holes are quite difficult par 4's, well over 400 yards long and are rated index 5 and 2, respectively. The 4th hole is a par 4 of 292 yards, theoretically a pushover. However, this section of the course is along the boundary fence to the neighbouring farms and the approach shot to the green requires placement to perfection in that you have to hit over the corner of the field that abuts the course. Any shot slightly left will cause the ball to kick away from the green, and anything slightly right is out of bounds.

Photos: David Worley

6th hole featuring the largest bunker in the UK

The 206 yard par 3, 17th hole

The 6th hole is a spectacular par 4 primarily because of the hazard that is in play with the second shot to the green. The tee shot has only a small landing area. Anything left of centre will be caught up in a nasty grass-covered dune and anything to the right requires an even more difficult line to the green. From the tee, the green is just visible but once you are playing the second shot, you are confronted by what is the largest bunker in the United Kingdom, if not the largest bunker in the world. In reality, it is a huge sand dune with the face completely eroded away. A wooden fence has been built inside the dune to hold the steep walls up so that, if you are able to get a decent lie, you then have to negotiate this fence over and above the height of the dune itself. Not surprisingly, this hazard is known as 'The Himalaya'. The degree of difficulty is such that you will be surprised to know this massive bunker is not treated as a hazard, so therefore it is possible to drop out of it with a one-stroke penalty. Assuming that you have avoided The Himalaya, then the shot to the green rather resembles that encountered on many Irish courses in so far as the green is tucked in a little valley totally surrounded by large dunes with very corrugated areas covered with the local grasses. Hit a good drive and an accurate second shot and it is an easy par 4. If you hit anything off-centre, then you name it and you can score it.

The 9th is a delightful par 4 of 393 yards with a crumpled fairway and wave-like rolling mounds across it. The green is on higher ground with the boundary fence and a lovely stand of pines behind. Sailing ships are a common sight as you look left to the harbour.

The 10th hole is rated the hardest on the course and deservedly so. It is a brilliantly configured par 4 of 457 yards in length. From the tee shot, the fairway is quite narrow with a stream hidden by large trees all the way along the left side and steep grassy banks along the right. Two really long and perfectly executed shots are required to hit this green in regulation figures.

The 13th and 14th holes provide a good view of the old 11th century church and adjacent cemetery which are literally right in the middle of the course. Apparently, at one stage the church was almost fully covered with sand and was gradually dug out many years ago. The small cemetery beside the church includes the grave of none other than the Poet Laureate John Betjeman. Looking back from the elevated 14th green, there is a magnificent view of the church, the previous four holes that have been played, and the entrance of the heads looking out to the ocean. It really is hard to concentrate on your golf with such amazing scenery.

The par 5, 16th is the closest to the water and is one of the prettiest parts of the links. The two finishing holes are in keeping with the excellent quality of the course in terms of the unusual nature of the holes and degree of difficulty. The 17th is a par 3 of 206 yards and requires an extremely accurate shot from the tee to the green, which is set amongst sand dunes with very nasty rough in particular on the right hand side.

If you are lucky enough to come off the green with a three, then whatever you do as you walk towards the 18th tee, remember to turn around and spend a few minutes looking at the view from the green to tee and ocean in the near distance. Take the wrong club off the tee, however, and this is double-bogey territory.

The 18th is a suitable finishing hole – a 446 yard par 4, and rated index 6 on the card. The fairway is particularly narrow and winds from right to left before approaching the clubhouse. Anything off line will be lost in the dunes, but an accurate shot will benefit from the hard, bouncy fairways, making a shot into the green considerably shorter.

St Enodoc is an absolute delight and is a must-play for any serious golfer. The club dates back to 1891 but it was not until 1907 that the course properly evolved. This is surely one of James Braid's greatest creations outside of Scotland. Braid returned in 1922 and 1935 and, fortunately, very little has changed since.

1st green and 2nd hole at dawn

Photo courtesy Phil Inglis/St Enodoc GC

BUDE & NORTH CORNWALL

ALTHOUGH THE COURSE DATES BACK TO 1891, IT WAS NOT UNTIL JANUARY 1949 THE NORTH CORNWALL GOLF CLUB AND THE BUDE TOWN GOLF CLUB MERGED AND THE BUDE AND NORTH CORNWALL GOLF CLUB WAS BORN. ORIGINALLY THE NORTH CORNWALL GOLF CLUB WAS FOR THE LANDED GENTRY AND SENIOR MILITARY PERSONNEL WHILST BUDE WAS VERY MUCH AN ARTISANS CLUB. WORLD WAR II DID MUCH TO BREAK DOWN SOCIAL BARRIERS AND MAY HAVE BEEN A CATALYST FOR THE COMING TOGETHER OF THE TWO CLUBS.

The course has the unusual aspect of being bordered by the town, the sea and the countryside. A feature is the undulating fairways and, in some cases greens, and a number of blind tee shots.

The 1st hole is a modest length par 4 of 348 yards but there are four fairway bunkers starting around 210 yards from the tee, and two bunkers at the right edge of the green. The 2nd is an even shorter par 4 but the drive is blind and three fairway bunkers on the right are very much in play.

The 3rd is a severe dog-leg left that favours a gentle draw from the tee. Anywhere right, especially near the green, is not the place to be. The par 3, 4th is only 144 yards but there are six bunkers and out of bounds to be avoided.

Five and six are similar length par 4's with the 6th being considerably more difficult. The drive is blind and the plateau green is narrow and has two bunkers on the left.

The 7th is another tricky medium length par 4. There is trouble, including out of bounds on the right and the green is a rather difficult slightly raised target. The front nine finishes with a very short par 5 that bends to the right.

The green can be reached in two but be wary of the out of bounds and then, near the green, a water hazard on the right.

The par 3, 10th is just 154 yards but is rated number 11. Do not miss the green as there is a burn at front and right, bunkers left and out of bounds at the back. The 13th is an even more demanding par 3. It is 201 yards in length and has out of bounds along the right.

Fifteen is a good par 4 featuring three cross bunkers about 170 yards from the tee. There is a burn that you can not see initially that is just short of the green and out of bounds is very close by if your approach is too bold.

The 16th is a very difficult long par 4 of 424 yards with the fairway in two sections. You need to drive to the left side to have any view of the green which can be hidden by a high mound. Another tough par 4 follows at the 17th, where there is internal out of bounds to the left and a burn running just before the green.

The 18th offers a little respite in that it is a short par 5 but you need to be conscious of out of bounds on the left of the dog-leg.

It might be only 6057 yards long but with so many out of bounds hazards you won't score well unless you drive the ball truly here. The greens are very good and are a change from the sometimes rather flat links greens. There are sea views but of course that also means it's usually fairly breezy.

ROYAL NORTH DEVON (WESTWARD HO!)

Sheep, burn and the 18th green

WESTWARD HO! ISN'T JUST A GOLF COURSE – IT IS A MUSEUM OF THE BEGINNINGS OF GOLF IN ENGLAND AND WITH A START DATE OF 1864 IT IS CERTAINLY THE OLDEST. J H TAYLOR WAS BORN AND DIED HERE AND THE HONOUR BOARDS LIST SO MANY OTHER ILLUSTRIOUS NAMES SUCH AS HORACE HUTCHINSON, HERBERT FOWLER AND HAROLD HILTON.

The town of Westward Ho! is essentially high up on the hills looking down over the relatively flat expanse of Royal North Devon. Your first impression might leave you feeling disappointed as you survey the flat rather featureless opening and closing holes. This may even lead to bemusement when you also notice the sheep around the burn in front of the 18th green and the horses nearby.

I have heard some rather unkind things said about these deceptively intriguing links, but these detractors perhaps did not appreciate that this land and layout was so perfectly suited to the golfing equipment of the nineteenth century. You may be surprised to learn that Royal North Devon measures a respectable 6665 yards from the normal back tees but is stretched to around 7000 yards for events such as the West of England Championship.

The 1st, 2nd and 18th holes together with the 17th green lie on the flat land on the clubhouse side of the narrow road that provides access to the beach for the public. All of these holes have a burn either running alongside or across or both. The long par 4, 2nd can be particularly tricky with its very small upturned saucer green.

From the 4th to the 16th holes Westward Ho! reveals its true self with crumpled fairways, penal bunkers and the dreaded tall and spiky sea rushes occupying large areas of the middle of the course. It goes without saying that the wind is always present.

The par 4, 4th hole is over the famous Cape bunker stretching across the whole fairway and supported by railway sleepers. This is a blind drive that should be directed over the upward arrow sign on the bunker face and you will need to carry the drive about 180 yards to be sure of clearing the hazard.

The 5th is a brilliant little par 3 of 136 yards. The word 'little' is perhaps figurative as this hole is usually into the 'sea breeze' and can play four clubs longer. The green is elevated and has six steep faced bunkers surrounding it. On a windy day you will be amazed how hard it can be to hit and hold the green.

Now that you are looking straight ahead from the 6th tee if you are still disappointed then I'll gladly refund your green fees. 'Alp' is a wonderful par 4 (index 1) of 408 yards of lunar landscape. To your left is the sea and the sandy dunes beyond

Photo David Worley

Cape bunker on the 4th hole

the out of bounds fence. Too far right and you will be in the rushes. There are also a number of fairway bunkers to avoid and the green has a big fall away to the right. But without doubt, the mesmerising feature of this hole is the fairway itself.

The 7th is another testing par 4 that dog-legs left. Avoid the rushes along the left as you have plenty of room right with only one bunker to avoid. Similarly on the short par 5, 9th you need to stay to the right away from the sea rushes.

If you still need to be convinced that this is not a mundane outing then wait until you survey the 10th hole. I did say hole, not fairway, because all you can see from the tee is the invasion of the sea rushes. Your drive can be right of the marker post but left is very dangerous.

The 11th tee presents similar problems but this fairway is somewhat wider than the last. The small green that is partly raised is the biggest obstacle to par at the 13th even though it is a very short par 5.

Fourteen is a long par 3 (201 yards) with five bunkers at the front and sides. Fifteen is a long par 4 that requires a very difficult semi blind second shot over three greenside bunkers.

The par 3, 16th is harder than it looks as the green tends to kick balls towards the bunkers or swales but I can't quite agree with Bernard Darwin who described it as 'perhaps the best short hole in the world'. There are rushes short of the green but they are only in play for a very poor tee shot.

Side view of the 5th green with the lunar landscape of the 6th fairway behind

The 17th is by far the longest hole at 555 yards over what seems a wide open fairway. The danger is the third shot to the green which is on the other side of the road and has a ditch that runs beside the road on the same side as the green.

The final hole has the road and ditch if you hook or pull badly to the left and to the right there is a burn that runs between the 18th and 1st fairways and then in front of the green.

There are no bunkers but the green is two-tiered so you need to finish on the right tier to avoid a possible three putt.

This may not be anywhere near the best course in England, but Royal North Devon has a wonderful charm that will add to the fun as you get a chance to briefly 'linger in the past' as Donald Steel so appropriately described it.

SAUNTON – EAST COURSE

18th green

This is a really top class course with plenty of challenges but all set out in a fair manner.

SAUNTON TOOK VARIOUS FORMS FROM THE 1890'S BUT THE COURSE OF TODAY REALLY STEMS FROM THE REDESIGN BY HERBERT FOWLER WHICH WAS COMPLETED BY 1919. TEN YEARS LATER THE CLUBHOUSE OPENING WAS CELEBRATED BY AN EXHIBITION MATCH BETWEEN J H TAYLOR, JAMES BRAID AND A YOUNG HENRY COTTON. IN 1935 FOWLER WAS ASKED TO DESIGN THE NEW 18 HOLE WEST COURSE SUCH WAS THE POPULARITY OF SAUNTON.

Much damage was done during World War II as this area was used as a training ground prior to the D Day landings. The damage was so great that the East Course did not reopen for play until January 1952.

Saunton East would be a wonderful venue for The Open, were it not for the geographical logistics. The turf here is of the lovely springy variety, the greens are very true and there is no escaping from any shot not on the fairway.

You can't get a much tougher start than a 478 yard par 4. The 2nd hole is not much longer and is a par 5 with several fairway bunkers that need to be avoided. Then follow two more par 4's over 400 yards. The second of these, the 4th, requires a very accurate drive down the left side (where there are four bunkers in a line) to a fairway that narrows significantly at about the 250 yard mark from the tee. The green sits attractively between two low dunes.

From the 6th to the 12th is a succession of seven par 4's but they are all quite varied and I did not for one moment feel any sense of monotony. At this stage there has been just the one par 3, the little 5th known affectionately as 'Tiddler'.

At thirteen you are relieved to find a par 3, 'Saddle', but this requires a well struck iron as the green is an upturned saucer in shape. Fourteen is a long tight par 4 with two fairway bunkers on the right making the fairway target even smaller. The 17th is a very tough par 3 of 207 yards with three bunkers and plenty of rough clad mounds. It will usually play much harder than its index rating of 16. The only place to miss is short and slightly left. The 18th is a glorious finishing hole, gently uphill and with a slight dog-leg right and then a fairly long second shot to a lovely large green framed by the clubhouse behind.

Considering there are only two par 5's, both relatively short, Saunton East is a formidable 6779 yards from the blue and 6427 yards from the white tees.

This is a really top class course with plenty of challenges but all set out in a fair manner. Everywhere there are low dunes which however tend to be dwarfed by comparison with the large seaside dunes of the adjacent West Course.

Perhaps I should leave the last word to Bernard Darwin who, when writing in the mid 1930's said: "Saunton is a most romantic place in which to play golf. It possesses everything on a fine big scale – gorgeous hills and wastes of sand to drive over, tall clumps of spiky rushes of the Westward Ho! brand but not quite so fierce and venomous, plateau greens perched defiantly on high where the wind does indeed 'play the tyrant' with the ball, greens nestling in dells, long narrow valleys and wide open stretches…It is almost impossible to describe true seaside golf to those who have never had the chance of playing it. If such a one was entrusted to my care, I would take him straightway to Saunton – yes, before St Andrews or Sandwich or anywhere – and say to him, 'Now here is the real thing'."[1]

1. *The Happy Golfer* –Bernard Darwin.

SAUNTON – WEST COURSE

FOLLOWING THE ORIGINAL DESIGN IN 1935 FROM HERBERT FOWLER, THE WEST COURSE UNDERWENT MAJOR CHANGES FROM FRANK PENNINK IN 1972/3. IN THE LATE 1980'S ALL GREENS WERE RE-LAID AND 30 NEW BUNKERS WERE ADDED.

Photo courtesy Saunton GC

The West measures 6403 yards from the blue and 6138 yards from the white tees. Its relative lack of length stems from having five par 3's, although four of these exceed 190 yards.

Club selection can be rather more difficult here as you negotiate some severe dog-legs and play alongside the tall dunes. The opening hole is a lovely dog-leg right to a green nestled at the foot of the tall line of dunes. Anywhere right of this green is not the place to be.

After a succession of different length holes, the 6th heads back to the dunes. The dangers are the grassy mounds jutting into the fairway and then the green which has two bunkers front left and which slopes from back to front.

The start of the homeward nine also provides for very varied holes but the finish is unusual with two par 3's in the final three holes. The 16th is rather like a slightly shorter version of the 17th on the East Course. There are two bunkers at the front but it is a large green so you can afford to hit one more club than you might think.

The par 3, 18th is somewhat tougher than the 16th and has plenty of gorse and buckthorn for a poor tee shot. The green has a number of mounds and anything too strong can finish in a bank with long grass.

You really need to think your way around the West Course which is a perfect day's golf when combined with the East. Everyone knows the reputation of Saunton East, but the West is also deservedly ranked amongst the best 100 courses in Britain.

1st green

BURNHAM & BERROW

Photo David Worley

1st green back to the tee and clubhouse on the right

WHEN THE CLUB WAS FIRST FORMED IN 1890 THEY APPOINTED THE 19 YEAR OLD J H TAYLOR AS THE FIRST GREEN KEEPER/ PROFESSIONAL TO LOOK AFTER THE NEW 9 HOLE COURSE. THIS WAS A TIME OF MASSIVE GOLF COURSE CONSTRUCTION IN ENGLAND. IN 1890 THERE WERE ONLY 110 CLUBS BUT THIS ROSE DRAMATICALLY TO NEARLY 1000 WITHIN JUST TEN YEARS. THE AREA AROUND BERROW PRODUCED A REMARKABLE NUMBER OF PROFESSIONAL GOLFERS WHICH INCLUDED THE BRAD-BEER BOYS. THEIR PARENTS, WHO WORKED AT THE GOLF COURSE, HAD FOURTEEN CHILDREN AND OF THE TEN BOYS NINE BECAME PROFESSIONAL GOLFERS. [1]

The course evolved over the next thirty years with input from Herbert Fowler and Hugh Alison but the main influence came from Harry Colt who at that time was also working in partnership with Dr Alister Mackenzie.

Burnham & Berrow has a wonderful array of holes with dunes, blind shots, elevated tees, greens in dells and even some flat marshland. The opening three and the two closing holes in particular are just superb tests of golf.

The 1st is a challenging narrow fairway with tall dunes on both sides. If you get a good drive away then this hole is not quite as tough as it looks. The 2nd is an equally good par 4 with a bumpy fairway through a valley amongst more gentle dunes. Bunkers are at the right for the drive and then along the left to catch your second. The 3rd is another wonderful par 4, a slight dog-leg left from an elevated tee to a punch bowl green almost completely surrounded by thickly grassed dunes.

The par 5, 4th hole bends right with the shoreline and here you get the first sea views. The 5th is a delightful par 3 of 158 yards to a raised green with three deep bunkers at the front.

Holes 6-8 are in flatter wetland. A new tee has been built on the right at the 6th which creates a much more difficult line with the water hazard.

The 9th is a good looking par 3 of 170 yards. The tee shot is over a slight valley with areas of long grass to a green with dunes behind and six pot bunkers, mainly around the front.

The par 4, 10th requires a blind drive over rough and a tall dune. This is quite a long carry for the average lady golfer.

The 13th is quite a difficult par 5 with real trouble if you miss the green anywhere right where there is a fall off to very unfriendly country. The par 3, 14th is not one of the most attractive holes from the tee but there are lovely sea views

Photo David Worley

The 3rd green is almost completely surrounded by dunes

from the green. It can be a difficult hole on a windy day. The tiered green is on top of a dune with run off on all sides.

The 16th is a short par 4 of 344 yards from a raised tee that tempts you to really go for it. Be careful of the wet area and then out of bounds which is only about 20 yards left of the green.

Seventeen is one of the best par 3's in the UK. The tee shot is 200 yards to a raised green that slopes left to right at the front and is protected by three bunkers and plenty of rough very close by. When I played there in 2006 the rough was thick but manageable but several years earlier, after a wet spring, the grass between tee and green was nearly waist high.

Eighteen is a tough finish that I would rate harder than its index of number 8. You need a long draw off the tee to reach this 445 yard hole in two. There is a line of low dunes all along the right almost to the green. A ridge angles across in front of the green and then there are four bunkers. Anything pulled left is in thick rough near the boundary fence.

I suspect that Burnham & Berrow would have been quite a challenge in its earliest years with the large dunes and plentiful rough. About the time that Darwin wrote his epic 'Golf Courses of the British Isles' (1909/10) there were no less than six blind par 3's.

The course of today represents a good test with accuracy, especially on the dune holes, being paramount. Even in the midst of a very dry summer the greens are amongst the best in England. Along with Saunton, these are the best dunes on any course in the South West.

1. *Between the Church and the Lighthouse (The history of Burnham & Berrow Golf Club)* – Philip Richards

Left: lighthouse and clubhouse from the 17th green
Below: the challenging par 3, 9th

Photos David Worley

WESTON-SUPER-MARE

THIS RATHER UNUSUAL COURSE IS ON THE COAST AT THE TOWN BY THE SAME NAME, ABOUT TEN MILES NORTH OF BURNHAM & BERROW. IN 1892 A PUBLIC MEETING DECIDED UPON FORMING A CLUB AND TOM DUNN (WHO HAD BEEN INVOLVED AT GANTON, SAUNTON AND DEAL) WAS ASKED TO CONSTRUCT THE LINKS.

In 1922, at a considerable cost of 1000 Pounds, the course was altered and modernised under the scrutiny of Dr Alister Mackenzie. From time to time holes have been modified but, in the most part, then later restored to the original Mackenzie layout.

This is a flat seaside course with about five holes running right along the shoreline. But the odd thing is, there is not even a glimpse of the sea. A wall of trees and tall buckthorn shrubs runs along the seaside boundary, no doubt planted years ago to help eliminate the problem of erosion and sand blowing on to the greens which plagued the club's early years.

Weston-Super-Mare is built on a small site but makes clever use of space with, for example, the 1st and 10th holes having semi shared fairways. A dominating feature is Uphill Church which sits above the far end of the course on top of a steeply angled hill.

The first four holes, 3 par 4's and a par 3, all run along the shore boundary with the buckthorn and then out of bounds on the right. The 4th requires a precise tee shot just left of the centre of the fairway to a green further right and protected by a large mound running right across the fairway and a tree if you are too far right with your drive.

Five and six are longer par 4's across the road near the caravan park (there seems to be one next to every seaside golf course in England). This area, known as Brean Downs, looks across to Uphill Church and its sheer drop at the back.

Coming back across the road there is a semblance of a dune but then the run home is on very flat terrain punctuated by a number of drains and small burns that increase the need for accuracy.

Weston-Super-Mare is worth a look because of the Mackenzie connection in particular. Its limitations are its modest length of 6245 yards and the flat terrain. The bunkers are quite shallow and the greens fairly flat so the feeling is more along the lines of holiday golf.

Clockwise from top right:
Par 3, 3rd hole – the sea is only a very short distance behind the trees;
Looking back from the 3rd green to the clubhouse;
Uphill Church from the 4th fairway

Photos David Worley

ROYAL LIVERPOOL

Photo David Worley

Classic revetted bunkers on the 18th at Royal Liverpool

BUILT IN 1869 ON LAND THAT WAS THE RACECOURSE OF THE LIVERPOOL HUNT CLUB, HOYLAKE IS SECOND BY JUST A FEW YEARS TO WESTWARD HO! (ROYAL NORTH DEVON) AS THE OLDEST OF THE ENGLISH SEASIDE COURSES. ACCORDING TO BERNARD DARWIN "HOYLAKE IN THOSE DAYS CONSISTED OF THE HOTEL...A FARM AND ONE OR TWO HOUSES, A RABBIT-WARREN AND A RACE-COURSE. GEORGE MORRIS, OLD TOM'S BROTHER, CAME FROM ST ANDREWS TO LAY OUT THE ORIGINAL NINE HOLES AND BROUGHT WITH HIM HIS SON JACK TO BE PROFESSIONAL TO THE NEW CLUB". [1] TWO YEARS LATER THE COURSE WAS EXTENDED TO 18 HOLES AND IN THE SAME YEAR IT RECEIVED ITS ROYAL DESIGNATION.

By the mid 1870's the horse racing moved elsewhere and Royal Liverpool began to immediately set a number of impressive precedents. In 1872 the first ever professional tournament in England was held there and was won by young Tom Morris. In 1885 the first Amateur Championship took place at Hoylake. In 1902 Hoylake hosted the inaugural International golf match played between England and Scotland. Hoylake also hosted the first International between Great Britain and Ireland against the USA in 1921 – this later became the Walker Cup.

Without doubt the most famous Hoylake member is John Ball who won the Amateur Championship eight times as well as the Open in 1890.

I played Royal Liverpool several years before the hype of the wonderful 2006 Open. I had been given the indication that it was flat and featureless. It may be lacking in tall dunes but it is anything but featureless. As I walked off the 18th I remarked that the player who wins the 2006 Open won't be using driver from the tees although it was not so much the bunkers I was thinking about but the heavy rough that ran along side the bending fairways following on from the wet early summer. The summer of 2006 reduced the ferocity of the rough but the firm fairways made the bunkers the biggest danger.

The opening and closing holes at Hoylake ('Course' and 'Stand') hark back to the early race course days. Some are opposed to any form of internal out of bounds but you can not have people driving across the practice ground. The 1st is a good par 4 of 427 yards which dog-legs right at 250 yards. Out of bounds is at the very edge of the right hand side including the green.

The par 4, 2nd runs to the furthest point away from the point of the triangle in the boundaries where the River Dee meets the sea. This is the last remaining green from the original design.

The 3rd is a short par 5 that bends left. The drive needs to avoid gorse on the left and bunkers on the right but for the shot into the green most of the bunkers are to the left.

On the visitors card, the par 3, 4th measures just 136 yards. From the championship tee it lengthens dramatically to 200 yards. The green falls away to the left and has four bunkers. The bunker at front right is the most dangerous.

The par 4, 5th is rated index 1. The hole dog-legs right with two bunkers at the corner. The shot into the green is over broken ground to an angled green with two bunkers at front left.

The lovely short par 4, 9th hole at Royal Liverpool

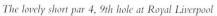

Par 3, 11th 'Alps' with the tide out on the Dee Estuary

It seems that nothing much has changed since 1910 when Darwin observed: "At Hoylake the golfing pilgrim is emphatically on classic ground".

The 6th is a par 4 that has a visually intimidating view from the tee. An out of bounds line in the form of a hedge skirts the edge of your line to the fairway some 190 yards away. On the par 3, 7th you hit over a marshy area but you can run your ball on from the apron as there are no bunkers in front of the green.

The 8th is a short but tricky par 5. Out of bounds runs along the left of the narrow fairway. The bunker at the front right of the green is deep and straight faced and should be avoided at all costs. Any approach slightly right of centre will funnel into this bunker.

The next four holes are probably the most picturesque as they run along side the Dee Estuary. The par 3, 11th 'Alps' is one of the best at Hoylake. At 193 yards from the back there is only the one bunker which is front right. However there

Par 3, 13th

18th green and clubhouse

are mounds along the front left and the green angles away to the left making the target even more difficult.

The last five holes are a tough finish with three long par 4's and two testing par 5's. Fifteen, seventeen and eighteen are littered with penal bunkers whilst the 16th (used as the 18th during the 2006 Open) runs back beside the practice fairway with out of bounds all along the right. The second shot must be played almost over the corner of the out of bounds line.

The 17th and 18th are relatively new greens and are much more undulating than the rest which are of a flatter nature. In more recent times a number of new bunkers have been added to these holes with Donald Steel completing the work in 2001.

The greens are somewhat larger than those of many of the nearby courses. The bunkers are deep but generally fair and the course is usually set out in beautiful condition. It seems that nothing much has changed since 1910 when Darwin observed: "At Hoylake the golfing pilgrim is emphatically on classic ground". "On a first view they (the links) are not imposing. Yet this place of dull and rather mean appearance is one of the most interesting and most difficult courses in the world, and pre-eminently one which is regarded with affection by all who know it well." [2]

1.   *A History of Golf in Britain* – Various Contributors
2.   *Golf Courses of the British Isles* – Bernard Darwin

WALLASEY

Par 5, 4th hole

TALL UNDULATING DUNES, A BEAUTIFULLY PRESENTED LINKS AND WONDERFUL VIEWS OVER LOOKING LIVERPOOL BAY AND THE IRISH SEA – WALLASEY HAS IT ALL. IF IT WAS PERHAPS 300-400 YARDS LONGER IT WOULD BE A MAGNIFICENT VENUE FOR THE OPEN, BUT FOR NOW IT WILL HAVE TO SETTLE FOR FINAL OPEN QUALIFYING STATUS.

Wallasey Golf Club started in 1891, during that frenetic period of activity when new clubs were being established all over England and Wales. Old Tom Morris prepared the first layout but in subsequent years there have been many alterations from Hilton, Hawtree, Braid and more recently, Donald Steel.

Wallasey can boast of two notable contributions to golf. Their past captain, Dr Frank Stableford developed the 'Stableford' system of points scoring which was first used in 1932. The club also has a wonderful signed portrait of Bobby Jones which was completed in 1930 when he qualified at Wallasey for the Open at Hoylake. A copy of this painting now hangs at Augusta.

The opening par 4 is not too demanding but then follows three very formidable holes. The 2nd is a long par 4 at 458 yards and the green is relatively small. The 3rd is an excellent par 4 to a raised and narrow green that provides the first views of the nearby sea below.

You will be suitably impressed by the magnificent view from the 4th tee high up in the dunes. This par 5 bends slightly left with the out of bounds fence and then the seashore all the way along the right hand side. It may be only 521 yards from the back, but this is an extremely exposed section of the course and there aren't too many still days in this region.

The elevated 11th green

The par 3, 5th heads directly toward the sea so club selection can vary dramatically to carry the 173 yards. The par 5, 7th is well bunkered for the drive and around the green which also has out of bounds very close to the right side.

The par 4, 8th dog-legs right with the out of bounds practice fairway all the way along the right. The entrance to the green is narrow with dunes on either side. The 9th is a par 3 that runs back to near the clubhouse. This is only 147 yards to a pretty green with just two bunkers and then woodland at the rear.

I love short but tricky par 4's and the 10th certainly fits that category. The hole bends almost at 90 degrees to the right after you first play your tee shot over the end of the trees. The second must be played up a steep hill to a bunkerless green. Anything too far right will be lost in the thick woodland.

The next two holes are a fine example of the wonderful bunkering at Wallasey. The 11th also plays uphill to a raised green with a severe slope at the front and is protected by some very deep bunkers. A three putt is always a possibility here so you are best to play to the back portion of the green. The 12th is the shortest of the par 3's at 143 yards but it is a classic hole in every sense. From the tee at a higher level there is a wonderful view. There is no fairway, no good place to miss, just a small green surrounded by five deep and straight-faced bunkers. With the prevailing wind being across the green this becomes a difficult target to hit and then hold.

An equally good hole is the 15th, a shortish par 4 to a green on top of a hill. Three large fairway bunkers occupy the left side of the upslope to catch a drive with a slight draw, which theoretically you would want to hit as the hole dog-legs a little to the left.

Sixteen is a long par 3 and seventeen is a long and demanding par 4 which may leave you with a blind second shot.

The 18th is a really majestic finishing hole. A par 4 through a valley between high dunes, the long hitters can attempt to carry the hill otherwise you need to play left. The rough is thickest along the right where there is also gorse and other scrub. The green is in a lovely amphitheatre setting below the attractive clubhouse.

Wallasey has no weakness and is in a great setting that adds to the drama of some of the holes. I'm not sure how many people from other countries realise just how many superb links courses are in the stretch from Royal Liverpool to Royal Lytham & St Annes. Wallasey is right up there with the best of them and should be a must play on your golfing agenda.

1. *Golf Courses of the British Isles* – Bernard Darwin.

Above: the par 3, 12th is a classic short hole with wonderful bunkering
Right: 18th green and clubhouse

"I do not think I have ever seen a course on which the contour of the hills and valleys was so infinitely picturesque." Bernard Darwin.[1]

Photo David Worley

WEST LANCASHIRE

THE CLUB WAS FOUNDED IN 1873 BY MEMBERS FROM ROYAL LIVERPOOL. AT ONE TIME SANDY HERD WAS THE PROFESSIONAL (1891) AND THEN TEN YEARS LATER HAROLD HILTON BECAME SECRETARY.

Photo courtesy Alan C Birch

Par 3, 12th hole

West Lancashire is located at Blundellsands, virtually midway along the marvellous stretch of links land that runs from Liverpool to Southport further north. Part of the course runs along the coast looking out across the shipping channels to the Irish Sea whilst the main inland boundary is the railway line.

You know right from the first hole that this is not an easy course. The opening par 4 measures 436 yards with a big dog-leg to the right. If you don't drive to the corner (255 yards) then you need to be left otherwise you will have a very dangerous line to the green.

The par 5, 2nd is aptly named 'Shore' as it runs alongside the low seaside dunes. There is rough and heather on either side, the fairway is narrow and the green has two well placed bunkers. The 3rd is an interesting par 3 with four bunkers in a line from the approach area to the right side. There is a swale on the left and the green runs away at the back.

The 4th tee presents the best views out to the sea. The hole dog-legs right where there is a large hollow. Out of bounds is all the way along the seaside left. The fairway becomes very narrow from 63 yards out and is made even more so by the two bunkers at the front right of the green.

Apart from the 13th green and 14th tee the rest of the holes are more inland. The par 4, 7th takes a big dog-leg right with bunkers and heavy rough for those who try to cut the corner. It seems hard to believe that the assistant professional holed in one here in 1972.

The 8th is another long par 4 that bends left with plenty of trouble if you miss the fairway. At 446 yards in length, this hole needs two really good shots to make the green. You need to drive very straight at West Lancashire. The 9th is a blind drive that will catch a down slope if well struck.

The long par 5, 11th (561 yards) runs straight alongside the railway line which is out of bounds on the right. There are three fairway bunkers on the left to trap any drive directed too far away from the out of bounds hazard on the other side.

Photo courtesy Alan C Birch

Par 5, 2nd at West Lancashire

Photo courtesy Alan C Birch

Par 5, 13th

The 12th is another very good par 3 of 179 yards. You have to carry the two bunkers at the front if you want to be on the green in regulation. The 13th tee is elevated and gives a lovely view down the valleyed fairway that bends left and heads back toward the sea. You need a slight draw with your drive but anything too far left will either catch one of the three bunkers at the corner or will be in thick rough.

The long par 4, 14th (447 yards) is just a plain difficult hole. From the tee in the duneland at the furthest point from the clubhouse only the longest of hitters has any hope of getting a full view of the green with their next shot. A long drive needs a hint of a fade to avoid running through the fairway into a wet ditch. A heavy stand of trees run along the right for the last 150 yards and also behind the raised green which is almost tucked in amongst the trees. This hole seems curiously out of character with the others and has a distinctly parkland course feel.

The 15th is another potentially dangerous tee shot with a dog-leg right. The stone wall beside the railway is along the left and thick trees are at the right for a sliced drive. The closing holes are a par 5, par 3 and a par 4 with the tee shot on the last hole being fraught with danger due to bunkers and a pond.

As a comparison, I would rate West Lancashire as being quite a deal more difficult than say Southport & Ainsdale. The rough at West Lancashire is very penal and is everywhere. It is essential that you keep your ball on the fairway. The greens are true and a number of them are raised. I found a most difficult aspect to be the bunkers which tend to be small and straight faced. Invariably my ball ended right up against the face with the only option being to attempt to play out sideways.

West Lancashire is a formidable test of golf that is quite long (6862 yards) and will penalize any bad shot.

I played it in the rain which was far more preferable to a howling gale.

FORMBY

Photo David Worley

The tight 7th hole – the green is around to the right

FOUNDED IN 1894, FORMBY PROGRESSED TO AN EIGHTEEN HOLE LINKS BY THE TURN OF THE CENTURY. THE FORMBY LADIES GOLF CLUB WHICH IS COMPLETELY INDEPENDENT BEGAN JUST TWO YEARS LATER IN 1896 AND HAS THE UNIQUE DISTINCTION OF HAVING ITS OWN 18 HOLE COURSE WITHIN THE BOUNDARIES OF FORMBY GOLF CLUB.

Willie Park designed the original layout and then in 1922 James Braid made changes to the last four holes. In the 1970's a change in the course of the River Mersey led to some loss of shoreline and a problem with shifting sand. As a result new holes at 7, 8 and 9 were designed by Donald Steel and were completed in the early 1980's. I never saw the old holes, but I would certainly rate the 'new' 7th and 8th as two of the very best at Formby. By 1998 some new back tees had extended the course to a very testing length of 6993 yards.

Formby is also quite unusual for the large areas of the famous Formby pines that run alongside many of the fairways. Several days before my last visit to Formby in early August 2006, an arsonist lit three fires simultaneously and destroyed many of these majestic specimens just back from the fairway edge in the vicinity of the 8th hole.

Apart from pines and lovely heather, Formby has a profusion of wildlife and plants and the whole estate of 470 acres has been declared a site of Special Scientific Interest.

Photo David Worley

You need a draw with your drive at the 8th, otherwise you will run out of fairway

Formby opens with two good solid par 4's with the railway line from nearby Freshfield station running close by along the right. There are large expanses of heather if you miss the fairway and the bunkers are predominantly on the same side as the railway. You need a slight draw from the tee of the par 5, 3rd hole. There are four fairway bunkers on the left for a pulled drive. There are also two bunkers in the middle of the fairway where your second shot might land.

The short par 4, 4th hole is a birdie chance provided you miss the fairway bunkers and hit accurately to the small green. The 5th is an attractive par 3, slightly uphill, to a green that is tilted from the back. There are sand hills on the right, pines at the back and a steep bank at the left where the ball will usually feed into one of the three deep bunkers.

The second shot is the difficulty at the par 4, 6th. If you haven't played Formby before then you really have no idea of the distance to the green set down below some sand dunes with a marker post well back.

The 7th is a stunning par 4 of 419 yards along a narrow fairway lined with pines. The hole dog-legs right so you need to keep your drive on the left side to be able to then go for the green that is up quite a steep hill. The green slopes severely from the back to the front and anything just short of the green will run back down the slope.

It says something for the degree of difficulty that the 8th is index 1 even though it is a very short par 5 of just 493 yards. This is another great hole played from a raised tee amongst the pines. The narrow fairway sweeps around to the left with a raised section on the right hand side. You need a draw from the tee otherwise you will run into the pines, but if you overdo the draw you will finish down an embankment. An accurate second shot will leave just a short iron into a raised and two-tiered green with a high mound blocking the entrance on the right.

Photo David Worley

8th green from 200 yards out

Formby is a stunning links with a slight heathland feel. Playing along more protected fairways amongst the pines is a nice change from the traditional exposed and wind swept links.

Accurate hitting is again needed on the long par 4, 9th hole which has pine trees, heather and bunkers on both sides. The straightforward par 3, 10th is followed by a lovely par 4 requiring a drive over low dunes to a fairway with four bunkers at the sides. The slightly raised green has no bunkers but is protected by sand hills on all sides other than the front.

The 12th to the 15th are par 4's all in excess of 400 yards. The 13th fairway is dotted with six bunkers before you play to a lovely bowl green with sand hills a little further back. Fourteen dog-legs left with internal out of bounds along the left. There are two greenside bunkers at the left which you may not see due to a dune which could partly obscure your view. The 15th is rated the second most difficult at Formby. There are no bunkers but the fairway is extremely narrow and the entrance to the green is between two sand hills.

The 16th is a very short par 3 with three deep bunkers toward the front. Do not miss long and left otherwise you may be looking for your ball in the trees and thick scrub.

Seventeen is a lovely par 5 that bends left with the pines running along the whole length of the boundary on the right hand side. The green slopes to the right toward a grassy hollow and a nasty bunker at the front.

The home hole is a good finish but is perhaps not quite as formidable from the tee as the earlier holes. When playing your second shot to the long green, watch out for the out of bounds car park at the right and the six bunkers, four of which are on the left side.

Photo courtesy Alan C Birch

Par 4, 11th with a narrow opening to the green

Formby is a stunning links with a slight heathland feel. Playing along more protected fairways amongst the pines is a nice change from the traditional exposed and wind swept links. The greens were first class and the whole course was in excellent condition even though the green keeper said the fairways in the summer of 2006 were the driest he had ever seen since starting there in 1963.

Don't miss out on observing the marvellous array of plant life including clove garlic, tufted vetch, reindeer moss, harebell, honeysuckle and roseby willowherb.

Formby is a joy to play. Despite the potential difficulties to be encountered from wayward shots, my wife and I were around the links comfortably in three and a quarter hours – as the Scots say – "a brisk game is a good game".

Formby clubhouse from behind the 17th green

SOUTHPORT & AINSDALE

Photo David Worley

The clubhouse at Southport & Ainsdale

S & A AS IT IS AFFECTIONATELY KNOWN, WAS A LATE STARTER HAVING BEEN FOUNDED IN 1906. THE JAMES BRAID DESIGN SOON GAINED A REPUTATION WITH THE RESULT THAT THE CLUB HOSTED MANY TOURNAMENTS INCLUDING THE RYDER CUP IN BOTH 1933 AND 1937. IT IS LOCATED NEAR THE TOWN OF AINSDALE AT SOUTHPORT, JUST NORTH OF LIVERPOOL. ITS IMMEDIATE NEIGHBOUR IN THIS STRETCH OF WONDERFUL LINKS TERRAIN IS ROYAL BIRKDALE.

S & A doesn't just start with a par 3, it starts with a very challenging 'short' hole that is 204 yards from the back tee. Nine bunkers guard the green so this can require plenty of club into the wind.

The par 5, 2nd can be intimidating with its narrow fairway and procession of bunkers. The next five holes are a succession of varying length par 4's. The hardest of these is the 448 yard 5th which has four fairway and three greenside bunkers. The 6th dog-legs right and the tee shot is blind. The big danger is in cutting off too much of the right hand corner. You then must negotiate a large number of bunkers so it is important to drive well to make the second shot a little shorter.

The par 3, 8th has no bunkers but the undulating green is raised and the tee shot is often into the prevailing wind. Out of bounds runs along the right of the 9th hole. The comparative lack of length of this par 5 (490 yards) is offset by the difficult shot to the green which is enclosed behind a semi circle of six bunkers.

The drive on the par 4, 12th is blind over gorse and rough. The slightly raised green has no bunkers but if you block your second shot right then you might be in the gorse. A wild shot on the par 3, 13th will leave you in a bunker, gorse, or maybe even in a pond if you overhit.

The hole most remembered at S & A is the 16th, 'Gumbleys'. At the 300 yard mark on this par 5 there is a large sleeper faced bunker set into the side of a large ridge. As you approach the green, bunkers are to the left and gorse awaits you to the right.

The finishing hole has a blind tee shot to a fairway which narrows at about 230 yards. The green is in a pretty setting with mounds and rough for anything short and right. There is a high bank behind the green and beyond this is the practice putting green and the clubhouse.

Despite the fact that there are twelve par 4's at S & A, they are all quite different. The course is enjoyable to play with some parts featuring heather, others gorse and there are the occasional stands of pines. Provided you stay on the fairway then you can score well but stray shots will be punished. There is a minor design weakness, mainly on the inward nine, where you frequently exit the green and then have to walk back towards the tee you have just played in order to get to the next tee.

Par 3, 8th hole

Par 5, 16th 'Gumbleys' with the distinctive sleeper faced bunker

HILLSIDE

HILLSIDE SITS ALMOST NEXT TO ROYAL BIRKDALE AND, ON THE OTHER SIDE OF THE RAILWAY LINE, SOUTHPORT & AINSDALE.

The club commenced in 1911 but the course of today bears little resemblance to the original layout. New land in the dune ridge was acquired in the 1950's and by 1967 the new back nine and changed front nine was completed by Fred Hawtree.

The opening nine holes are a tough test, especially in the wind, but then the flatter holes give way to the large dunes and stands of pines that makes the second nine really special.

Your ability to hit the ball straight is tested immediately with out of bounds in the form of the railway line running the full length of the par 4, 1st hole and par 5, 2nd. The 2nd also features water by way of a ditch on the left and a pond at the right for the drive. The same pond is along the right edge of the green on the dog-leg par 4, 3rd hole.

The par 3, 7th runs into an area of fir trees which attractively line both sides around the green. The front nine ends with two good par 4's, the 8th dog-legging to the right and the 9th bending left to a slightly raised green with five bunkers.

The back nine starts with a most attractive short par 3. Pine trees jut out on the left side and there is a steep grassy bank on the right edge of the green which also has four bunkers, mainly towards the front. The tee is elevated at the par 5, 11th which curves slightly to the left through dunes on either side. A large bunker needs to be avoided at the front right of the green.

Par 4's at thirteen and fourteen run through dunes and then follows a very sharp dog-leg left at the par 4, 15th. The fairway is very narrow at the corner and there are four bunkers on the left if you risk trying to cut off part of the dog-leg.

The attractive par 3, 10th hole

The par 5, 17th is 548 yards and almost dead straight. It features a wonderfully undulating fairway with dunes and thick rough running along both sides. It has a Royal Birkdale feel which is not surprising since it is so close to this part of Hillside.

The 18th is a testing par 4 of 440 yards from the back tee. From the raised tee the hole bends right with dunes on the left and bunkers along the right.

Photo courtesy Alan C Birch

It is probably just as well that the two nines are in their present order because the back nine is so good anything else would seem an anti-climax. Greg Norman gave the highest accolades when he apparently wrote to the club and described the back nine holes as the best in Britain.

Photo David Worley

Above, left:
the par 4, 15th dog-legs left with 3 bunkers
at the corner

Left:
Hillside – 18th green and clubhouse

ROYAL BIRKDALE

Photo courtesy Alan C Birch

Across the 10th green and the beautiful dunes at Royal Birkdale

BIRKDALE GOLF CLUB BEGAN IN A VERY LOW KEY MANNER AS A NINE HOLE COURSE AT SHAW HILLS. THEN IN 1897 THE CLUB MOVED TO BIRKDALE HILLS AND AN EIGHTEEN HOLE LINKS WAS CONSTRUCTED.

In 1922 a seven year plan was put into place to bring the course up to championship standard. F W Hawtree and J H Taylor were awarded the contract. They wisely decided to lay out the holes in valleys between the dunes rather than over them. Apart from creating a tough but fair test of golf, this also provides for excellent crowd viewing from the dunes. The now famous art-deco style clubhouse was part of this planning and was completed in 1935.

After the Open of 1991 (won by Ian Baker-Finch) all the greens were redesigned and relayed which at the time was considered a very brave decision.

Royal Birkdale starts with three tough par 4's each running in a different direction. The 1st is probably the most demanding at 449 yards and with out of bounds down the whole of the right hand side. Whilst the 2nd is some 28 yards shorter, it is usually into the prevailing wind and the green is very well bunkered. The 3rd features a narrow entrance to a green protected by grassy sand hills at the right and the rear.

Only a very good strike will reach and hold the green on the 203 yard 4th hole. Four bunkers are at the front and woodland lies further back behind the green.

The 6th is a monster par 4 at 480 yards. The hole turns right at 262 yards where there is a large bunker at the corner. The green is at a slightly higher level and is flanked by large dunes and thick rough very close to the right hand edge. The green on the short 7th is lower than the tee but it is totally surrounded by seven pot bunkers.

The 9th can be a dangerous hole. The tee shot is blind and the hole then dog-legs right. There is thick rough and gorse if you miss the fairway. The green is slightly raised and there is plenty of trouble if your approach is too long.

The par 4, 10th dog-legs to the left. There are five fairway bunkers and nasty rough if you don't keep to the short grass. The 12th is the most attractive of the four short holes.

Par 4, 3rd hole

Photos courtesy Alan C Birch

The green at the short 7th is surrounded by 7 pot bunkers

Photo courtesy Alan C Birch

The 183 yard 12th is one of the best par 3's at Royal Birkdale

View from behind the two-tiered green at the par 5, 17th

The unusual art deco clubhouse at Royal Birkdale

The plateau green is nestled amongst the dunes with four deep bunkers at the front. At 498 yards the 13th must be the longest par 4 on any course in Britain. The fairway has its share of bunkers and, as with most holes at Birkdale, if you spray the ball around you will be walking through long grass or scrub. Particularly if you pull your long second shot left then you will not find your ball.

The long par 5, 15th is equally as demanding mainly due to the thirteen bunkers that inhabit this hole. Most of them are dotted around the area your second shot will finish so laying up for your third shot on this hole is not an easy task.

The 16th dog-legs right and is also very heavily bunkered starting with three bunkers about 55 yards out. For the members this is a short par 4 of 347 yards but the championship tee is 130 yards further back creating a long carry over the rough.

The par 5, 17th starts with a drive that must be threaded between two large sand hills and ends with a two-tiered green with sand hills, long grass and willow scrub almost surrounding it. The finishing hole at Birkdale is just about the toughest on the Open rota. A par 4 of 472 yards, there is out of bounds down the right and a large bunker in the centre of the fairway at about 225 yards. Sand hills with long grass run along the right of the snaking fairway to a green with a narrow entrance and three bunkers.

Royal Birkdale is a most imposing links with its huge dunes and very thick rough close by the fairways' edge. At around 7000 yards from the Championship tee it is now a real brute of a par 70 with only two par 5's. Furthermore the four par 3's have an average length of over 191 yards. In horrible conditions on the Saturday of the 1998 Open the average score was 77·49. The eventual winner, Mark O'Meara, was rumoured to have lost six balls in one of his practice rounds when a wet summer had left the rough long and thick.

I don't want to deter you from playing Royal Birkdale. From the normal tees it is a little more forgiving and you will enjoy the walk down the valleyed fairways of this beautifully presented course.

HESKETH

Par 3, 2nd hole at Hesketh

SET IN A LOVELY PART OF SOUTHPORT, HESKETH IS HALF LINKS AND HALF PARKLAND ALONG THE RIBBLE ESTUARY. I HAVE INCLUDED IT IN MY LINKS CATEGORY AS IT IS POSITIONED AT THE NORTHERN END OF LANCASHIRE'S SAND DUNE SYSTEM AND IT IS THE OLDEST CLUB IN SOUTHPORT WITH A START DATE OF 1885.

The English Golf Union owes it existence to Hesketh; it was a former captain who was behind its formation and became the first Union President.

Although the best holes at Hesketh are in the area between the sand hills and the clubhouse, one of the most photographed is the par 3, 2nd hole. There is a gully between tee and green and hollows with thick rough lie on either side. A steep bank is at the back and further behind is a row of trees with the clubhouse clock tower just visible.

The par 4, 388 yard 14th is a dramatic looking hole. The tee shot is somewhat daunting with out of bounds along the right and thick heather in front of the clubhouse on the left. Low dunes and thick grass line the two sides with houses on higher ground framing the picture at the back of the green. A large mound runs across the fairway to catch the second shot and set into the side of the mound are three bunkers.

After you have played the 18th, a great finishing hole, be sure to look out for the famous fir tree outside the clubhouse. It was originally given to Arnold Bentley along with his prize at the 1936 Berlin Olympic Games.

You will enjoy Hesketh and its historical links including the famous Bentley Room which contains memorabilia of the Bentley brothers' achievements.

In 2008 whilst Royal Birkdale is hosting the Open, Hesketh will be staging the Junior Open Championship.

Top: well bunkered 4th hole
Bottom: the very interesting par 4, 14th

Photos courtesy Alan C Birch

ROYAL LYTHAM & ST ANNES

Photo courtesy Alan C Birch

18th fairway and, from right to left, the clubhouse, dormy house and professional's shop

LYTHAM SIMPLY WREAKS OF HISTORY BOTH ON THE COURSE AND IN THE CLUBHOUSE. THE CLUB WAS ESTABLISHED IN 1886, THE FIRST PROFESSIONAL BEING GEORGE LOWE. OVER THE EARLY YEARS THERE WAS ALSO SOME ARCHITECTURAL INFLUENCE FROM HARRY COLT AND HERBERT FOWLER.

Lytham hosted the inaugural Ladies Amateur Championship in 1886 and has held ten Opens and two Ryder Cups amongst a long list of prestigious events.

Bobby Jones won his first Open title here in 1926. In the final round he lay equal at the 16th with Al Watrous who had made the 17th green in two. Jones pulled his drive into sandy scrub. From 175 yards out and with rough, bushes and bunkers blocking his view, Jones nipped the ball perfectly and finished inside his rival's ball. He then went on to win. A plaque sits on the left of the 17th fairway to commemorate the shot and his mashie-iron hangs in the clubhouse below his painting.

Par 3, 1st hole as seen from the members' balcony

Royal Lytham is a par 71 that measures 6882 yards from the Championship tee. The card for visitors and normal play for members is substantially shorter at 6360 yards. With 3 par 3's, the first nine is where the scoring is a little easier.

This is the only course used for the Open that begins with a par 3 – probably now best remembered after the 2001 Open when Ian Woosnam started with a birdie 2 and then found there were 15 clubs in his bag.

The 2nd and 3rd are two par 4's running alongside the railway on the right where the rough is also thickest against the grassy bank next to the boundary fence. The preferred line from the tee is right on the 2nd and left at the 3rd, in each case requiring you to play close to the fairway bunkers.

The next four holes all run in different directions. The par 4, 4th hole sweeps around to the left and has five small but steep faced bunkers beside the green. The long 7th (555 yards) is one of the best holes at Lytham. A big slice will mean lost ball. The fairway is lined with bunkers as it bends right towards a green that is partly hidden by the highest sand hills on the course.

The par 4, 8th is a wonderful looking hole with a classic use of hazards. Your drive must be on the fairway. To the right there is rough, trees and then the railway. Any drive pulled left is in long grass or a bunker. The green is perched much higher up on a plateau but 40 yards in front is a grassy ridge with three bunkers which cover most of the fairway. The green tends to slope to the front left where a deep bunker awaits your visitation.

I love the closed in feel of the par 3, 9th which, in keeping with true traditional links design, is at the furthest distance

Photo courtesy Alan C Birch

The short 9th, one of my favourite holes at Royal Lytham

from the clubhouse. There is gorse and then trees if you are too far left or right and the raised green is accompanied by nine bunkers at the front and sides. This is one of those greens where there is a wonderful satisfaction in being there with the tee shot.

The 10th is a short but tricky par 4. If you slice your second shot you will be in very long grass. If it is just a little short and offline to the right then you may finish in a nasty deep pot bunker. You will then have to play over another pot bunker to get on the green or risk playing sideways where anything a little strong will be in one of two bunkers on the left. Sometimes you just have to take your penalty and play out backwards – but it sure hurts.

The par 3, 12th is slightly longer than the 9th and has a very similar configuration of greenside bunkers. Out of bounds is dangerously close right of the green. The 13th is a short par 4 that is a definite chance for birdie. Just drive straight and then you have a very short iron to the green. If you want to know the prevailing wind direction then have a look at the lean on the stunted trees at the left of this green.

Fifteen, rated index 2, is a very long par 4 of 467 yards from the Championship tee. Only a drive with a very brave line will give you a chance of getting to the green in two.

After you retrace the footsteps of Bobby Jones on the 17th you stand on the 18th tee and wonder how you can avoid the sea of large fairway bunkers. If you push your tee shot too far right you will be in gorse and thick scrub. For the long hitter you need to take the line over the first two bunkers on the right side of the fairway. As you

prepare for your shot to the green there is the magnificent panoramic vista of the clubhouse, dormy house and professional shop. The green is narrow at the front, bunkered on both sides and runs away at the back.

There are 197 penal pot bunkers, the rough is thick and the greens are difficult to hold as they tend to be slightly higher in the centre. For a links course the fairways are unusually even and are always in wonderful condition. Visually, Lytham is different in that it is surrounded by red brick housing on one side and the railway line on the other. It is a mile inland and you can't see the ocean, but make no mistake this is a genuine links and a great one at that.

The 12th provides a great example of the bunkering at Royal Lytham

Above: 17th green from the right hand side
Left: this plaque sits on the left of the 17th fairway to commemorate the shot played from 175 yards out by Bobby Jones in the 1926 Open Championship

ST ANNES OLD LINKS

ST ANNES OLD LINKS STARTED IN 1901 WITH GEORGE LOWE, THEIR FIRST PROFESSIONAL, DESIGNING THE ORIGINAL NINE HOLES. THE CLUB SOON HAD TO MOVE, DUE TO ENCROACHING HOUSING, TO THEIR PRESENT SITE WHERE SANDY HERD WAS ALSO INVOLVED IN THE DESIGN.

Photo courtesy of Stuart Hogg

Par 3, 9th is the signature hole at St Annes

The links occupy a rectangular piece of land which is now bordered at the perimeters by housing, a railway line and Blackpool airport. All holes but for three of the par 3's run in a parallel fashion at 90 degrees from the clubhouse.

After a fairly easy par 4 to start, the 2nd is somewhat longer at 403 yards and features six bunkers to catch the drive and three cross bunkers some 30 yards before the green. Anything just a little too strong through the green is in danger of finishing out of bounds.

The par 3, 3rd runs to a corner of the property and has out of bounds coming in at an angle on both sides of the green. There are seven bunkers so you have to go for the flag – there is no bail out area.

Index 1 is the long par 4, 4th hole which is 442 yards from the back tee and usually plays into the prevailing wind. The two fairway bunkers 35 yards short of the green are a frequent cause of poor scores on this hole. The 5th and 6th are consecutive par 5's. Each has their difficulties with the 5th featuring out of bounds along the right and the 6th fairway being peppered with bunkers.

This is a tough stretch of holes with the par 4, 7th measuring 447 yards from the back. There is a gully and broken section of fairway 62 yards from the green and from here to the front of the green there are nine bunkers.

The 9th is the signature hole at St Annes. This par 3 of 169 yards plays back to the clubhouse with the green in a bowl with large mounds on either side. Four bunkers guard the front and another four are at the sides of the green. Bobby Jones is supposed to have liked this hole so much when he played St Annes in 1926 that he took measurements so as to reproduce a similar hole in the United States.

Ten, eleven and twelve are par 4's with the first two being tricky but possible birdie holes. The 13th is a long par 3, and the 14th and 15th are medium length par 4's punctuated by a large number of bunkers.

The par 3, 16th and the two finishing par 5's each have out of bounds along the right hand side. Of these the 17th is probably the most demanding with its length of 552 yards, railway line to the right and mounds and bunkers along the left.

St Annes is certainly a challenging layout which offers little protection from the strong westerly. One of the landmarks that is very visible from the links is the Blackpool Tower built back in 1894 as a half size copy of the Eiffel Tower.

Whilst it is not as long as its illustrious neighbour, St Annes Old Links is used as a qualifying course when the Open is played at Royal Lytham & St Annes.

CASTLETOWN

Early morning dew on the 12th hole

YOU CAN SEE THE SEA FROM EVERYONE OF CASTLETOWN'S 6707 YARDS ALONG THE LONGNESS PENINSULA AT THE SOUTH EAST END OF THE ISLE OF MAN. THE ISLE IS ITSELF LOCATED IN THE IRISH SEA ALMOST MIDWAY BETWEEN NORTHERN ENGLAND AND NORTHERN IRELAND.

Although originally laid out in 1892 by Old Tom Morris, Castletown needed substantial rebuilding after World War II. This was done with great care by Mackenzie Ross who at the same time restored Turnberry and built Southerness – both nearby as the crow flies.

The 1st is a straightforward short par 4 of 253 yards uphill. The 2nd is a longer par 4 and has a tricky undulating green with a ridge running across near the centre. The par 5, 3rd hole dog-legs to the left. As you approach the green there are large mounds and rough along the right.

There is plenty of gorse and scrub on both sides of the 4th which also turns sharply left. You may not need driver from the tee as you can run out of fairway. The bunkers here are mainly at the back of the green. Accuracy is essential on the 5th, a par 4 of 423 yards that bends right following the shoreline. Out of bounds is all along the right and thick gorse is on the left. A large bunker sits in the middle of the rippling fairway 70 yards out from the green.

The drive at the par 4, 6th is over gorse to a wide fairway. Only chronic slicers need fear the out of bounds or stone wall on the right. Fairway bunkers need to be avoided on the long 7th (572 yards). The three on the right are very much in play for the second shot.

The 8th is the first of only three par 3's at Castletown. There is rough and one deep bunker well short of the green. You will find trouble if you miss the raised green on either

Right: par 4, 5th with out of bounds along the right

Below: the green at the 16th is one of the most scenic parts of the links at Castletown

Photo courtesy Alan C Birch

Photo courtesy Alan C Birch

side but right is worst as this could leave you down a bank and near the seashore. Nine, ten and eleven all follow the shore line which is on the right. Each of these holes necessitates a drive over the corner of the bank beside the sea and out of bounds at the right. The 11th is by far the longest (446 yards) of these three par 4's and has a fairway bunker at 263 yards from the tee. Your drive needs to be between this bunker and the grassy ridge on the left of the fairway.

The picturesque par 5, 12th has most of the trouble as you approach the green. Bunkers are on both sides and a bank with heavy rough runs all around the rear of the green. The 13th is a very dangerous little hole of a mere 133 yards. Large deep bunkers are at the front of the green which is set into the side of a slope. Left will be in rough up the bank below the 6th tee and right will finish down the slope.

The par 4, 15th needs a well placed drive to avoid out of bounds on the right and two fairway bunkers at the left. The green on the par 3, 16th is one of the most scenic parts of the links. At 185 yards with gorse and a very large bunker on the right, this can be a dangerous hole into the prevailing wind. Castletown has just the one tree and virtually no dunes so you bear the full force of any wind that is blowing here.

Like many other holes at Casteltown, the tee shot on the 17th needs to be a very slight fade to follow the bend in the hole from the tee. The difference on this hole however is the chasm, with rocks and sea below, that you must drive over. Keep left as even a long hit over the chasm might end up in the rough and heather if it tails a little too far right. The second shot is then fairly straightforward with the lovely setting of the hotel in the distance.

Your good score can still be ruined by the wonderful, but scary, 18th . The fairway again slopes left to right with the coastal cliffs along your right. The blind drive needs to be left, away from a bunker and gorse. This will then give you the best line into the green which has a deep ravine just in front.

Castletown is a delightful links with the added beauty of the isolation and quietness that comes from island golf.
Having said that, I don't recommend you time your golfing visit for early June when the famous motor cycle event is staged.

Photo courtesy Alan C Birch

17th hole and clubhouse in the distance

SILLOTH ON SOLWAY

Photo courtesy Silloth on Solway GC

The very wind exposed 5th green

I FIRST DISCOVERED SILLOTH IN 1996 WHILST SPENDING A WEEK IN THE LAKE DISTRICT. IT WAS A TEDIOUS DRIVE INTO RATHER DULL COUNTRY WITH INDUSTRY SPOILING THE FEW GOOD OUTLOOKS. BUT THE DRIVE WAS CERTAINLY WORTH THE EFFORT. I HATE TO USE THE EXPRESSION, AND I HAVE AVOIDED DOING SO TO THIS STAGE IN THE BOOK, BUT THIS IS A HIDDEN GEM OF THE FIRST ORDER. BACK THEN, HARDLY ANYONE I SPOKE WITH HAD EVER HEARD OF SILLOTH ON SOLWAY BUT NOW QUITE RIGHTLY IT IS BEGINNING TO RECEIVE ITS LONG OVERDUE RECOGNITION.

Photos courtesy Silloth on Solway GC

Top: undulating fairway and green at Silloth's 14th
Bottom: clubhouse, Silloth on Solway

On my first two golfing visits to the UK I played nearly 90 courses. Silloth has the distinction of being my worst score so I have the utmost respect for it. If you can't handle the wind then be prepared to spend plenty of time in the rough or looking amongst the plentiful gorse.

Silloth on Solway Golf Club was started in 1892 by the North British Railway Company. It was first laid out by Davy Grant with later input from Willie Fernie and Willie Park. Historically, Silloth is famous for producing Cecil Leith a trail blazing lady golfer who dominated womens' golf around the time of the First World War.

Right from the outset you realise the necessity of straight driving at Silloth with heather and gorse along the left of the 1st. The 2nd dog-legs right in a valley with gorse lined banks. The 3rd, another par 4, dog-legs left to a plateau green.

After one more par 4, you come to the very good 5th hole, 'Solway'. The tee is elevated and the drive is to an angled fairway along the shoreline. Keep your shots low when the wind is blowing otherwise you will be amazed how your ball can go off line once it gets above the height of the dunes.

Two more par 4's along the shoreline and then the short 9th, Silloth's version of the Postage Stamp 8th at Royal Troon. Hitting down from the raised tee the green appears an easy target, but there are plenty of bunkers at the front of the green which slopes away to the right.

Ten and eleven are par 4's that alternate with a dog-leg left and then right. The shot into the 11th green is picturesque with the green surrounded by gorse and the church steeple standing in the distance. The green at the long par 3, 12th is similarly framed but also has a heathery bank at the front left.

The hole you will always remember after playing Silloth is the par 5, 13th which is appropriately named 'Hog's Back'. Although only 485 yards, the second shot is through a narrow gully to an elevated ridge which falls away on both sides into either heather or gorse. The totally exposed green is at the top of the hill with many approaches running tantalisingly to the edge of the green before falling away.

Fourteen is a rather less difficult short par 5 and fifteen is a good driving hole from an elevated tee to a reasonably wide fairway. The gorse lined par 3, 16th is slightly uphill to a raised green with twin bunkers at both sides.

The final hole requires two good straight hits to be on the 401 yard par 4 in regulation. The drive is the key as you need to be aware of fairway bunkers on the right and a fall off towards heather and gorse along the left. The green is long and narrow and has a bunker on each side as well as just short of the apron.

Silloth on Solway is a terrific course that never lets up. Especially with the usual windy conditions, you will need to play very good golf to beat your handicap here.

The short 9th – Silloth's version of the 'Postage Stamp' at Royal Troon

Photo David Worley

WALES *Nefyn GC, view from beside the 11th tee*

WALES

ROYAL PORTHCAWL

Royal Porthcawl's opening hole is hard to match anywhere

THE TWO PRE-EMINENT LINKS IN WALES ARE QUITE CLEARLY THE TWO 'ROYALS' NAMELY ROYAL PORTHCAWL AND ROYAL ST DAVID'S FURTHER NORTH AT HARLECH.

I must plead guilty for having a strong affection for Porthcawl after spending three nights in the Dormy House and having three balmy days to wander around playing and photographing along the attractive shoreline of Rest Bay. Where else can you sit on the verandah of the clubhouse just a few yards from the water's edge and at the same time look down those first three engaging holes right beside the sea.

After a rather primitive start in 1891 as a 9 hole course, the club moved to its present location four years later where 18 holes were laid out. The original 9 holes was by a fellow named Gibson, the professional at Westward Ho!, but it is not clear if he too completed the new 18 holes. In any event, the new course underwent alterations by Harry Colt in 1913 and Tom Simpson in 1933.

In 1909 the club received the Royal prefix and a good relationship developed with the Prince of Wales who became the patron of the club in 1923 even though it was not until 1932 that he first played there.

Photo David Worley

5th hole, a dog-leg uphill par 5

Royal Porthcawl's opening hole is hard to match anywhere. The drive is across the 18th to a fairway that slopes left towards the sea. Thick heather and gorse will be your reward if you play safe too far right. Anything even a little too far left is likely to end up in one of the four deep bunkers. A wild hook will be out of bounds on the beach or rocks.

The 2nd can be a brute at 451 yards to a green only a few yards from the out of bounds fence. Anything long and right will fall into a hollow with long grass. The 3rd is a similar length par 4 but with more of a dog-leg left following the shore. There is a long bunker at the right of the raised green which is also only a few yards from out of bounds. The fairways are a series of humps and hollows so you won't have had too many level lies so far.

The 4th is a long par 3 of 212 yards with two bunkers well short of the green and four closer by. This hole runs inland so you will often have the sea breeze at your back making it difficult to stop the ball.

The 5th is rather unusual. This par 5 is a dog-leg around heavy rough and gorse at the corner and then runs up a steep hill to a small plateau green. A stone wall marks out of bounds all along the left and is within just a few yards of the green. This hole is tough enough at 486 yards from the white tees but for the blue markers there is a tiger tee which lengthens the hole to 611 yards. When playing to the green you are conscious of out of bounds being so close to the left, but anything right will kick into a thick bank of gorse.

From one extreme to the other with the 7th being just 122 yards. This is a pretty little hole on high ground at the furthest point from the clubhouse. The green is an island surrounded by rolling mounds and six bunkers.

Eight is a very tricky short par 5 with out of bounds left, gorse on the right and a succession of fairway bunkers as you head uphill needing controlled draw shots to keep out of the rough. The 9th has a slightly raised tee giving you a good view of all the gorse on the right. A draw is required here also with your second to a well bunkered green. It is the difficult second shot that makes this hole index 1 on the card.

It is impossible to get on the 11th green unless you land your ball there, 180 yards from the tee. The green is raised and slopes left to right. There are five bunkers starting from the front and then in a line along the left and there are two bunkers at the right. Anything long will run down a bank so not surprisingly the hole is rated the eighth most difficult.

Thirteen is a long par 4 (475 yards from the blue and 421 from the white) that can wreck your score if you don't know the course. The second shot is semi-blind downhill but what you can't see is that the fairway narrows at about 80 yards from the green with a big fall off on either side into deep hollows with thick rough. There are also five bunkers that may catch your approach to the green.

The 14th is a fairly short par 3 downhill but the greenside bunkers are quite deep and are very straight faced. Fifteen and sixteen are tough par 4's playing uphill for the second shots. From the 16th tee all you see is a line of cross bunkers at the foot of a ridge running across at about 265 yards out and 155 yards short of the green.

Seventeen is a short par 5 but it is uphill with a blind tee shot and heavy rough and gorse before angling left to another well bunkered green.

The par 4,18th is as good a finish as the 1st is as an opening hole. From high up the drive is straight down towards the sea with the green right beside the clubhouse. Although downhill, you are usually into the wind. The fairway disappears about 100 yards short of the green where a grassy hollow runs across. Unless you can hit the green on the full then you have to aim your second left, rather dangerously close to the 1st tee, in order to counteract the slope of the fairway and green.

This is a totally exposed seaside links and the weather can quickly turn for the worst. In a howling gale in 1961, Peter Thomson won the Dunlop Masters by eight strokes from a quality field. The club history paints a wonderful word picture of Thomson's play on the 410 yard 18th, which was directly into the wind: "He hit a very good tee shot on this par 4 down to the sea. He then hit a one iron, straight as an arrow, which rose no more than ten or fifteen feet and seemed to go on forever, to finish on the green amidst astonished applause." [1]

Royal Porthcawl is a terrific course with no easy holes. It is substantially longer from the blue at 6829 yards which is nearly 400 yards more than the distance from the white tees. I felt the second nine was the more difficult partly because of the number of blind shots. A feature of Royal Porthcawl is its beautifully presented bunkers, as well as the very friendly members.

"Links they may worthily be called, for the golf at Porthcawl is the genuine thing – the sea in sight all the time, and the most noble bunkers." [2]

1. *Royal Porthcawl Golf Club 1891-1991* – Leo McMahon
2. *Golf Courses of the British Isles* – Bernard Darwin

Top: the short par 3, 7th has an island green surrounded by mounds and six bunkers
Centre: par 3, 11th requires a carry all the way to the green
Bottom: 18th green

SOUTHERNDOWN

Photo David Worley

Clubhouse and 10th green from side on

SOUTHERNDOWN IS INCLUDED UNDER THE CATEGORY OF CLIFFTOP LINKS EVEN THOUGH IT IS A MILE OR TWO INLAND. OVER MANY CENTURIES SAND HAS BEEN BLOWN UP FROM THE EXPANSE OF BEACHES BELOW THAT ARE CLEARLY VISIBLE FROM THE COURSE. SO MUCH SO THAT THERE ARE NOW SOME PARTLY EXPOSED SAND DUNES HIGH UP IN THE HILLS. THE LAND HERE IS ALSO FULL OF LIMESTONE WHICH FURTHER IMPROVES THE DRAINAGE AND HELPS PROVIDE FOR TYPICAL LINKS FAIRWAYS.

Writing earlier in the twentieth century, Darwin comments that Southerndown 'is perched high aloft and looks down on Porthcawl'. Not being at shore level 'it has many of the characteristics of the typical downland courses…but it has not, curiously to relate, the typical down turf. The winds of the centuries have blown so much sand up from the seashore that they have practically succeeded in imbuing the turf of the downs with a second sandy nature.'[1]

In 1905 Willie Fernie (not the same Willie Fernie who won the Open in 1883) designed the first layout. Later on changes were made by Herbert Fowler, Willie Park and Harry Colt but not much has really changed since those early days.

The 1st hole is always remembered by Henry Cotton's famous quote 'bracken to the left, bracken to the right and a fairway rising to the sky'. This fairway also slopes left to right so when the ground gets firm in summer just keeping your ball on the fairway is not easy.

The 2nd, a long par 4 of 439 yards, is one of the most spectacular and most difficult on the course. Playing into the green there is a mound on the left, a bunker on the right and two bunkers a little further back also on the right to where the fairway slopes. From the green there are

Caution!
Golfers may be out of sight but still within range
Please take care!

magnificent views for miles over the Ogmore River Valley and Bristol Channel. The four par 3's at Southerndown are all good holes.

The 5th is well bunkered and needs an accurate tee shot. The slightly longer 10th has gorse to the right and then a ridge in front of the entrance to the green. Most of the bunkers are left which is the side of the natural fall of the land.

The finish is a long one with three long par 4's and a par 5. The 15th is the toughest at 466 yards but the 18th can be tricky with a tee shot over gorse, usually into the wind, on to a split level fairway and then to a green with a large bunker on either side at the front.

After you have played Southerndown you will remember the views, the bracken and gorse, the hills, the sheep, and of course the wind. In 2006 the Welsh Open Amateur Strokeplay at Southerndown was completely abandoned due to the wind and rain.

As the seagull flies, Southerndown and Royal Porthcawl are neighbours but they provide a complete contrast which you should enjoy.

1. *Golf Courses of the British Isles* – Bernard Darwin

Top: 2nd green and the Ogmore River Valley at the right
Above: par 3, 10th hole

PYLE & KENFIG

Photo David Worley

Bracken everywhere at the par 3, 15th

I CAN ONLY COMMENT ON A COURSE BASED ON MY EXPERIENCE AND OBSERVATIONS THERE, AND I AM CONSCIOUS OF NOT BEING INFLUENCED BY WEATHER CONDITIONS OR HOW GOOD, OR BAD, THE STANDARD OF GOLF MAY HAVE BEEN.

Photo David Worley

1st green, Pyle & Kenfig

I played Pyle & Kenfig on a fine summer's day in July 2006. This was by far the most disappointing of the 97 courses I visited this particular trip. It is often said that Pyle & Kenfig is in the shadow of its neighbour, Royal Porthcawl. In my opinion they are a long way apart in both design and condition. Having said that, there are four or five good holes on the back nine but even these suffered from the fact that the fairways were one step away from becoming dustbowls in large areas.

The first nine, designed by Harry Colt in 1922 is the original nine holes. The inward nine which is in the more interesting duneland is the work of Mackenzie Ross.

The two opening holes are straight forward par 4's heading uphill. The 3rd is a short par 4 that is a real birdie opportunity as long as you avoid the greenside bunkers. The 4th and 6th are each fairly straightforward par 3's.

The par 5, 5th hole is not long and is another birdie chance as long as you stay away from the thick bracken along the left hand side.

The 7th is a good par 4 which runs uphill with a dog-leg to the left. A draw shot from the drive makes it an easier hole but you need to avoid the bunkers that seemed to me to be more or less in line with the marker post.

Nine is a good par 5 running downhill back towards the clubhouse. The main obstacle is the deep fairway bunkers in place for your second shot and then the tight corner where the green is located. With the fairways so hard and dry, avoiding bunkers was something of a lottery.

You cross the road for the second nine which starts with an uphill par 4, similar to the 1st. The par 5, 11th dog-legs left to a green on higher ground at the start of some more interesting terrain. Fairway bunkers are the only real danger here.

Holes twelve to fourteen are the three best at Pyle & Kenfig. The 12th is a somewhat intimidating par 3, 190 yards and uphill. There is no fairway, only bracken on all sides and a small landing area in front of the green which is well bunkered. On a windy day this could be lost ball territory. I am surprised that it is rated the second easiest on the course. Thirteen is a par 4 that dog-legs right to a green higher up amongst the dunes. Be careful not to drive too far right unless you are a big hitter.

The elevated 14th tee also asks the question as to how much of the right hand corner you should take on. If you hit straight then you can run out of fairway and finish in thick bracken. To the right are dunes so the ideal tee shot is a long fade. You then play uphill to a steeply sloping green with one very large straight faced bunker at the front left.

The 15th is a long par 3 of 206 yards but it is all downhill. There are several large bunkers all at the front section on the green. The background is a mass of thick bracken and shrubs which makes the hole look a little harder than it really is.

The final three holes return to the less interesting land and each is a par 4 of over 400 yards. Sixteen and eighteen are birdie chances if you get a good drive away whilst the 17th is rather more difficult with its sloping green and greenside bunkers.

I'm sure Pyle & Kenfig would look much better after some summer rain but having no fairway sprinklers whatsoever leaves them very vulnerable in a hot and dry spell. I can only conclude that this is no where near as good a course as its past ranking in some surveys might suggest.

PENNARD

Photo David Worley

Wonderful views from the 8th tee

WHEN YOU BOOK YOUR GAME AT PENNARD, MAKE A NOTE TO BRING YOUR CAMERA. THIS IS CLIFFTOP LINKS AT A SPECTACULAR LEVEL WITH SUPERB VIEWS ACROSS THE GOWER PENINSULA. PENNARD IS EIGHT MILES SOUTH WEST OF SWANSEA AND IS NOW OFTEN REFERRED TO AS THE 'LINKS IN THE SKY'. THE CLUB HAS AN OFFICIAL START DATE OF 1896 BUT IT WAS SOME YEARS LATER BEFORE THE LINKS DESIGNED BY JAMES BRAID WERE LAID OUT.

Pennard starts with a long par 4 where a good drive with a slight draw is needed and then it is just a mid iron to the green. Anything sliced right will be in thick rough or out of bounds.

The 2nd is a pretty little short hole with the green in a dell and featuring only two bunkers. The par 4, 3rd requires a draw from the tee as does the par 5, 4th hole. This is the first real taste of the bumpy fairways that give almost a lunar landscape. The second half of the 4th has out of bounds along the right where there is a public walkway to the beach below the cliffs.

The par 3, 5th is only 165 yards in length but it offers you some real problems if you don't hit the green. The green is built up on the down slope of a hill so anything left, right or long will run down a bank into the rough. There is one bunker at the front left and two are at the front right.

The 6th is another dog-leg left par 4. The tee is right beside the cliff edge with sea views and below the meandering river and flood plain amongst the cliff and dunes. The green is situated in a dell with a narrow gap between two small mounds.

Seven and eight are short par 4's. The 7th runs past bracken and the old castle ruins on the right and the 8th requires a solid draw to take on the dog-leg. The views to the sea from the 8th tee are even better than those from the 6th.

The par 4, 9th (445 yards) is index 1 on the card and it too bends to the left. The second shot here is quite difficult and there is a deep bunker about 60 yards out on the left side which is right where you want to land your ball in the firm summer conditions. The index rating of 4 on the very short par 5 (492 yards) 10th gives a clue that there are some

hazards to avoid. The drive is down hill but there is a burn on the left that is very much in play. The fairway then bends left and uphill to a green surrounded by six bunkers. The area short of the green is very bumpy and will often kick balls off to the right.

The par 3, 11th is 180 yards uphill with a large hollow, a burn and rough ground just past half way to the green. There are mounds on the left of the green and a bunker at front right. On a windy day you won't see too many hit this green with their tee shot.

Photo David Worley

7th hole with the ruins of the old castle on the right

The 12th is a short par 4 of 298 yards but it is very hard to hold your blind second shot to the green cut into the side of a hill. It is easy to roll off the green and finish 30 yards away lower down on the next tee.

Into the sea breeze the par 3, 13th is a tough hole at 207 yards. From the tee it appears that the correct line is over a mound blocking the view to much of the green, however there is a bunker hidden in this area.

The 14th is yet another par 4 that dog-legs to the left. Although there is no sense of repetition on the course, it is very much set up for those who favour a draw with their drive.

The three closing holes require some adventurous shot making to match the superb views. Sixteen is a par 5 that this time bends to the right. The elevated tee demands a big drive but watch for the two bunkers at 250-260 yards on the left. As you get nearer the green everything runs left

From green to tee on the very difficult par 3, 13th

Photos David Worley

There is no margin for error if you miss the green at the 16th

Photo David Worley

towards the 17th. The green slopes steeply from the back but the view almost compensates for a three putt.

The 17th is another par 5 but I found it to be almost unplayable from the tee because of the hard and quite bare fairways. The hole runs along the cliff edge with the fairway sloping steeply from left to right. Theoretically the drive is straight but only a draw has a chance of staying on the fairway. There is then a big dog-leg left uphill so your second shot is semi-blind over gorse and heather towards a green with a narrow landing area in front.

Eighteen is a good par 4 of 415 yards and slightly uphill. There is thick heather on both sides from the tee. You can't risk a draw because the fairway slopes left so a slight fade is ideal. You then have a straight shot to the green with a few small mounds but no bunkers to worry about.

Unfortunately Pennard was very dry the day I was there and the greens were a little patchy. But this really is quite a unique links course. Apart from some hilly and unusual holes you will also have to share the scenery with the wild ponies and cattle which graze on the links. You can't play golf in Wales without putting Pennard on your list.

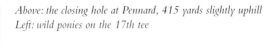

Above: the closing hole at Pennard, 415 yards slightly uphill
Left: wild ponies on the 17th tee

Photo courtesy Pennard GC

TENBY

Photo David Worley

12th green

SITUATED ON THE PEMBROKESHIRE COAST WITH VIEWS ACROSS TO THE ISLE OF CALDEY (HOME TO THE CISTERCIAN MONKS FOR OVER A THOUSAND YEARS), TENBY IS THE OLDEST GOLF CLUB IN WALES. THE CLUB WAS ESTABLISHED IN 1888 AND, THANKS TO JAMES BRAID, BECAME AN 18 HOLE COURSE BY 1907.

Finding the course can be tricky first time round as you divert from the busy streets of Tenby and follow the railway line to the lower ground where the links land is set out to the west.

The 1st is a really cracking opener, a par 4 of 476 yards. Mounds and heavy rough run along the left so it is easy to block your drive and finish beyond low mounds to the right and onto the 18th fairway. With so much potential danger there are no bunkers needed on this hole.

You cross the public walkway to reach the 2nd tee for what is another straight long par 4. The 3rd is a shorter par 4 and is one of the best holes at Tenby. 'Dai Rees' has heavy rough and dunes along the right. The entrance to the green is quite narrow with dunes to the right and a bunker on the left. The small green slopes steeply from the back to the front. Although it is a tricky hole, I am a little surprised it is rated index number 1.

The 4th is a tough par 4 of 440 yards that can ruin your scorecard. The tee shot is very tight with a fair carry to the fairway and then the second shot is to a green hidden down in a dell. All along the left side is a bank with thick rough and creepers that make finding a ball here nearly impossible. The hillock to the right of the green provides the first of some sea views.

The par 3, 6th is only 118 yards but it is not without its difficulties. There is thick rough and what can be a wet area short of the elevated green and three bunkers are placed to catch anything a little long and wide. The hole name 'Lifter's Cottage' relates to the cottage and its occupiers who operated the railway gates.

The 7th, a par 4 of 415 yards has the railway line along the right. There are four fairway bunkers to trap the drive and another in the fairway centre 46 yards out from the undulating green.

In 2006, the 8th was a par 4 with a slight dog-leg left. The tee shot is over a public walkway and as a result of a young child being hit by a ball, this hole is being moved further up the hill with a green that is surrounded by bracken and gorse.

Nine is a super par 3 of 185 yards over a deep gully of thick rough. If the wind is behind you may want to land short of the green but there is a bunker hidden in this area. Missing the green left will leave you with a difficult recovery shot.

The 10th 'James Braid' is rated the second hardest at Tenby. The line is tight from the tee but if you get a good drive away down the hill then this hole plays easier than its rating. The 12th is another very good, and difficult, par 3. There is no fairway and no bail-out area anywhere. From the back tee the 197 yards is virtually all carry over the two deep grassed gullies to the green on a flattened plateau. The walk to the 13th tee reveals a beautiful vista looking across the sea to Caldey Island.

Thirteen is a short par 4 downhill. Big hitters might go for the green (305 yards away) but you need to miss the two fairway bunkers on the left and two greenside bunkers at the right.

Top: lovely par 4, 3rd hole 'Dai Rees'
Middle: the green is hidden for the second shot into the 4th, a tough par 4 of 440 yards
Bottom: 14th green from side on

Fourteen may be a short par 5 but you had better stay on the fairway. The left is a line of rough, gorse and scrub. The fairway is littered with bunkers and then near the green there is a deep gully at the left edge.

You then walk across the railway bridge to three holes on slightly higher ground on the other side. The 15th is a good par 4 with the railway line, thick rough and gorse all along the left.

The 16th is an unusual hole. The first part of the fairway narrows just before a burn runs across about 270 yards from the tee. You then hit up a very steep hill with the green perched at the top. With the dry conditions I layed up with a 3 iron from the tee and then played a 5 wood to the green.

The par 3, 17th is the sort of hole you either get to love or hate. The high tee provides wonderful views for miles across the country side. The green is at the bottom of the hill with a bunker on either side at the front. It is very difficult to hit and then hold the green and there is plenty of trouble by way of trees if you are too strong with your shot.

The 18th is an unusual finishing hole that I must say I rather liked. There are two tees, one being elevated high in the rocky outcrop that otherwise stands behind the white tee area. The secret to this hole is the drive. The railway line and out of bounds runs along the left and there are two fairway bunkers to the right. A straight drive will leave you with a simple mid iron second shot, but a blind one, to the flat green. About 80 yards out the fairway virtually disappears where there is a mound and hidden fairway bunker. That area should not be in play if you hit a good drive and, as there are no greenside bunkers, you can afford to land just short of the green. One final caution – do

not over club as there is out of bounds and the car park very close behind the green and a line of conifers.

Tenby is a very good links course with excellent greens and some first class par 3's. If there is a weakness then I would suggest that it is a little short at only 6373 yards from the back tees and the condition of the bunkers could be improved.

Photos David Worley

Par 3, 17th – you will either love it or hate it

1st green back to the clubhouse with the 18th fairway at the left

ASHBURNHAM

ASHBURNHAM, AT BURRY PORT ON CARMARTHEN BAY, TAKES ITS NAME FROM THE 5TH EARL OF ASHBURNHAM WHO ONCE OWNED THE LAND AND WAS THE CLUB'S INAUGURAL PRESIDENT IN 1894. LIKE MANY OTHERS, ASHBURNHAM STARTED OUT AS 9 HOLES BUT BY 1902 THE FULL 18 WERE IN PLAY. SIGNIFICANT ALTERATIONS TOOK PLACE IN 1910 AND 1913 BASED ON THE SUGGESTIONS OF J H TAYLOR.

Photo courtesy Ashburnham GC

Gower view

Whilst it measures 6624 yards from the normal white tees, it is a good test in the wind from the very back tees which add a further 286 yards. Ashburnham is very much an out and back course with the ninth being the furthest point from the clubhouse.

The first two and last two holes run in the opposite direction to the other holes and are more of an inland character. The other fourteen are quality links with some big dunes and the sea in close proximity. Based on the prevailing wind, the first nine is usually into the wind and the second nine is wind assisted.

The opening hole will certainly test your nerves. It is a par 3 of 185 yards with five greenside bunkers and out of bounds down the right hand side. The long par 4, 2nd (444 yards) heads out towards the links land and it too has out of bounds all along the right. There are also a number of bunkers to contend with.

Holes three to sixteen more or less run parallel with the sea shore. The layout can become a slicer's nightmare with holes 3, 4, 5, 7, and 8 all featuring out of bounds along the right. The par 3, 6th moves away from the boundary but is still demanding at 189 yards and with five bunkers around the green mainly on the right.

Index 1 is the par 4, 9th (438 yards) which dog-legs left. There are trees if you slice right and a large bunker if you try to cut too much of the left hand corner. The fairway then narrows with two more bunkers along the left and closer to the green.

The next six holes are the closest to the dunes and the sea although the sea views are not a constant. Apart from dunes and mounds there is gorse to be avoided on the 12th and 13th. The par 5, 14th has a broken fairway and a lovely dell green surrounded by mounds.

Photo courtesy Ashburnham GC

16th green

18th green and clubhouse

14th green

The 15th, index 2, is a very long par 4 requiring a drive over the nearby 14th green. The second shot into the green is somewhat intimidating. There are no bunkers but the narrow fairway is bordered by a large dune on each side about 50 yards out and then a wall of thick bushes. Behind the green is also heavily treed.

The par 3, 16th is from a raised tee to a green that slopes away to the back behind which is a high grassed mound that is almost a wall. Two large bunkers are at the front and one each side so only a lot of luck would allow you to run the ball on to the green.

Two tough holes in heavier soil conclude the round. Seventeen is a long par 4 with a burn on the right and bunkers down the left. The par 4, 18th is a fairway in two sections. The drive is straight ahead then the second is left and uphill over broken ground to a tightly placed green with mounds and rough very close at hand. On a windy day a pulled drive or second shot could finish out of bounds.

Ashburnham can be a tough proposition in the wind. The greens are very good and there is some first class links golf to be had with quite a variety which is not always the case with out and back designs. Whoever said "all links courses are the same" should come and visit Wales.

CARDIGAN

AFTER SEVERAL SHORT LIVED EFFORTS AT NEARBY LOCATIONS, A COURSE WAS EVENTUALLY BUILT AT GWBERT-ON-SEA IN 1905 AND WITHIN A YEAR OR TWO A CLUB WAS FORMED. THE ORIGINAL DESIGN CAME PRIMARILY FROM A MR DAY WHO WAS THE PROFESSIONAL AT TENBY AND HAD BEEN THE WELSH CHAMPION IN 1903. THIS COURSE WAS KNOWN AS THE CLIFF HOTEL LINKS. HOWEVER IT WAS NOT UNTIL THE 1930'S THAT A PURPOSE BUILT CLUBHOUSE WAS COMPLETED AND IT WAS NOT UNTIL THE 1960'S, WHEN MEMBERSHIP BEGAN TO GROW, THAT CARDIGAN GOLF CLUB FINALLY HAD 18 HOLES.

This is a rather hilly and very wind exposed course. The fairways have a good links feel and the greens are true. Gorse and bracken line many of the fairways especially the 1st, 3rd, 6th, 12th and 18th holes. For a hilly course it is also reasonably long at 6687 yards.

Most of the course is clifftop links and on virtually every hole there are views across Cardigan Bay and the Teifi Estuary at Gwbert two miles from Cardigan.

The round starts with five par 4's. The 4th has a pretty green setting with just the one bunker at front left but anything too strong can finish well down a bank.

Then follows an unusual combination where the next five holes alternate as par 3, 5, 3, 5, 3.

The par 4, 15th has a lake in play on the right and a sloping green with two bunkers left and one large bunker on the right side.

The short par 4, 17th needs no bunkers near the green as everything runs to the right including the treacherous green.

The par 5, 18th is lined with gorse on the left and right and has a very bumpy fairway. There are two bunkers near the green but there is a reasonable gap between them if you want to play a running shot onto the green.

Cardigan is an interesting clifftop links but I wouldn't want to be there in a howling wind. Personally, I think that well constructed and well maintained bunkers can raise a course to another level. I feel that Cardigan falls a little short in this aspect.

Photo David Worley

17th green

BORTH & YNYSLAS

12th green with 5th green behind

View from above the 6th green – the best of the dune area at Borth & Ynyslas

Photo David Worley

Do **NOT** drive off when
cars are approaching
along the road.
The responsibility is **YOURS!**

PEIDIWCH TARO EICH
PÊL OS BYDD CEIR YN
GYRRU HEIBIO.
EICH CYFRIFOLDEB
CHI YDYW.

THE LINKS ADJOINING BORTH BEACH DATE RIGHT BACK TO 1885. AFTER WORLD WAR II SOME CHANGES WERE MADE UNDER THE DIRECTION OF HARRY COLT WHILST AT THE SAME TIME CARE HAS BEEN TAKEN TO RETAIN THE ESSENTIAL CHARACTER OF THE COURSE.

The first hole and the last three lie on exposed flat land, marshy in parts, on the clubhouse and inland side of the road. The remaining fourteen all run parallel with the shoreline on the narrow strip of sandy land bordered by the road on one side and some interesting dunes and the beach on the other.

The opening hole, a par 4, is straight forward but if you are inaccurate you need to remember that the road is on your left and a wet area starts on the right about 75 yards short of the green.

After you cross the road you face index number 1 in the form of a 455 yard par 4. Accuracy is essential with the road running all along the right and the beach on the left. From the 3rd onwards the land is slightly wider so at least you then only have one of these hazards to contend with at any time. Whilst the par 4, 3rd is much shorter than the 2nd, there are four bunkers along the right to be avoided.

Whilst still heading away from the clubhouse, the 4th to the 8th holes move from the shoreline and are on the road side of the thin strip of land. A wet ditch runs along the fairway

edge on five and six, just inside the boundary fence beside the road. The par 4, 6th has a tall grassy dune right behind the green which is itself half way up the dune. Anything right is in heavy rough or a drain. Cutting into the fairway on the right and just short of the green is a car parking area for beach goers which is out of bounds.

The 8th is a super par 5 that dog-legs right following the road. Bunkers, rough and then out of bounds are on the right so the temptation is to keep left in the lighter rough between the 8th and 10th fairways.

From the 9th to the 14th the holes are more or less along the shoreline. The par 4, 10th is rated the second hardest hole, partly because of the tight drive to a fairway that narrows at about 210 yards from the tee with the intrusion of an out of bounds fence. The par 3, 11th has no fairway and three bunkers guard the front of the green so the 170 yards is almost all carry.

Twelve is a short but tricky par 4. There are mounds everywhere here with the small flat green virtually hidden by them. A small bunker lies between the mounds that guard

the front of the green. A marker post at the back gives you your correct line. The 5th green sits side by side with the 12th so that it creates the impression from the distance of a double green.

The most difficult of the par 3's is the 204 yard 14th. Out of bounds and the beach run close by on the right and there are two fairway and two greenside bunkers.

On the clubhouse side of the road, the par 3, 16th has marsh along the left and a wet ditch that runs across the flat fairway about 35 yards from the green. The final two holes are shortish par 4's that are straightforward provided you are accurate. If you don't stay on the fairway then seventeen has a marsh on your left and the road to your right whilst eighteen has out of bounds along the left.

Borth & Ynyslas is an easy walking sporty holiday course with some good holes near the dunes. Lack of length at 6116 yards and rather shallow bunkers tends to reduce the degree of difficulty somewhat but the humps and hollows create plenty of variety in the shot making. Ignore the caravan park and the flat holes near the clubhouse – the rest is pretty good.

ABERDOVEY

"If you are not strong, be cunning" Aberdovey Golf Club motto

Photo David Worley

Attractive duneland at Aberdovey

NORTH OF BORTH & YNYSLAS AND ON THE OTHER SIDE OF THE DOVEY ESTUARY, ALMOST HIDDEN AWAY FROM CIVILISATION, IS THE DELIGHTFUL ABERDOVEY IN THE MIDST OF THE SNOWDONIA NATIONAL PARK.

From the rocky hill above the links, the Trefeddian Hotel looks over a layout that encompasses the spirit of the early days of golf. The border on one side is the railway line, and on the opposite side is a line of large coastal dunes and then the sea.

It is impossible to separate Aberdovey Golf Club from Bernard Darwin. His uncle Colonel Ruck was a pioneer of the club and even laid out the first primitive nine holes. Darwin's grandmother lived nearby at Machynlleth. He learnt his golf first at Aberdovey and became their inaugural Captain in 1897, five years after the official beginning of the club.

So much did Darwin write about his beloved Aberdovey that in 1996 the club published a whole book of these articles and reflections. Here are just a few of my favourite brief extracts that hopefully will entice you to retrace Darwin's footsteps:

> "Travelling by train to Pantlludw and Aberdovey was a journey to paradise. If I had a book on the trip, I scarcely turned a page of it; I just thought of the joys ahead of me and looked up at the rack to see that my clubs were safely there" [1]

> "There never was such a romantic, exciting, deliciously anticipated journey as that one to Aberdovey…In short, about this one course in the world I am a hopeless and shameful sentimentalist, and I glory in my shame." [2]

Darwin even extolled the virtues of the climate there. "It is part of history that on two successive New Year's days Mr Ted Parry played there in his shirt sleeves". [3]

The links have undergone changes with input from James Braid, Herbert Fowler and Harry Colt. When the original 18 was first played the home hole ran from its present tee then across the railway line to somewhere near the cricket pitch on the sports oval. In the early 1930's the members objected to the lengthening of several holes. Finally, the members won and the committee was forced to reduce the length of some holes, especially one which was over 600 yards and usually played into the wind.

The opening hole can be a tough introduction to Aberdovey if you are into the wind or it is blowing across the links. As you head towards the taller dunes there is trouble if you miss the fairway on either side. The 2nd is a short par 4 but the fairway is a very narrow target between the dunes.

One of the most famous holes at Aberdovey is the blind par 3, 3rd hole, 'Cader'. This hole was much more ferocious in

Photo David Worley

16th green with the railway line (not in picture) just a few yards below

Darwin's day when the dune blocking the view of the green was decidedly higher. Caddies would stand on the hill and yell "on the green" or "in the rough" in a more disapproving tone.

Six, seven and eight all run beside the railway line where the land is much flatter. The 10th and 11th are long par 4's, the 11th being a dog-leg right around a large area of high rough and patches of gorse.

The par 3, 12th is one of the best holes and is much more dangerous than its index rating of 18 would suggest. Into the wind this is just about the longest 149 yard hole you will ever play. The green is at the top of a high sandhill just a few yards from the out of bounds fence and the beach. Anything slightly left will run down the steep bank and anything right is in the dunes or even on the beach.

After a few holes on fairly flat terrain, you then encounter the mischievous 16th, a par 4 of just 288 yards. Mounds and small dunes are to the right of the approach to the green and

the railway line is precariously close to the left. The 17th and 18th are equally treacherous for hookers, particularly the 18th which is bordered by water channels and thick waist high reeds.

All the greens at Aberdovey are bordered by a simple electric fence – usually one or two strands of lightweight wire. They are effective at keeping the large cattle from the greens, but you will frequently have to share the tees and fairways with them.

Given half decent weather this is 6454 yards of bliss for any serious lover of links and the history of this wonderful past time.

1. *The Darwin Sketchbook – Bernard Darwin Green Memories* – Bernard Darwin.
2. Ibid.
3. Ibid.

ROYAL ST DAVID'S

Photo David Worley

18th green, clubhouse and Harlech Castle from the 14th tee

ROYAL ST DAVID'S AT HARLECH WAS FOUNDED IN 1894 AT THE END OF THE 10 YEAR GOLFING BOOM. THE TWO MEN MOST RESPONSIBLE, WILLIAM MOORE AND HAROLD FINCH-HALTON WANTED A GRAND COURSE FOR WALES AND SINCE SCOTLAND HAD ST ANDREWS AND ENGLAND HAD A ST GEORGE'S THEY DECIDED UPON THE LOGICAL (WELSH) CHOICE OF ST DAVID'S. KING EDWARD THE SEVENTH GAVE THE CLUB THE ROYAL PATRONAGE IN 1908.

The links are in a magnificent seaside setting with Harlech Castle immediately behind the clubhouse and the Snowdonian Mountains further in the distance.

It is considered by many good judges that Royal St David's is the toughest par 69 you will find anywhere. Eight par 4's over 400 yards is one of the main reasons why this may be true. The opening two holes each have a wet ditch in play, mainly on the left for the drive. The first hole is a particularly difficult start at 443 yards and with plenty of bunkers.

The 3rd is a brute of a par 4 of 468 yards and rated index 2. A wet ditch runs along both sides to the 270 yard mark and there is thick scrub and gorse particularly on the right side. Just to add to the danger, out of bounds also runs for the entire length along the right and is quite close to the green.

The par 3, 4th heads closer to the beautiful rolling coastal dunes. This is a reasonably long par 3 (188 yards) to a raised green with three bunkers. The par 4, 5th changes direction and is the first of seven holes which feature the treed hillside as their backdrop. This is another hard hole with wet ditches

There is no respite on the back nine as the 10th turns towards the sea.

View over part of the back nine

10th hole and Snowdonian mountains in the distance

Par 3, 14th from the ladies tee

and gorse on both sides. Bunkers along the left dictate your approach. The 6th is even more heavily lined with gorse and features a cross bunker about 60 yards short of the green.

Seven and eight are demanding par 5's. A wet ditch runs nearby on the left side of the 8th but this is the side of the fairway you need your drive to finish. Out of bounds is not far behind the green guarded by two bunkers at the entrance.

There is no respite on the back nine as the 10th turns towards the sea. This par 4 is rated the most difficult of all the holes It is long (453 yards) and has a stream and marshy area along the left for the drive, on the right for the second and runs across the fairway about 70 yards before the green.

Eleven is a good little par 3 where the green can be hard to hold when the wind is assisting you. There are dunes either side of the green and three bunkers at the right.

The 12th is a good driving hole, back towards the clubhouse, from a tee nestled in a dune. The drive needs to avoid four bunkers on the left and two small ones at the right edge of the fairway. There are a further six bunkers as you get closer to the green. Thirteen is a similarly difficult par 4 where a hooked drive will be dead in the rushes.

The 14th is a wonderful par 3 that is almost a totally different hole from the ladies tee some 90 yards closer. The hole is 222 yards for the men, from a low tee to a hidden green in a dell surrounded by dunes. The ladies tee is elevated and from there the hole is visually far more attractive, but considerably easier.

If you are waiting for some easy holes…then keep waiting because there aren't any. Fifteen is a great par 4 that looks very difficult from the tee – mainly because you are struggling to find much in the way of a fairway. The drive is

very tight with grassy mounds everywhere and a very narrow fairway after about 260 yards. The green is surrounded by low dunes.

The 16th tee gives wonderful views to the sea and Harlech Castle. Your drive needs a carry of 160 yards to be over the dunes and reach the fairway. There are three bunkers 30 yards out and another four around the green. Bunkers and dunes make the drive on the 17th a very demanding shot. A very large cross bunker makes the second especially difficult for all other than long hitter.

The par 3, 18th is probably the only weak hole on the course. It is flat and not particularly interesting in appearance but it is 201 yards in length and there are six greenside bunkers. The approach from the left is somewhat blocked by low dunes so the four bunkers on the right of the green are a popular resting place.

This is a most exacting test of golf. Not surprisingly, it has been the venue for many major tournaments on a constant basis since 1922. Royal St David's is links golf on a grand scale so much so that you are surprised that it is only 6591 yards from the championship tees.

PORTHMADOG

Photo David Wortley

Above: the picture postcard short par 4, 12th hole – the tee is on the right beside the rocks

Right: stunning view of the beach from the 12th fairway

Photo David Worley

The par 3, 13th – the tee is at the top of the dunes above the wooden steps

PORTHMADOG IS A JAMES BRAID DESIGN AND DATES BACK TO 1905. IT IS SITUATED JUST PAST THE MODEL VILLAGE OF PORTMEIRION AND TWO MILES SOUTH OF THE BUSY LITTLE TOWN OF PORTHMADOG.

Before going to Porthmadog I was undecided as to whether it would meet my criteria to be included in the book. The first nine is heathland but with good firm linksy fairways. The back nine is an absolute gem with some really outstanding links holes amongst the duneland which left me in no doubt as to its inclusion.

From the 3rd to the 9th you are on slightly higher ground on the inland side of the entrance road. The 3rd is a par 5 lined with fir trees on both sides. The 4th is a difficult par 4 of 451 yards with out of bounds all down the left side and a pond at the right that will catch any sliced second shot.

The par 4, 5th dog-legs right with ponds on either side starting at around 160 yards from the tee. The short 6th has no bunkers but is almost an island green surrounded by water.

There is quite a walk from the 9th green, past the clubhouse and 1st tee to reach the 10th which heads straight out towards the dunes and seashore. This is not a long par 4 (377 yards) but you are in serious trouble if your drive is not accurate. There is thick gorse on the right and heavy rough followed by out of bounds down the left side. The shot into the green needs to avoid a bunker on each side of the fairway 50 yards out and another two at the front sides of the green.

It is not often that a par 3 is rated the third most difficult hole on the course. The 11th green is tucked away in the corner of the course with only the back tee of the 12th before out of bounds and Samson's Bay. Heavy rough and the out of bounds boundary is also along the left side with thick gorse near the tee. A steep bank is short right making it very hard to get up and down if you block the tee shot out in that direction.

The short par 4, 12th is picture postcard material. Measuring 275 yards from the normal tee but 358 from the back, the hole bends left around the shoreline to an elevated green in the high dunes. There is a small lay up area of only about 60 yards starting at 208 yards from the back tee. The drive needs to be over the edge of the beach with a slight draw. Too far left and you will be on the beach. If you are long and right you will be lucky to find your ball in the dunes and heavy rough. If you have the wind behind and are tempted to go for the green you would need a draw but anything even slightly short will be in a hollow with long grass or one of the two bunkers in front of the green. Don't let the adrenalin get the better of you here otherwise you might be playing three from the tee. On a calm day the view across Samson's Bay from the green is really wonderful.

Into the wind the par 3, 13th is a real challenge at 202 yards. Although the green is on much lower ground you can hardly see it due to numerous sandy dunes. The 14th ,'Himalayas', is only 387 yards but it is justifiably rated index number one. The drive is blind over the dunes and then five bunkers are scattered around the fairway and green making the second shot very difficult. If you hook left of the mounds then you might finish out of bounds.

The 15th is of similar length to the previous hole and has a very narrow opening to a green with mounds on each side. The short par 4, 16th presents another blind drive and then a green with three bunkers, one of which runs right across the front, and the out of bounds boundary very close to the rear.

Seventeen is a danger hole if you stray from the fairway which is lined with gorse on both sides. It is not a long par 5 but there is a big dog-leg left at about 225 yards from the tee. The fairway bends left again near the green and there is a wet ditch on the right about 25 yards out.

The 18th is a slightly more straightforward finish, a par 4 of 404 yards that bends just to the right. The green lies between the 1st and 10th tees with a bunker on either side and out of bounds through the back. Apart from levelling the tees and greens, the inward nine holes is very natural through the dry sandy landscape.

Porthmadog is a very interesting course with good greens and a wonderful back nine which presents some really chall-enging links golf.

PWLLHELI

Photo David Worley

10th green and the now derelict Tanbwlch cottage

IF YOU ARE HEADING NORTH WEST TO NEFYN FROM EITHER HARLECH OR PORTHMADOG THEN YOU WILL BE DRIVING THROUGH PWLLHELI ON THE SOUTH COASTLINE OF THE LLEYN PENINSULA.

Although a nine hole course briefly existed for a few years after 1891 at nearby South Beach, the Pwllheli Golf Club official start date is 1900 when Tom Morris of Hoylake designed nine holes in the dunes at the present site. Nine years later the course was extended to 18 holes by James Braid.

Some of the new nine is on terrain that is more parkland than links, but I have included Pwllheli because holes 8 to 16 are the real thing when it comes to old fashioned links golf.

Based on Braid's original plans the 1st and 2nd holes ran perpendicular to the beach with the current 1st hole being more or less where the 2nd hole was and the present 7th hole being on the site of the old 1st. Braid then had holes 3-7 along the dunes and coastland. Now it is the 8th hole, with the tee right beside the clubhouse, where the links holes begin.

The 8th is a lovely par 4 of 350 yards along the edge of the dunes with thick gorse on both sides. The green is slightly angled and has three bunkers including one that is right in the middle of the fairway 26 yards out.

The tee for the 400 yard 9th hole is the nearest to the beach of any part of the links. The drive is over gorse and rough but then the fairway has plenty of room on the right with the 15th fairway running alongside but heading in the opposite direction. Anything pulled left will be in the dunes.

Ten is a picturesque and quite demanding par 3 of 197 yards. The dunes are along the left and there are four bunkers around the green. The two at the front are deep and straight faced and are a real danger. Behind the green is the now derelict Tanbwich Cottage which was the birthplace of a former captain of the club.

The short par 4, 11th is at the furthest point beside the duneland. The elevated tee will tempt you but there are seven bunkers including two that are almost in the middle of the fairway.

The thirteenth to the sixteenth head back to the clubhouse. A burn meanders along on the left and this forms the boundary of the holes that are a little more inland. Index 1 is the 15th, a long par 4 of 455 yards. The hole takes a big dog-leg left so you need a long draw with your drive. If you cut off too much of the corner there is gorse and the burn. A topped drive will find a wet ditch that runs across the fairway and a slice will find gorse that is also on the right hand side.

The 16th is a shorter par 4 that again bends to the left. There is gorse immediately in front of the teeing ground before the very bumpy fairway commences. If your drive is straight, rather than a draw, you could run out of fairway at about 200 yards and you will then either finish in gorse or a wet area. You can't run your downhill second shot onto the green as there is a large bunker blocking most of the front entrance.

Seventeen and eighteen run more or less parallel with the 1st hole. Each is a medium length par 4 in more of a downland area although the 18th green returns to the area of sandy links land.

Pwllheli has good greens and some interesting holes from the 8th. However, only half the holes are pure links and the course is flat and rather short at only 6108 yards.

8th green from left hand side

13th green

In summary, worth playing but this is in my 'holiday golf' category.

NEFYN

Photo David Worley

Tee for the par 3, 5th

Photo David Worley

Behind the 12th green – at the right is the 16th tee with green beyond the grassy ravine – 17th tee is at the top of the rocky mound right of the ravine

NEFYN & DISTRICT GOLF CLUB STARTED IN 1907 AS A NINE HOLE COMPLEX AND WITHIN FIVE YEARS HAD EXTENDED TO 18 HOLES. IN 1933 A FURTHER 9 HOLES WERE ADDED AND NOW 26 OF THESE HOLES ARE USED. THE FORMAT IS A FRONT 10 HOLES FOLLOWED BY TWO ALTERNATIVE 8 HOLES. THE 'NEW' COURSE INCLUDES THE 8 INLAND HOLES WHILST THE 'OLD' COURSE ENCOMPASSES THE UTTERLY SPECTACULAR HOLES THAT RUN ALONG THE NARROW HEADLAND TO THE VERY EDGE OF THE CLIFFS.

The 1st tee is high up and gives a perfect perspective of the good golf holes and superb scenery that is to follow. Although it is downhill, the 1st is a long par 4 of 458 yards. Bunkers are mainly on the left for the second shot to a green that is side by side with the 17th green.

The next three holes border right on the edge of the high cliffs. The 2nd is a par 4 that dog-legs left and uphill. There is no need to try to cut the corner and risk seeing your ball disappear down the steep cliff face. There is plenty of room left and then you have a straight shot to the elevated green. You also should keep left on the 3rd but you need to keep away from the one fairway bunker that is on the left side.

Although the 4th is a short par 5 of only 477 yards, it is rated index number one. A draw is needed for the first two shots as anything near the cliff may run further in that direction. There are two fairway bunkers along the left close to where you need to land your first two strikes. Be careful as the cliff encroaches into the fairway just short of the green which has two bunkers short and right and another two at the left. This is a really pretty hole that sweeps along the clifftop to the far corner of the course. The sea views are as good as it gets.

The 5th is an uphill par 3 of 156 yards from a small tee on a very narrow section of cliff that juts out over the sea. Anything sliced right is lost forever down in the sea inlet. The green is protected by five bunkers and can be hard to hold with a following wind.

Holes 6–8 run back beside holes 2–4 whilst the New Course holes are higher up on the right hand side. Bunkers come into play more on these three par 4's.

There is a fairly long walk from the 10th which is on the inland side of the clubhouse to the 11th which is on the other side of the clubhouse near the car park. This is the start of a stretch of holes that must rate as being nearly as spectacular as Old Head at Kinsale in southern Ireland.

The 11th is theoretically an easy short par 4 of 323 yards. The drive is downhill with cliffs along the right side. There is then an area of rough just short of a hill with the cliffs still on your right and a very steep fall away left or through the back of the green. The second shot to this small green is blind. Better to be short than long on this approach.

The 12th is an intriguing hole. It is a short par 5 but is rated index 2 because of all the dangers. The fairway is extremely narrow with the public walkway along the left and a high ridge with rough all along the right. The shot into the green must also be very precise as there is a deep grassy ravine short and left. If you block it right you will be lucky to find your ball higher up in the long grass.

Thirteen is a potential card wrecker. This long par 4 dog-legs left around the cliff to a green protected by dunes on either side. If the wind is blowing in from the left then you have to hit over the edge of the cliff and let your ball drift back to the fairway. If you aim just a little too far left you are on the rocks and if you fade it right then you will run right across on to the 15th fairway.

At the end of the headland is a high tower which you climb and then play from an artificial grass tee to the 14th green 165 yards away at the other corner of the cliffs. The green is well below the tee so judging distance can be very tricky. Even one club too much may run your ball across the green and down the cliff along the back right. The safe line is to the left edge of the green but there is a large bunker along this side. It helps if you are not hitting first here and you can learn from the mistakes of those before you as you enjoy the views over Lifeboat Bay and beyond.

The 15th is uphill and dog-legs left following the cliff face. A hook here will mean lost ball. Your biggest risk is to avoid errant tee shots coming across from the 13th tee.

The 16th is an interesting par 3 that plays a little shorter than its 188 yards might suggest. A deep ravine is front left and a high mound that is also the 17th tee is on your right and very close to the cliff edge. There are three greenside bunkers – two on the left and one at the front right hand side.

The 17th is a shortish par 5 that presents a birdie opportunity provided you hit two very accurate shots, preferably with a slight draw to keep away from the cliffs along the right. The walkers on your left, heading to the beach, can be a bit worrying as they are almost on your preferred line.

The 18th is an uphill par 4 of 327 yards. Nefyn has a major problem with the public walkway which runs in front of the 18th tee. There were so many using it on the day in early August when I played there that they had to close the men's tee for safety reasons and we had to hit from the ladies tee on the other side of the path. You need a slight draw so even from the ladies tee you are still playing very close to this walkway. I'm sure this is a real worry to the club and it is certainly quite distracting whilst you are playing.

David Williams Golf Design has been employed in 2006 to try to solve the safety issues as well as the congestion that occurs with both courses using the same first ten holes. One of the changes will be to re-configure the layout into three groups of nine holes.

Apart from this public safety problem, you will really enjoy the challenge and wonderful holes at Nefyn. The fairways and greens are first class and the views are never ending. Although the back eight holes has a number of rather scary tee shots, if you hit the ball straight it is easier than the earlier holes.

2nd green with the 12th green in the distance

Par 5, 4th hole rated index no.1

There is no other way to describe Nefyn other than to say it is a fabulous example of clifftop links at its most exhilarating.

Photo David Worley

Par 3, 14th as seen from the artificial tee on the concrete tower at Nefyn

CONWY (CAERNARVONSHIRE)

Photo David Worley

17th green

In 2006 Conwy had the distinction of being the first Welsh club to hold a Final Qualifying Round for the Open.

CONWY IS SITED IN A LOVELY SETTING ON LAND THAT HAS BEEN KNOWN FOR HUNDREDS OF YEARS AS THE MORFA. SOME HOLES HAVE THE CONWY ESTUARY AS THEIR BACKDROP WHILST OTHERS HAVE THE MOUNTAINOUS GREAT ORME LOOKING DOWN UPON THEM.

Conwy (originally known as Caernarvonshire) Golf Club officially began in 1890 but it was fifteen years earlier that a group of members from Royal Liverpool Golf Club organised for a professionally designed 12 hole course. By 1895 the links had extended to 18 holes and by 1899 they had staged the Welsh National Championship. In 2006 Conwy had the distinction of being the first Welsh club to hold a Final Qualifying Round for the Open.

The 1st heads straight towards the sea and is a tougher hole than the length of 375 yards would suggest. The par 3, 2nd is only 147 yards but has an index rating of 13. In the wind the green is a difficult target with pot bunkers running along both sides.

The par 4, 3rd is the only hole that actually follows the shoreline. There is plenty of rough on either side as you play to a plateau green with two deep bunkers at the front. The 4th is a par 4, dog-leg left with plenty of gorse if you drag anything left.

Index 1 is the long par 4 (442 yards) 5th which bends to the right with the Great Orme dominating the view beyond the green. Accuracy is needed here with a fairly narrow fairway and a bunker on either side to catch an errant drive.

The 7th is a similar shaped hole to the 5th but runs in the opposite direction. At 441 yards you need a good long draw

Photo courtesy Aled Jones, Conwy GC

7th green from behind

to have any hope of reaching the green in two. From the tee there is plenty of rough along the left and there are bunkers on the right. This is a tough stretch of long par 4's. The 8th, index 3, offers no respite at 435 yards. The tee is near the sea with the hole bending right towards the green of the par 3, 6th hole. The front nine ends with a par 5 that runs back toward the sea with the green perched up above the fairway and very wind exposed.

The 10th is the second of four par 5's over the six holes commencing from the 9th. If you are playing Conwy for the first time then you will be somewhat confused here as the drive on the 10th is across the start of the 4th fairway. Fairway bunkers are the principal danger on this hole.

The par 3, 13th is at the far end of the course heading away from the sea. There are four deep bunkers around a sloping and two-tiered green. The final holes are all on the inland side and it is here that the thick gorse presents itself as a major hazard, especially when the wind is blowing. The 15th is a lovely little par 3 with gorse in front of the tee and a cluster of bunkers just short of the green.

Sixteen, seventeen and eighteen have much lusher and less linksy fairways. These three par 4's are a very tough finish with very tight fairways lined with gorse. I'm sure many a promising stroke round has been ruined by a lost ball or two in this closing stretch. The 18th is probably the most heavily bunkered green at Conwy with a line of bunkers running along both sides.

Conwy is a very solid test of golf where the wind places great demands on your ability to hit accurately. The day I played there I could hardly stand on the tee as a cold squall hit the course and it became very difficult to play any sort of reasonable golf. To be fair to Conwy I revisited the next morning when the sun shone, conditions were far more pleasant, and the course looked very inviting.

The imposing Great Orme

18th green and clubhouse

Conwy GC with North Wales GC on the other side of Conwy Bay

NORTH WALES

Photo courtesy Gren Jones, North Wales GC

The green at the par 3, 16th is hidden once you walk from the raised tee

NORTH WALES GOLF CLUB IS BESIDE LLANDUDNO'S WEST SHORE ON THE OPPOSITE SIDE OF CONWY BAY TO CONWY GOLF CLUB. WHILST IT IS PERHAPS NOT QUITE AS TOUGH AS ITS NEIGHBOUR, IT HAS SOME LOVELY DUNELAND AND IS LITERALLY BORDERED BY THE SEA ON ONE SIDE AND THE RAILWAY LINE ON THE OTHER.

North Wales owes its start in 1894 to a Manchester businessman, Tancred Cummins, who immediately recognised the site as ideal for a golf course. He influenced both John Ball and Harold Hilton to visit and give advice on the course layout. Cummins was both club Captain and Secretary for 38 years from 1894 to 1933.

The 1st is a gentle par 4 that dog-legs left, the only real danger being out of bounds down the left. The 2nd is a little longer and requires a good draw from the tee. There are quite a few bunkers to be avoided with the second shot. All the danger is left on the par 4, 3rd where there is both a water hazard and out of bounds.

The par 3, 4th is 193 yards in length and usually plays into the prevailing wind. The railway line is right along the left side and there are two bunkers at the right of the green. Short but straight is a safe option.

The 5th and 6th holes each have water ditches that are in play, particularly on the par 5, 5th which dog-legs left. Seven and eight are the last of the holes that run alongside the railway line which is all along the left. The 8th is quite a tricky par 4 which also has a very narrow fairway about 60 yards short of the green. The placement of the drive is the key as the thick rough along the railway line forces you to play slightly out to the right from a blind drive.

North Wales is not a course for hookers. Nine, ten and eleven run close to the sea along the left side. The 11th is a particularly tight tee shot and at 415 yards, par 4, is rated the hardest hole on the course.

The 13th 'Hades' is an excellent par 3 of 177 yards running through a valley with thick rough at the back of the green. There is also plenty of heavy rough here if you hit a wide tee shot. The elevated 14th tee is right beside the beach. This par 5 heads back to the clubhouse and has trouble by way of grassy mounds on both sides for the drive. The green is well guarded by three bunkers.

A draw around the left corner will give you a birdie opportunity on the 330 yard 15th hole. Sixteen and seventeen are both interesting short par 3's. The 16th green is set in a bowl surrounded by rugged dunes. One of the two bunkers is set into the mound running across the front which blocks the view to the green once you walk from the raised tee. The 17th tee shot is to a dell green with some rugged steep dunes very close by. Both the 16th and 17th have elevated tees and can be tricky with regard to club selection, especially when the wind is blowing.

The par 4, 18th has bunkers down the right and out of bounds the whole way down the left side. Two very straight shots are needed to hit the green which is open at the front but has bunkers at the back and sides.

North Wales is an interesting links, not overly long, and with very good greens. I would love to revisit when it was not quite so dry, especially around the duneland between the 14th and 18th holes. This would be a much tougher track if the bunkers were a little more penal. You will enjoy the golf and peaceful atmosphere on these genuine old fashioned links.

Top: 10th hole – not the place for a hook
Below: don't be short at the par 3, 17th

PRESTATYN

PRESTATYN IS THE MOST NORTHERLY LINKS COURSE IN WALES AS YOU JOURNEY ALONG THE COASTAL ROAD TOWARD THE ENGLISH BORDER. IT WAS ESTABLISHED AS A NINE HOLE LINKS IN 1905 AND THEN 18 HOLES ONE YEAR LATER. IN 1921 THE ORIGINAL NINE WAS TAKEN FOR DEVELOPMENT SO A NEW NINE WAS DESIGNED BY W J LEAVER OF MANCHESTER AND WAS IN PLAY THE FOLLOWING YEAR. SOME CHANGES, INCLUDING LENGTHEN-ING THE COURSE, WERE COMPLETED IN THE EARLY 1990'S UNDER THE GUIDANCE OF DONALD STEEL AND TODAY IT MEASURES A VERY HEALTHY 6825 YARDS FROM THE CHAMPIONSHIP TEES.

A feature at Prestatyn is a very wide burn known as the Prestatyn Gutter which runs parallel with the sea and railway line, effectively cutting the course in two. It is 30–40 feet wide for the most part so it is a very real hazard. The entrance road runs through the course to the clubhouse in the middle of the layout but, despite this, the 9th is almost at the furthest extremity of the boundaries.

The 1st is theoretically an easy short par 4 of 307 yards that dog-legs left around the Gutter with a wet area of long grass and a drain further along. This wet area is all out of bounds starting at the beginning of the fairway proper about 150 yards from the tee. There is plenty of room to the right towards the 6th fairway but a slight draw with your drive is preferable.

Photo David Worley

Seven bunkers protect the green at the 13th

The 13th is another par 3 but much more difficult.

The long par 5, 3rd (553 yards) is the last of the opening holes into the prevailing wind. A solid drive is needed so that the second shot around the left hand dog-leg can clear the wet ditch. If your drive is not long then you will have to decide whether you can carry the ditch with your next shot. The ditch angles from the left and then across the fairway about 150 yards from the green. Out of bounds is also along the left and at the back of the green.

Holes 4-8 run along side the lovely coastal dunes but they are not really in play along the left as each of these holes angle away from the shore.

There are some very demanding par 4's at Prestatyn. Seven are over 400 yards, six of them well over this mark. Whilst the par 4, 4th is 470 yards and is index 2, the 10th which is 450 yards is the more difficult. It is into the prevailing wind and has the Prestatyn Gutter along the left and out of bounds by way of the practice ground along the right side. Two fairway bunkers just right of centre at 183 yards and 223 yards are also a danger. You need two very straight hits along this narrow fairway.

The par 3, 11th is visually challenging with the Gutter running across the fairway and four bunkers in front of the slightly domed green. The 13th is another par 3 but much more difficult. To hit the green requires carry for most of the 177 yards as there are four bunkers in front. There are two more bunkers at the left side and one at the right edge of the green.

The 14th to the 17th all run beside the railway line on the left. Fourteen is probably the most difficult as this long par 4 has plenty of rough left and three bunkers for any drive slightly right. There are also two bunkers short of the green

at the right for those playing safe away from out of bounds. Fifteen is a shorter version of the 14th and sixteen is a long version which bends to the right.

After the 17th, a medium length par 3, the 18th is a short par 5 with eight bunkers dotted along the right edge of the fairway. Out of bounds runs along the left, beside the entrance road, from about 220 yards forward of the tee. The green slopes from left to right and runs away at the back with out of bounds by way of the clubhouse surrounds not far away.

As with all the other courses I visited in the south of England and all through Wales, Prestatyn's fairways had been badly affected by the hot dry summer of 2006. The greens were quite large, generally fairly flat and were excellent. This is another course I would like to revisit when there is at least a tinge of green on the fairways. This is not the most scenic part of Wales but Prestatyn is worth the stop if you are journeying north to the superb courses in the Liverpool area.

18th green and clubhouse during the hot dry summer of 2006

IRELAND *Royal Portrush 5th green*

IRELAND

NORTHERN IRELAND

IRELAND

ROYAL COUNTY DOWN

Photo courtesy Gary Prendergast

3rd hole Royal County Down

ROYAL COUNTY DOWN IS AN ENCHANTING GOLF COURSE OF THE HIGHEST ORDER. LOCATED AT NEWCASTLE IN NORTHERN IRELAND, THE COURSE IS ALMOST AT THE FOOTHILLS OF THE MAJESTIC 3000 FEET HIGH SLIEVE DONARD AMONGST THE MOUNTAINS OF MOURNE. TO ADD TO THE BEAUTY OF THE SETTING, THE FIRST THREE HOLES RUN ALONGSIDE DUNDRUM BAY.

Old Tom Morris was paid the princely sum of four guineas to design the original layout which opened in 1889. Harry Vardon made some modifications in 1908, the same year in which Edward VII bestowed the Royal patronage.

The course is just picture perfect with acres of purple heather, gorse, broom and bracken. The bunkers are quite severe but are even more hazardous due to the long rough or eyebrows that run along the top of many of them. In some cases this effectively raises the height you need to hit to exit the bunker by a further two feet.

But don't let the beauty of Royal County Down cause you to lower your guard. This can be a very unforgiving course once you miss the fairway. There are a number of blind drives over steep dunes. You have no idea where your ball has finished if you stray even marginally from the marker posts. This is also a long course – 7181 yards from the championship tees and 6881 yards from the medal tees.

The 1st at Royal County Down is a lovely par 5 that runs through a valley. The fairway narrows about 60 yards out with grassy mounds making the entrance a tighter line unless you are playing into the green from the middle of the fairway. The 2nd is the first of nine par 4's that are all over 430 yards. The long second shot has to carry mounds and bunkers that run right across the fairway at about 46 yards short of the green which is bunkered at the left and has a grassy hollow on the right. The 3rd is a long par 4 of 477 yards along a narrow fairway that is slightly valleyed. Thick rough and bunkers are on both sides. The steep banks of the dunes encroach right to the fairway's edge along the latter half of this difficult hole.

Distinctive bunkers at Royal County Down

The par 3, 4th is a wonderful par 3 of 213 yards. From the elevated tee you must carry a forest of gorse to a green with seven bunkers at the front and a further two at the back right. From the lower tee these bunkers are almost invisible. The green is raised with run off on both sides and at the back.

The 5th and 6th are both par 4's with blind tee shots. Seven is a very picturesque short hole of 145 yards. The view to the green is dominated by the larger bunker at the front with its whispy eyebrows. The 8th is a super looking par 4 that heads back to the clubhouse. The fairway edges have

Photo David Worley

The short par 3, 7th hole

The 10th is another first class par 3. The raised tee is back at the clubhouse. A long strike of about 190 yards is needed through a slight valley with four bunkers at the front sides. A straight hit will run on as there are no obstacles at the front.

Eleven requires a blind drive over a high dune. There is gorse to the left and heather and gorse at the right. Another long second shot is needed to reach the par 4 in regulation.

There is some respite at the par 5, 12th but the 13th is a very difficult par 4 measuring 444 (422 medal) yards. The hole bends right to a green in an amphitheatre setting. Very thick rough will swallow up any errant shot here. Fourteen is a long par 3 that is visually the least interesting of the short holes. Another long par 4, the 15th is followed by a lovely short par 4. The fairway at the 16th is beautifully shaped and is narrow for the drive. The dunes on the left are covered in thick gorse. The best view on the 16th is from the green looking back to the elevated tee.

I remembered the 17th from my previous trip as being a rather odd, out of character, hole with a large pond in the centre of the fairway starting at 106 yards from the green. By good fortune the groundstaff were working there on my second visit. I queried the concept of the pond with them and I was advised that prior to the pond being built the water always ran to the rough on the right side of the fairway which became a permanent wet area. Since the pond has been built this problem has been resolved.

several dangerous bunkers and large expanses of heather. There are no greenside bunkers but anything slightly off line will run off the raised green.

The par 4, 9th is one of the most photographed golf holes in the world. Despite its beauty, it can be a real beast. The drive is over a huge dune covered in long grass and heather. As the hole

is 486 yards (428 medal) yards, you are probably playing a long second. The fairway narrows at 47 yards out where there are two bunkers. Dunes on the right will block a shot to the green from that side and there are three greenside bunkers. In 2006 the sides of the approach area was normal grassy rough but when I played Royal County Down in 2003 this area was all tall bracken which made the shot very intimidating.

I can't think of too many more difficult finishing holes than this par 5 of 550 yards. The fairway slopes to the right but bends slightly left. There are a massive twenty four bunkers running along the edges beyond which is ample rough and heather. The green is one of the most treacherous with a big slope from back to front.

Photos David Worley

The 9th hole from the dune about 250 yards from the green – in the distance is the 3000ft high Slieve Donard

Narrow fairway of the short par 4, 16th

Royal County Down is beautifully maintained and has just about the
best greens in Ireland. The blind drives make it a difficult prospect
first time round where you are liable to lose a few balls.
I imagine that the number of blind drives is the only possible reason why
County Down has never been used as a venue for the Open Championship.
It would be criminal to visit Ireland and not play this majestic links.

ROYAL PORTRUSH – DUNLUCE COURSE

Short 3rd hole, 'Islay'

STARTING OUT IN 1888 AS THE COUNTY CLUB, IT WAS GIVEN ROYAL STATUS JUST FOUR YEARS LATER BUT BY 1895 THE NAME WAS CHANGED TO THE ROYAL PORTRUSH GOLF CLUB.

The Dunluce course as it exists today is largely the work of Harry Colt who re-designed the course over the period from 1929 to 1932. Further alterations took place in 1946/7 when two new holes, the 8th and 9th, were built to replace the old 1st and 18th. Whilst the Dunluce course is on higher and more open ground, the club is fortunate to have an excellent second links known as the Valley Course.

This is a good test at 6304 yards and features many fairways that are sheltered by tall lines of dunes on both sides.

The Championship course has a never ending variety of holes punctuated by thick rough and bracken which will usually result in a lost ball from any wide shots.

Photo: David Worley

The brilliant par 4, 4th hole with some well placed bunkers

Photos David Worley

5th green, 'White Rocks'

View from the back of the 5th green

The opening hole is an uphill par 4 with internal out of bounds on both sides. The par 5, 2nd continues on to higher ground. There is a large bunker at 215 yards and then three cross bunkers short of the green on the left. Bracken and thick rough is uncomfortably close to the green.

The next three holes are at the highest point and are amongst my favourite holes. The par 3, 3rd 'Islay' measures just 155 yards but it is totally exposed to what is usually a cross wind. A dangerous small pot bunker is at the front left behind which the ball tends to run into a hollow with some potentially unfriendly lies. Anything long will suffer a similar fate and a duffed tee shot will be in very thick rough.

The 4th is a brilliant par 4 of 457 yards heading towards the seaside cliffs. Out of bounds and a wall of trees runs the entire length of the right hand side. The fairway has some mesmerising undulations with a bunker just left of centre to catch the drive. Grassy hillocks create a narrow entrance to the green which is slightly left of the line of the fairway.

The dog-leg 5th 'White Rocks' is much photographed and is a very memorable par 4. The drive is downhill with a temptation to cut off the corner. If you don't pull it off then enjoy the walk in the bracken whilst you search for your ball. If you miss the undulating green on the right you will be in a deep hollow and if you are more than a few feet too long you will be out of bounds and possibly on the beach fifty feet below. The view from the green reveals the white cliff face on the right and the Isles of Islay and Jura in the distance.

Into the breeze the par 3, 6th is a very long 189 yards where there is heavy rough everywhere. Seven and eight are very good par 4's with a dog-leg left at the 7th and right at the 8th. The shot into the green at the 8th needs to be over the corner of rough hillocks which makes club selection harder to judge. There is no margin for error anywhere near the green other than just short.

The 9th and 10th are both relatively short par 5's but they are dangerous holes. The green at the 10th is nestled amongst

bracken covered dunes so accuracy is paramount. The par 3, 11th is from an elevated tee amongst the bracken to a green below that is surrounded by bunkers. In a cross wind I saw plenty of balls finishing at the edge of the 12th tee.

The drive on twelve must avoid bunkers on the right and then an accurate second shot is needed to hold the plateau green with a very formidable bunker at the left.

The tee shot is uphill at the par 4, 13th 'Skerries'. The fairway approaching the green is very undulating and tends to run to the right. There are two bunkers waiting for you if you try to hug the left side.

Each time I have played Portrush the weather has been rather unkind but it has always saved the worst for my arrival at the tee of the wonderful par 3, 14th 'Calamity Corner'. The brave line is over a deep ravine but a long fade might be a little safer. The hole is 210 yards uphill and into a 4-5 club gale when I was last there. If you are just slightly right

Photos: David Worley

The 13th green is a difficult target for the second shot

Don't miss the green to the right at the 14th, 'Calamity Corner'

then you could finish at least fifty feet lower down in unforgiving rough.

After the downhill 15th comes the potentially treacherous 16th. Short of the green the fairway becomes very narrow, made even more so by several deep bunkers. Anywhere left or through the elevated green is dense bracken while along the right the rough is as thick as it gets at Portrush.

The par 5, 17th is always remembered for the enormous bunker facing you on the right at the edge of the Valley course. A strong draw is needed from the tee to miss the bunker and then give you a chance of reaching the green in three into a strong wind.

The 18th is probably the only really flat hole on the whole course. The main danger here is the considerable number of fairway bunkers and out of bounds close to the clubhouse side of the very large green.

Royal Portrush is best described as 'the golfer's links course'. It is tough and unrelenting, especially in wind and rain, but it is still a very fair course with a wonderful backdrop of the lines of dunes and the Valley course. This is the only venue to have hosted the Open outside of England and Scotland when Max Faulkner won in 1951. Why it has never returned to such a great layout is a complete mystery to me.

PORTSTEWART – STRAND COURSE

Photo David Worley

Amazing dunes at the 2nd hole

PORTSTEWART IS SITUATED BESIDE THE RIVER BANN ON THE EDGE OF LOUGH FOYLE MIDWAY BETWEEN PORTRUSH & CASTLEROCK.

The club started in 1894 but it was not until 1908 that it moved to its present location at the opposite end of the town. All that seems to be known of the origins of the course is that it was laid out by a Mr Gow of Portrush. Changes did not take place until the 1960's when further land was purchased.

The Strand Course as it is today is a mixture of some of the old and seven new holes. The new layout which incorporated more of the duneland was designed by Des Giffin and opened for play as recently as 1992.

If you could combine the front nine at Portstewart with the opening nine at Royal County Down then this would surely be the most spectacular links course on the planet.

The 1st is an absolutely stunning introduction that takes you straight into the tall duneland. This lovely par 4 sweeps downhill and to the right. There are no bunkers but there is thick scrub or buckthorn along the right for the sliced second shot.

The 2nd is an even more outstanding hole. From an elevated tee you look down a valley between huge dunes, especially on the left and then a green that is higher up at the foot of some more dunes. This hole is only 366 yards but is rated index 7. Position off the tee is more important here than length. The fairway is only about half width at 102 yards short of the green which has just the one bunker at front right. A hooked drive will spell disaster.

Index no. 1 at Portstewart is the 5th, a par 4 of 461 yards

The 3rd is a long downhill par 3 of 218 yards with the largest dunes at the left. The green is reasonably open but has rough at the right and bushes close to the back. The green also slopes severely from the back so short and left is the only place to be if you are not on the green.

The 4th is a good par 5 that dog-legs right. Heavy scrub and bushes will catch a slice off the tee. You don't want to be short with your third shot as there are two bunkers on the right and a dune is just before the green on the left side of the fairway.

Index 1 at Portstewart is the 5th, a long par 4 of 461 yards (449 from the white tee). An accurate drive with a slight draw is needed on this very picturesque but narrow fairway. The green is in a raised dell with dunes running along both

Plateau green at the par 3, 6th

The 7th is another great hole that runs through the dunes

sides. From behind the green there are pretty views to the River Bann at the left.

The par 3, 6th is only 143 yards but unless you land on the green the ball will run down from the plateau. Two pot bunkers are set into the side of the hill at the front of the green.

The 7th is another stunning drive through the dunes. It is further than you think if you try to cut the right hand corner. You need to stay left for a straight second shot. The fairway narrows and at 60 yards from the green the fairway drops away at the right hand side approach area.

The 8th is a tough par 4 of 427 yards. The hole bends sharply to the left around very tall dunes. Anything to the right or back of the green will fall away sharply. Nine, ten and eleven

are all good par 4's followed by a par 3 at the 12th. Two relatively short par 5's give some respite as does the short 15th which has five bunkers out front but no danger at the back.

Three different par 4's conclude the round. On a windy day the second shot to the exposed 17th green is very testing. The 18th is the most heavily bunkered hole on the course. A strong drive is essential but watch out for the cluster of three bunkers at the left corner starting at 220 yards from the tee. At 461 yards uphill all the way and with eleven bunkers to avoid, this seemed to be much harder than index number 8.

Purists will be delighted that, as was the case at Portrush, there are no distance markers at Portstewart. It is hard to follow up such a brilliant first nine holes but even with the slight let down on the back nine, Portstewart is a very good golf course with more than its share of memorable holes.

CASTLEROCK

A FEW MILES WEST OF PORTSTEWART ON THE NORTHERN COAST OF IRELAND YOU WILL FIND THE UNDERRATED LINKS AT CASTLEROCK.

Par 3, 4th hole with danger on both sides

Par 4, 7th hole

Seven years after the club started in 1901 Ben Sayers expanded the layout to 18 holes. Subsequent changes were made in 1925 by Harry Colt and then later by Fred Daly who was appointed as professional there in 1952.

The holes away from the dunes are all quite good but those amongst the dunes, notably 1, 7, 8, 9, 17 and 18, are really wonderful links holes with some dramatic dunes especially around the 18th tee area.

The 1st is a lovely par 4 that winds to the right through the dunes to an elevated two-tiered green. The 2nd is uphill and dog-legs sharp right into land that is more of a farmland nature. After such a promising start this is a real let down.

The par 5, 3rd has out of bounds down the right and three bunkers almost in the middle of the fairway starting at 275 yards from the tee and then 130 yards and 44 yards short of the green.

Whilst not being amongst the dunes, the par 3, 4th 'Leg O'Mutton' is one of the best holes. From the elevated tee you play 200 yards straight along side the railway line on the right. The out of bounds stakes are some five yards further in and are only just off the fairway. A burn angles along the fairway from in front of the tee to the left of the green that has two bunkers on each side. You can run a straight shot on from the apron. The 5th is a short par 5 that also runs alongside the railway line. Six is a straightforward short par 4 until you get closer to the green. There is a burn that is difficult to see that

Par 3, 9th from behind the green

runs in front of the green which is narrow at the front and is bunkered at both sides.

Index 1 at Castlerock is the par 4, 7th (418 yards) which bends left and then uphill. The view from behind the tee looks towards the sea and tall dunes on the right nearer the green. The 8th dog-legs right to a green amongst the dunes. The green slopes to the right but if you aim too far left you will run down a bank with light rough.

The par 3, 9th is another very good hole in the duneland. It is 200 yards to the front of the green and there is no fairway whatsoever. There are no bunkers so with a bit of luck you can run your ball on from the front or slightly left.

Ten is a good par 4 with an undulating fairway at the approach to the green. There is also a deep swale just short and to the right of the green which needs no bunkers. Eleven is a par 5 with a tight tee shot and then bunkers in front of the green and a burn at the back.

At the par 3, 14th (192 yards) you need to negotiate a burn short and left and then five bunkers, two of which are about 25 yards short of the green. The 15th is a tough par 5 that runs uphill all the way. The drive is over a marker stone that is almost in the rough on the right. The fairway slopes left toward several fairly large bunkers. Anything even slightly left of the centre of the apron or the green will run down a bank.

On a windy day the par 3, 16th looks quite daunting. Everything slopes right but if you try to come in from the left you will almost certainly be bunkered with a tricky shot to a green that runs away from you to a steep bank at the right edge.

Seventeen is an excellent looking par 5 from an elevated tee looking out over most of the course and then the sea. The narrow fairway has the unusual feature of two bunkers on top of each other in a mound about 120 yards out from the green which is slightly raised and is back amongst the dunes.

The par 4, 18th is a spectacular finish. Although the fairway bends to the right only very long hitters should take this side of the fairway otherwise your shot to the green will be in thick rough and will be blocked by large dunes. There is plenty of room left to then enjoy the approach up the steep hill to the green which appears to be alarmingly close to the clubhouse windows. If you are a bit timid with your second then be prepared for your ball to roll back to the bottom of the hill.

Behind the 18th tee is the nine hole Bann Course which has several very good holes with dunes and the sea nearby. If some of these holes could be incorporated into the eighteen hole Mussendon Links then this would further improve what is already a very good course.

Castlerock has good greens and in true links tradition has no fairway sprinklers or distance markers other than 150 yard marker posts. Pick a quiet day and I'm sure you will enjoy this friendly club and its challenging layout.

10th green from the 17th tee

5th at the 9 hole Bann course

View from beside the 18th green back to the tee

PORTSALON

PORTSALON IS SOMEWHAT OFF THE BEATEN TRACK TO THE NORTH OF LONDONDERRY. ON THE WAY THERE I LOOKED AT NORTH WEST AND THEN DUNFANAGHY LINKS. BOTH LOOKED QUITE FLAT AND UNINTERESTING AND WERE ONLY PARTIALLY LINKS COURSES SO, APOLOGIES TO THE MEMBERS THERE BUT THEY DIDN'T MAKE IT INTO THIS BOOK.

M y reviews use the measurements adopted by the club so please note that the card for Portsalon is in metres not yards.

Portsalon has been around since 1891 stretching along the shores of Lough Swilly with the mountains of Donegal to the north and west. The original design was from a Portrush professional by the name of Thompson. By 1905 Portsalon had already hosted its first major tournament – the Irish Ladies Championship.

As recently as 1986 the club finally ceased to be in private hands and became owned by the members. Pat Ruddy was given the task of redesigning eight of the holes. This was completed in 2002 after which Portsalon now has a formidable length of over 6400 metres.

There are some interesting holes beside the sea, alongside dunes and there is the natural hazard of the very wide burn that runs in front of the 2nd and 16th greens. The mounds and rolling fairways have largely negated the need to have many bunkers.

2nd hole where you must skirt the beach with your drive and then negotiate the river in front of the green

The opening hole is quite a tester from a high tee down to a fairway that skirts the sand and water along the left. The second shot is uphill with just the top of the flag visible on the green.

The long par 4, 2nd hole invites you to take on part of the beach at the left corner and then you must decide whether to go for the green or play up short of the river which runs across at 30 yards out.

Holes 3-9 are all amongst low dunes. The 3rd and 9th each share a double green. The par 5, 4th is an attractive hole running along a valley between dunes on both sides. The distant mountains form a backdrop behind another double green.

The par 3, 5th comes back in the opposite direction and has a green that is tilted from the back so as to feed any weak shot into a bunker or grassy swale.

Index 1 at Portsalon is the 6th, a very good par 4 of 435 metres (407 from white tees) that runs right beside the ocean. A slight draw is needed down the very narrow fairway with the tallest dunes and heaviest rough along the left. The 7th is the last hole that runs along the shoreline. This is a medium length par 4 of 352 metres that dog-legs to the right. There is a deep grassy valley in front of the well-bunkered green.

The 9th is a very good long par 4 (435 metres) which runs back in a valley beside the 4th fairway. The 10th is an attractive but fairly easy par 3 and the 11th is a good par 5 that also has a valleyed fairway through the dunes.

Thirteen is a short but potentially treacherous par 4. The fairway dog-legs left just before the green where there is very thick rough, especially along the left. Near this green and virtually under the elevated 14th tee is the location where Mass was celebrated in secret during the oppressive years when Oliver Cromwell ruled.

Par 3, 5th with its steeply sloping green

The 14th is another attractive but potentially dangerous hole. From the high tee the fairway twists and turns downhill with nasty rough in a hollow to the right.

The two finishing holes are also potential score wreckers with the burn and out of bounds. The drive at seventeen needs to be a slight draw but beware of out of bounds on the left. The fairway is split level and leads to an elevated plateau green with a small bunker and steep drop away at the left.

If you pull your tee shot at the 18th then chances are your next shot will be blocked by the wire mesh that protects the nearby house and street car park. The green is not an easy target as it is surrounded by bunkers and swales.

Portsalon has found an innovative way to solve the public liability problem with the public using the course to access the beach. The walkway is below ground with a cage like structure running across the 1st and 18th fairways.

This is a very well maintained sporty course with some excellent holes in the dunes and along the shoreline. It is also a very solid test of your golfing skills.

BALLYLIFFIN – OLD LINKS

BALLYLIFFIN STARTED OUT AROUND 1947 AS A PRETTY ORDINARY NINE HOLE COURSE. SUBSEQUENTLY, LAND CLOSER TO THE DUNES WAS PURCHASED AND IN 1973 THE NEW 'OLD' COURSE WAS READY. DESIGN FOR THIS MAY BE ATTRIBUTED TO EDDIE HACKET, CHARLES LAWRIE AND FRANK PENNINK. THE TOTAL AREA OWNED IS APPROXIMATELY 365 ACRES OF PRIME DUNELAND.

When Nick Faldo first set foot here in 1993 he described Ballyliffin as the most natural golf course he had ever seen. Faldo was engaged to upgrade the Old Links with new revetted bunkers, new tees and several larger greens. This work was finished in 2006.

With its very natural crumpled fairways the Old Links certainly look much older than they are. The 3rd is a wonderful example of a good short par 4. The hole heads toward the ocean along the narrowest of fairways.

The 5th known as 'The Tank' is a memorable and rather unusual par 3 of 176 yards. The tee shot is uphill to a plateau green set between two large sand hills.

The 10th is back at the clubhouse. The hole dog-legs right with the crumpled fairway typifying this layout. The 14th returns to the sea at Pollan Bay. The dunes are flattened but they manage to eat into the fairway along the right hand side. After the 17th you move away from the sea as the 18th heads back to the clubhouse. This is one of the best holes with its meandering fairway amidst the low dunes.

Photo: courtesy Larry Lambrecht

5th hole, 'The Tank', Ballyliffin – Old Links

Now that the Old Links has been renovated by Faldo, Ballyliffin can justifiably boast to have two first class examples of links golf at its best.

BALLYLIFFIN – GLASHEDY LINKS

BALLYLIFFIN IS THE MOST NORTHERLY LINKS IN IRELAND. IT IS SITUATED ON THE BEAUTIFUL INISHOWEN PENINSULA OVERLOOKING POLLAN BAY AND THE SMALL ISLAND GLASHEDY ROCK.

The Glashedy Links were completed in 1995 after two years of work under the guidance of Tom Craddock and Pat Ruddy. This is now the premier course at Ballyliffin with the Old Links being relegated to a very good second choice.

The Glashedy is long at 7226 yards from the black tees. The back nine is considerably longer and tighter and has just the one par 3. The course is very well laid out, every hole is different and the rough is not ridiculously long unless you are very wide. The ladies tees have also been thoughtfully placed. Another feature of the course is the deep and generally quite large revetted bunkers, most of which are below the fairway level and without any lip so they can't be spotted from the distance. On the dog-leg holes where you want to cut the corner with your drive there are often bunkers hidden in the light rough right on your preferred line.

The opening holes are three long par 4's with a large bunker guarding both the 2nd and 3rd greens. The 5th is a most attractive short hole of 177 yards with the Atlantic Ocean in the background. Five bunkers surround the green. The 7th is also a par 3 with a spectacular view over the Old Links from the tee high up on a large dune. The green is 100 feet lower down so judging distance is very difficult. A large pond awaits anything pushed right and short.

The par 4, 11th can play much shorter than the card (419 yards) would suggest. My wind assisted drive some how

6th hole through the low dunes

Photo courtesy Larry Lambrecht

travelled 345 yards along the green fairway but the next two holes are considerably longer. The 12th is a dog-leg par 4 and the 13th is a magnificent par 5 that heads uphill away from the sea to a narrow entrance at about 50 yards short of the green. If you run through the back there are several small pot bunkers that are hidden from view. If you miss the bunkers then the rough is only a few feet away. The view from the back of this green is simply wonderful with Glashedy Rock in the distance.

At the par 3, 14th the green is like a small island amidst a sea of low rolling dunes as you stand on the tee and head back in the line with Glashedy Rock.

Fifteen, sixteen and seventeen all require very precise shots into the green. The par 4, 18th runs through a corridor between the dunes and two lovely revetted bunkers. This hole is relatively short at 382 yards from the normal tee but is considerably more difficult at 455 yards from the back tee.

Photo courtesy Larry Lambrecht

The green at the short 14th is an island amidst a sea of rolling dunes

There are some big greens at Glashedy and they are sometimes two-tiered. This is a really fun course that has few weaknesses and is in first class condition. I think it would be a pretty tough test in the wind and playing from the very back tees – at 6897 yards from the gold tees, that's long enough for me.

Another feature of the course is the deep and generally quite large revetted bunkers, most of which are below the fairway level and without any lip so they can't be spotted from the distance.

ROSAPENNA – SANDY HILLS LINKS

Photos courtesy Aidan Bradley www.golfcoursephotography.com

*Far left: don't be short at
the par 3, 3rd hole*

*Left: the par 4, 6th is rated index
No1 and is one of the best holes*

THE PAT RUDDY DESIGN OPENED IN 2003 AND IS THE PREMIER COURSE OF THE TWO AT THE ROSAPENNA COMPLEX WHICH INCLUDES AN EXCELLENT HOTEL ALMOST BESIDE THE 1ST TEE. THE HOLES RUN THROUGH A NEVER ENDING CHAIN OF DUNES WHICH AT TIMES ARE QUITE HIGH BUT GENERALLY THEY HAVE A LOVELY COMPRESSED LOOK ABOUT THEM.

Sandy Hills is a really interesting links with one good hole after another. Almost every green is set in a dell dwarfed by dunes. Many of the drives are through a narrow fairway twisting amongst the sandhills. The greens are quite good but if there is a minor weakness it is the bunkers which lacked any character.

The two opening par 4's make for a tough start. The 1st is 495 yards from the back (461 yards from the white tee) and requires a very difficult second shot through a narrow gap in the dunes with a bunker right in the middle of the fairway just short of the elevated green. The 2nd is nearly as long and has lots of trouble around the green. There are deep hollows and bunkers that will catch anything not hit into the centre of the green.

The par 3, 3rd is 188 yards (162 white) over a gully to an exposed raised green with just the one bunker in front. You do not want to be short here. The 4th is another good par 4 that twists to the right about 75 yards short of the green. If you play your second shot in with a draw you are hitting to a dangerous area with three bunkers so a slight

The 9th hole from green to tee

fade is the best option. The fourth is long at 438 yards but is reduced to only 346 from the white tee. All the trouble is along the right hand side.

One of the best holes at Sandy Hills is undoubtedly the 6th, a par 4 which is rated the hardest hole on the links. The drive is through the dunes and then down hill for the second to a green framed by the sea inlet not far behind. Whilst you need to miss the bunker at the front of the green, be careful not to be too strong as there is thick rough close by.

A feature of the holes around this part of the course is that they are all high up on a virtual plateau with compact dunes overlooking a number of the fairways on the Old Course.

The short 7th is downhill to a slightly domed green with just the one bunker at the right. Although it measures 196 yards (182 white) it plays at least one club shorter. Keep to the left with your drive on the par 5, 8th so that you can play into the green hitting away from the deep gully to the left.

The 9th is another of the very good holes. The drive needs to be right of the bunker at 250 yards from the back tee and 201 from the white. You then need to be very precise with your second. There is a large area of broken fairway and rough starting about 60 yards before the green which is at the top of a low hill. Anything a little short will run into the greenside bunker. The best view is from the green looking back across the bumpy landscape to the tee area.

Although the 9th is far away from the pavilion, this is not an out and back design. All the holes run in a variety of directions so the wind is never behind or into you for more than two or three consecutive holes.

The par 4, 10th provides a small target for the drive with its twisting fairway bordered by very thick rough. The backdrop behind the raised green is quite contrasting with previous holes as now there is a mountain range in the distance.

The key to the par 3, 11th is, don't be short or right. This hole also plays a little longer than the distance of 186 yards would suggest. There is a challenge at every hole and the par 4, 12th is no exception. The landing area for the drive is generous but the second shot is very tricky. The fairway is narrow and there are two very large bunkers, one at the front and the other at the right edge of the green.

Hole 13 is a shortish par 5 that is possibly a birdie chance but first you have to remain on the narrow fairway that dog-legs right. At the half way mark the fairway is at its narrowest and long grass and mounds are only a few feet away.

Fourteen is the shortest par 4 and is then followed by the second longest. The 14th green has the sea close at hand whilst the 15th green is in a pretty setting almost surrounded by low dunes. Wildflowers are in abundance in the rough along these fairways. The short 16th is carved through fairly rough terrain on both sides. A large bunker is at the front of a green that is two-tiered and slopes steeply from the back.

The 17th is a short par 5 but the rough here is very severe on both sides of the fairway and at the right and back of the green. Sandy Hills ends as it starts – with a rather demanding long par 4. The 18th is 487 yards (394 white) and is rated index number two. The hole bends left so the drive needs to be to the right side for a long straight shot to the green in front of which are bumps and hollows and two bunkers.

The 11th plays a little longer than its 186 yards.

Photo courtesy Aidan Bradley www.golfcoursephotography.com

From the back tees you will be unlikely to play to your handicap. At 7155 yards it is long and it is equally punishing for any shot hit off line. Despite the bending fairways and the encroaching rough, there is little in the way of blind shots and most tees are elevated – a deliberate and attractive design feature from Pat Ruddy.

This is still a relatively new course but it is right there with the best of them and well worth the journey.

ROSAPENNA – OLD COURSE

Photo David Worley

8th hole of the new 9 designed by Pat Ruddy that will soon form part of the Old Course

The story of golf at Rosapenna is a fascinating one and is very much a case of the old and the new. In 1891 Lord Leitrim engaged Old Tom Morris who staked out the first links here. Early in the 20th century Harry Vardon lengthened several holes and re-designed the present 4th, 6th and 7th. Some time later James Braid changed the 5th and 8th and it is uncertain as to whether Braid or Vardon altered the 13th hole.

The first ten holes are very links like and run between the sea and the dunes in an area known as The Valley. Holes eleven to eighteen are on higher ground and unfortunately nearer to recent housing developments. This is more like meadowland terrain.

Pat Ruddy, the designer of Sandy Hills at Rosapenna, was asked to design and build a new nine holes in the duneland beside the Sandy Hills course. This nine, temporarily known as the Strand Links, will eventually replace the meadowland holes on the Old Course. In 2008 the Strand and Valley nines will become the Old Tom Morris Links. The new layout will measure 7100 yards from the championship markers compared with 6450 yards on the current Old Course.

The Strand nine is already a good looking set of holes with a very similar feel to Sandy Hills. The 6th has a very impressive green setting with a huge dune at the back creating an amphitheatre effect. The 8th winds down hill through low dunes. Anything slightly right will kick into the rough. The green has two pot bunkers at the front and is hard to hold as everything slopes to the back. The fairways should have matured nicely by the time the new configuration is in play in 2008.

ROSAPENNA IS NOT ON THE NORMAL TOURIST ROUTE BUT IT IS IN A PART OF NORTHERN IRELAND THAT IS WELL WORTH A VISIT – EVEN IF YOU ARE NOT A GOLFER. THIS IS A REALLY PICTURESQUE SETTING AT THE EDGE OF SHEEP HAVEN BAY BESIDE THE LITTLE VILLAGE OF DOWNINGS.

DONEGAL

Photo David Worley

5th green from the 6th tee

FROM 1959 TO 1973 DONEGAL EXISTED AS A NINE HOLE COURSE NEAR THE TOWN. THIS WAS NOT REALLY GOOD LINKS SOIL WHICH LED TO THE SECURING OF A LEASE OVER 180 ACRES OF SANDY DUNELAND SEVERAL MILES AWAY ON THE COAST JUST OUT OF THE TOWN OF MURVAGH. THE EDDIE HACKETT DESIGN OPENED IN 1976 AND A NEW CLUBHOUSE WAS BUILT IN 1998. FURTHER IMPROVEMENTS HAVE RECENTLY BEEN COMPLETED WITH THE REMODELLING OF SEVEN GREENS BY PAT RUDDY.

Donegal is longer and harder than it appears. The card is in metres – only the Irish would know why half the courses in this region use yards and half use metres.

The first four holes are all on uninspiring flat land that has a distinctly inland feel. Out of bounds and wet ditch runs along the right of the first three holes whilst at the long par 4, 4th out of bounds is still along the right but the ditch runs across the fairway at 167 metres from the tee.

At last we are alongside the dunes. The par 3, 5th is a wonderful short hole of 179 metres. There is a large bunker short and right and three smaller bunkers at the sides of the green. If you block your shot right you will be in rough down a bank so left edge of the two-tiered green is the target.

The 6th is a short par 5 with the line of dunes set back along the higher right hand side with the sea not too far away. This is a straightforward hole except for the three fairway bunkers starting at 50 metres out from the green.

Donegal manages to throw in some unusual design features just when you least expect them. The par 4, 7th starts off as a rather bland looking hole with the dunes not really in play along the right but then you suddenly come on to some broken ground 70 metres out from the green. The fairway then drops away to a green set at the foot of a dune. Short and left will put you in a nasty hollow with a large mound lying between this hollow and the green.

The par 5, 8th is a great looking links hole that is almost out of character with what has so far come before. The rolling fairway is not far from the shoreline with everything tilted left towards an area of light rough with mounds and swales. The 8th tee is one of the best locations for views around the course. Rough ground breaks the fairway 84 metres from the green. The fairway recommences and runs to a bunker in the centre and then, above a bank, lies the plateau green.

The par 4, 9th is a change of character with a thick pine plantation and out of bounds at the right and running to the back of the green. Between the green and the pines is a mass of wildflowers. The 9th returns to the clubhouse as the front nine is virtually an anti-clockwise loop running around the outside of the back nine which runs in the opposite direction.

After two medium length par 4's you are faced with the tricky 12th hole. This is a long par 5 at 543 metres from the back. Your drive needs to stay out of the five bunkers that lie

Looking back at the clubhouse from the 8th tee

on the fairway's edge between 188 and 244 metres short of the green.

Thirteen is a good par 3 with two greenside bunkers and a mound in front. Fourteen, like the 12th, is a par 5 on flat land with a burn snaking across the fairway starting at 116 metres from the green.

From the elevated tee at the 17th you will be tempted to go for the drive on this short par 4. A powerful slight draw is needed but a little right is not too bad a position. However, if you pull or hook your tee shot then you are in very long grass and with your view to the green partly obscured by a thickly grassed dune.

At the par 4, 18th the burn just before the start of the fairway should not be in play. There are three bunkers at the right and one on the left side that will make it difficult to reach the green in two if you drive into them. Whilst they are needed to give the fairway some definition, to me they look rather artificial set at the front of some man made mounds. Some traditional pot bunkers at fairway level and without the mounds would be more attractive and more penal. The green is in an imposing setting with four bunkers at the front and sides and a ring of grassy mounds around the back.

Donegal has excellent greens that are amongst the fastest in Ireland. There is a mixture of some very interesting holes and some that are really quite ordinary. The drive to the club is some distance from the main road and as a result this is one of the most peaceful settings you could ever imagine. The water views over the sheltered inlets add to the serene atmosphere. Donegal is a very enjoyable round of golf, it is just a pity there aren't a few more really standout holes.

COUNTY SLIGO

Photo David Worley

The par 4, 10th is a good driving hole

COUNTY SLIGO IS SITUATED AT ROSSES POINT A FEW MILES NORTH WEST OF SLIGO TOWN. THE ORIGINAL NINE HOLES WERE LAID OUT IN 1894 BY GEORGE COMBE, THE FIRST SECRETARY OF THE GOLFING UNION OF IRELAND. BY 1906 THE COURSE HAD INCREASED TO A FULL EIGHTEEN HOLES.

It was here at County Sligo that the West of Ireland Championship began in 1923. The course was substantially revamped by Harry Colt with work completed in 1931. The new bunkering was then attended to by Colt's assistant at the time – Hugh Alison who later became noted for his deep bunkers.

The measurements at County Sligo are in metres. The opening hole is a medium length par 4, uphill, and with a generous fairway. Make sure you miss the bunker that is 10 metres short of the green on the right. The 2nd is a shorter par 4 of 278 metres that bends right near the out of bounds corner. The shot to the raised and well bunkered green is tricky. From this green there are superb views over Sligo Bay and the famous mountain, Ben Bulben.

After a short par 5 that is a good driving hole comes the scenic par 3, 4th with its raised but bunkerless green. With a bit of a breeze blowing, hitting this green is one thing but holding it is quite a deal more difficult.

Out of bounds and a wet ditch runs along the right of the par 5, 5th and the par 4, 6th hole. The 7th is index 1, the main danger being the drain that angles across the fairway between 10 and 20 metres short of the green. At 393 metres this can play quite long so you may have to lay up with your second shot. The 8th is also a solid par 4 with the drain again in play at 30 metres before the green.

The picturesque short 9th features a green that is almost encircled by six bunkers. Anything right or long will run down a steep bank. Ben Bulben provides a scenic backdrop with the resting ground of the poet W B Yeates in the distant churchyard.

The par 4, 10th is a good driving hole that is slightly downhill. Keep right on the high side of the fairway and you will then have only a fairly short approach into the flat green.

The 4th green is difficult to hold

One of the most photographed holes is the aerial view of the par 5, 12th which runs down to the sea and lighthouse further out. You need a draw from the tee provided you avoid the bunker at the left corner.

The par 3, 13th (162 metres) throws up a variety of hazards which probably make the hole seem a little harder than it really is. The tee shot is over the corner of the sandy beach to a green that is at lower ground. There are five bunkers at the front and left and a burn runs close by at the back right. Fortunately the green is fairly flat and is reasonably large.

Fourteen is a lovely par 4 on lower ground near the sea.

The fairway bends right and has a drain running across. Ideally you need a slight draw off the tee and then a slight fade into the green. The rough is thicker around these holes particularly if you go right at the par 4, 15th or long par 3, 16th.

The 17th is a really attractive par 4 of 414 metres that dog-legs left over broken ground and then heads uphill to a bunkerless green with a steep slope at the very front. The 18th is a rather less engaging par 4 where you need to keep left away from the line of fairway bunkers along the right side. The uphill drive is a blind tee shot but a good strike will leave you with a fairly short approach.

Aerial view of the 12th hole and Sligo Bay

The 17th is an attractive par 4 that dog-legs left and then heads uphill

Photos courtesy Co.Sligo GC

I found that the course played a little longer than the distances on the card would suggest, but that may have been due to the relatively lush fairways which took away something of the real links feel. The greens were generally flat and perhaps a little uninteresting. Even though there are no dunes to create spectacular settings there are some very good holes at County Sligo with the best occupying the stretch from the 9th to the 17th.

ENNISCRONE

View from the 11th green to the 12th tee beside Scurmore beach

A MEETING IN 1918 MARKED THE FORMAL BEGINNING OF GOLF AT ENNISCRONE WHICH IS A LITTLE OUT OF THE WAY JUST NORTH OF BALLINA IN THE NORTHWEST. IN 1974 EDDIE HACKETT EXTENDED THE LINKS TO EIGHTEEN HOLES BUT DUE TO MONETARY CONSTRAINTS AT THE TIME MUCH OF THE DUNELAND WAS LEFT UNTOUCHED.

Some radical changes made by Donald Steel were completed in 2001. Six new holes were built among the towering dunes, some over one hundred feet high, and other holes were re-routed. In 2003 the 18th was completely redesigned and features Steel's trademark revetted bunkers. The relinquished six holes in the flat terrain were added to three new holes to create an additional nine hole course.

This is a beautiful setting beside Killala Bay with views across the Moy Estuary and out to Bartra Island now owned by Nick Faldo who intends to develop a new links course there.

I had not visited Enniscrone until 2006 and I was simply amazed by the size of the dunes and how cleverly the holes have been carved through them without disturbing their structure. The biggest dune is one hundred and fifty feet high and resembles a grassed pyramid.

Photo David Worley

The second half of the twisting downhill 13th

It only takes half of the first hole before you enter the magnificent duneland. The opening drive can be a little daunting in a strong wind. Out of bounds is right (the clubhouse) and left (the practice fairway) along a fairway that dog-legs hard right. It then narrows to a significantly raised green amongst the dunes.

Next you face a very testing par 5. The drive must be dead straight through dunes with thick rough. The fairway then dog-legs right with a very narrow opening between more dunes. The green is on a plateau with superb views over the Atlantic Ocean. The uphill long par 3, 3rd hole has rough everywhere and a multi-tiered green so there is no need for any bunkers – this hole is already difficult enough. The 4th

necessitates another very straight drive through rough and dunes at either side.

The only weak holes at Enniscrone are in the flat area containing holes 6 to 8. The 9th is the last of the holes on the low land but this is much more dangerous than it might first appear. Scurmore Beach is beside the left edge of the fairway and there is thick rough if you slice. The hole is almost dead straight and is only 395 yards from the back tee but it is rated index number six. Apart from the need for great accuracy

Photo Gary Prendergast

The author on the green of the magnificent 14th hole – 'Valley of Diamonds'

you must also avoid the three pot bunkers in a line across the fairway about 20 yards short of the green.

The 10th is an excellent par 4 with the elevated tee overlooking the Moy Estuary. The par 3, 11th is uphill and with the sloping green being amongst the dunes this is another short hole that does not need any bunkers.

The next few holes play through the most dramatic dunes you could ever imagine. The par 4, 12th is a mere 345 yards but is rated the third hardest at Enniscrone. The fairway rolls around like the "big dipper" with the green cut into the side of a steep dune. If your approach is even a fraction short you will run down into a deep hollow. The 13th is virtually the same length as the 12th but it is an entirely different hole. The tee is high up above the low lying part of the course and looks down the twisting fairway that bends right and around the dunes. If you play for the white marker stone your ball will run for miles following the shape of the fairway. The green lies in a dell with two bunkers and low dunes at the sides and rear.

The par 5, 14th showcases the magnificent pyramid shaped dune that towers over the fairway. This dune is the famed 'Cnoc na gCorp'. Local lore has it that a company of Vikings once landed here around 789AD. They were met by huge opposition from the O'Dowda Clan who were the Chieftains of the area. The victors piled the bodies of the slain in one great mound and covered them with earth and sand – hence the name 'Cnoc na gCorp'. This is also the area where General Humbert and the French invasion landed in August 1798. A strong drive is needed to run uphill to the

Photo David Worley

Photo Gary Prendergast

The 15th runs beside low dunes on a plateau on top of the course

Looking back at the 16th, a superb par 5 with tall dunes on the left and Killala Bay along the fairway right

first landing area. The fairway twists left and then right to the sloping green set below more dunes. To say this is an attractive hole is somewhat of an understatement.

Index number one is the 15th, a par 4 of 421 yards that bends left and feels as though it is on a plateau on the top of the course. The par 5,16th is my pick as the most attractive hole. The fairway bends gently to the right around a line of craggy dunes. To your left are some low dunes and then Killala Bay. The best view here is from behind the green looking back.

The 17th is potentially a sensational par 3, were it not for the horrible caravan park that is located in the near distance directly behind the green. The tee is high up over a valley with long rough and then the raised green is set amongst some lower beachside dunes. With the wind whipping off the sea from your left I'll guarantee it will take you a few minutes to decide on club selection.

The 18th is a long par 4 with out of bounds on both sides. This hole is somewhat out of character with numerous and quite large revetted bunkers, especially down the right side for the drive and on both sides of the green. I understand that eventually most of the other bunkers at Enniscrone will also be revetted.

There are so many good holes here it is hard to single out individual ones but certainly the stretch from around the 12th to the 16th is dramatic. The par 5's are not overly long but they are all made difficult by the winding fairways through steep dunes and often ending with sloping or split level greens. This is a thrilling course to play but you must be able to get your drive away accurately to stand any chance of playing to your handicap.

CARNE

CARNE IS WELL AND TRULY HIDDEN
AWAY ON THE BELMULLETT PENINSULA
ABOUT 50 MILES WEST OF ENNISCRONE.
IT WAS WITH GREAT ANTICIPATION THAT
I PLAYED CARNE IN AUGUST 2006,
ESPECIALLY SINCE I NOTED THAT IN THE
JULY 2006 ISSUE OF GOLF WORLD IT HAD
BEEN VOTED AS NUMBER 43 IN THE LIST
OF THE TOP 200 COURSES IN BRITAIN AND
IRELAND. SINCE ENNISCRONE WAS LISTED
AT ONLY 115 I THOUGHT IT WOULD HAVE
TO BE INCREDIBLY GOOD.

13th green from the 10th tee

Rating golf courses can inevitably become subjective but I really think they have got it horribly wrong. In fact I wonder how many of the judging panel have actually played the course. At present Carne has some wonderful holes amongst the tall dunes, but they are virtually all on the back nine. The front nine is nowhere near as good. I didn't particularly like several of the early holes and I felt the 18th was just a bit too wild. The par 3, 14th is a really good short hole by the sea but the green is tilted on such a steep angle putting on it is like playing "mini golf".

However, Carne has the prospect of being very highly rated when the new holes are built. There are some potentially fantastic holes just lying there amongst the dunes in the area behind the present 15th to 17th holes. I was told that they intend to have nine new holes here so when they are added to the existing holes 10-18 then Carne will be really something.

Hitting into a strong breeze the opening hole, a par 4 of 366 metres, can be rather tricky. There are lots of mounds, heavy rough if you miss the fairway and then a partly hidden green. There are some low dunes but some of the next few holes have less of a links feel with farmland running along the left side.

The par 4, 3rd is the best of the early holes. The fairway runs through a slight valley to a green with grassy mounds to the right and a pond at the left. The main hazard at the 4th, a short par 5, is out of bounds and a wet ditch that runs along the left and then also behind the green. The second shot at the par 4, 5th is partly obscured by low dunes that block the low route to the green. Six is a somewhat more difficult par 4 with a difficult recovery if you miss the green.

The 7th is a rather plain short hole of 162 metres uphill with out of bounds at your left. From the 8th hole onwards you enter the duneland where the quality of the holes improves very quickly. At the 8th you can easily drive to the left of a mound with light rough in the near middle of the fairway, but this will then leave you with a difficult angle over the large dunes which are all around the green except for the front where there is one bunker. This second shot into the green is downhill for the last part but is a little longer than it looks.

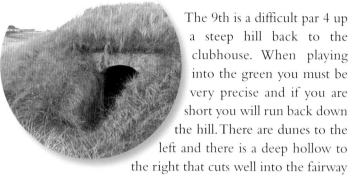

The 9th is a difficult par 4 up a steep hill back to the clubhouse. When playing into the green you must be very precise and if you are short you will run back down the hill. There are dunes to the left and there is a deep hollow to the right that cuts well into the fairway at 42 metres from the green.

Although the 10th is a short par 5 (465 metres), getting on the green in two is made difficult by the side of the large dune which projects across the left side where there is also a bunker around where your preferred line would be.

The par 4, 11th is a wonderful challenge requiring two very accurate shots through towering dunes. A good drive will take you to the dog-leg where you will have only about 85 metres uphill to a plateau green. A huge dune with scarified ridges patrols the right and anything left will be in the rough down a steep bank.

I really like well designed short par 4's and the 11th and 12th are perfect examples of how much fun they can be. The twelfth is the reverse of eleven where here the hole dog-legs sharply to the left. If you drive straight over the big dune on the left then you will run across the lower fairway and you will either finish against the fence or be out of bounds. What you need from the tee is a strong draw or a straight hit of no more than 215 metres. It is only when you walk to your drive that you then see the green hard left perched near the top of a big dune. The thought of being short or right with your approach is bound to put you in the back left corner of the green.

The 13th is a beautiful par 5 that conjures up a feeling of great tranquility. The fairway sweeps down to the sea, seemingly with relief from any dangers. You may not notice

Photo: David Worley

The slope on the 14th green is quite extreme

it from the tee but there is a gully with a burn at 270 metres on the low side of the fairway on the right. Farmland and out of bounds runs along the right hand boundary fence all the way to the sea shore. This hole has an interesting two-tiered green with really lovely views across the sea and along the deserted beach.

From the par 3, 14th tee beside the shore you need a slight draw to the green which is uphill 137 metres away. This could be a good hole but the slope of the green is quite extreme. If you are long and finish at the back of or just through the green then it is almost impossible not to putt off the green – and that is on a comparatively still day.

The par 4, 15th is uphill all the way and looks ferocious from the tee. The bumpy fairway is narrow and falls away to a gully on the right starting at 170 metres. The second shot passes over an even more narrow strip of fairway to a green high up in the dunes. There is no bail out area – you must be straight. Anything left will be down a steep bank and short right is in a deep grassy hollow. This is a difficult hole, especially for the ladies.

The "wow" factor is certainly present at the par 3, 16th. You head off the 15th green to the right and up to the top of the massive dune. Way below is a green with three bunkers but plenty of open space at the front. It is easy to be fooled and come up short with your tee shot.

The 15th is a tough par 4

Top: the par 3, 16th with the tee at the top of the dune
Above: the par 5, 18th is a difficult finishing hole

The run of brilliant holes on the back nine continues at the 17th which is rated index one. This is a long par 4 of 399 metres but uphill all the way. The landing area for the drive is generous but it becomes quite narrow from 150 metres short of the green which is cut into the side of a dune. If you pull your second you will be in rough on the dune face and if you cut your approach you will run down the steep bank.

Eighteen is a tough par 5 to finish. You need a strong drive through the dunes. Even the first cut of rough is thick but if you are wider than that you could be walking in the rough for hours trying to find your ball. There is a deep valley full of bumps and hollows about 130 metres short of the green which is high up on a wind exposed plateau.

This Eddie Hackett creation was not completed until 1993 when he was over 80 years of age. It is already very good with some really dramatic holes. I look forward to revisiting when the new nine holes are built after which Carne could become an outstanding statement of links golf.

CONNEMARA

CONNEMARA IS NEAR THE TOWN OF CLIFDEN ON THE CENTRAL WEST COAST. THE ORIGINAL EIGHTEEN HOLES WAS DESIGNED BY EDDIE HACKETT AND OPENED IN 1973. IN 2000 A THIRD NINE, PARTLY DESIGNED BY HACKETT BEFORE HE DIED, WAS COMPLETED WITH THE TWO OPENING HOLES RIGHT BESIDE THE SHORELINE.

I have read all the quotes in the brochures, including the comment that the back nine "was the equal of any in the world". Well, I'm sorry but I must have visited a different golf club called Connemara. The whole place was a great disappointment after what I had come to expect.

There are virtually no dunes and the only holes near the sea are the first two on the new nine. There are few standout holes amidst the landscape of rocky outcrops.

The opening hole of 381 yards (369 from the medal tee) tended to play longer with the big dog-leg left and the last 50 yards being uphill to the wind exposed green. The second is a straight ahead par 4 leading to higher ground.

The par 3, 3rd is 164 yards with the out of bounds fence along the left side and then close to the back of the green. There are three large bunkers in the approach area. Behind the green, on the other side of the road, is a large lake that is not in play but famous for its swan population.

The more interesting holes are on the back nine. The 12th is index number 1. It is a par 4 of 445 (429 from medal tee)

The par 3, 13th from beside the green

Photo courtesy Gary Prendergast

yards that dog-legs right at about 210 yards. There are three bunkers short of the raised green which has a big run off on the left hand side.

The 13th is one of the best holes. It is a long par 3 of 212 yards (200 from medal tee) across a valley to a tilted green with a small pot bunker at either side of the front of the green and one at the back. Short or left will be in thick rough, whilst a really bad slice could find wetlands or a lake further right. The backdrop behind the green typifies the landscape which is covered in rocky outcrops. This par 3 has the high difficulty rating of index number five.

The par 5, 14th features another elevated green with three bunkers in a line on the right between 68 and 17 yards from the green. The 18th is an interesting finishing hole. Although it is a fairly short par 5 of 526 (512 from medal tee) yards, there are a number of dangers. Out of bounds runs along the right and is very close to the fairway from around the 275 yard mark. A wet ditch runs across the fairway 102 yards

18th green from side on

The 9th hole on the new nine and clubhouse

short of the green. There are four bunkers at the front and one at the right side of the green that is elevated and tilted from the back to the front.

Numerous holes follow a similar pattern along flat fairways that then rise up over the last 50 yards to an elevated green. This makes them very wind exposed but there is a sense of sameness.

There are some good holes on the new nine. The 1st is a lovely shortish par 4 that bends left following the shoreline.

The green has a narrow entrance that is protected by mounds at the left and a bunker at the front right.

The 2nd is a fine looking par 3 of 222 yards from the championship tee but only 152 from the medal tee. The green has two levels and is at an angle to the fairway. You walk under the roadway to the 3rd hole which runs away from the sea into a wetlands area. When this nine is played with one of the others this hole is rated only index 14 which is surprising given the potential for disaster. It is a short par 4 of 322 (252 medal) yards but there are wetlands at the left and then encroaching right into the fairway so

you can only play an iron from the tee. You then hit left over water to the green which is almost at 90 degrees to the tee.

The last two holes run amongst the holes from the original back nine. The 9th is a good finishing hole with a ditch 20 yards short of a steep bank and then yet another raised green with a fairly steep slope.

18
512 Yards
Index 13
Par 5

Connemara has too much flat ground to ever be a stand out course and there is a real lack of variety amongst the holes. If the quotes in the brochure hadn't been so full of praise I might have been a bit less harsh in my appraisal.

LAHINCH

TWO YEARS AFTER LAHINCH GOLF CLUB OFFICIALLY STARTED (1892) OLD TOM MORRIS WAS ASKED TO REDESIGN THE LAYOUT. ONE OF THE FEW REMNANTS OF OLD TOM'S WORK IS THE FAMOUS PAR 3, 5TH HOLE 'THE DELL'. IN 1907, GEORGE GIBSON, THE PROFESSIONAL FROM WESTWARD HO! INTRODUCED FIVE NEW HOLES ON THE SEAWARD SIDE OF THE ROAD.

The course of today owes much to the work of Dr Alister Mackenzie in 1927. The committee of the day subsequently decided in 1935 that Mackenzie's greens were too undulating and should be flattened out. Fortunately, in 1999 the club made the decision to have Lahinch restored to the original Mackenzie concept. This work has now been completed by Martin Hawtree and also included re-routing some holes and building two new par three holes.

On a windy day you won't find many holes harder than the 3rd at Lahinch

The links at Lahinch occupy a wind exposed triangular plot of land bordered by the Atlantic Ocean on one side, an estuary and a road. I may be influenced by the fact that each time I have played Lahinch it has been wet and windy, but I would rate the layout as one of the toughest courses I have encountered.

There are no weak holes but, personally, I do not like the concept of the 4th hole 'Klondike'. This hole invariably takes ages to play and sets the scene for a slow round. The hole itself is a testing par 5 of 475 yards. The drive is uphill to a narrow fairway in a valley. A huge dune blocks the second shot so unless you are a long hitter you need to lay up.

The shot over the dune to the green is totally blind and is also over the start of the 18th fairway. As a result, a marshal is stationed at the top of the dune and signals you with either a red or green flag.

The opening hole is uphill and is usually into the wind so it plays longer than its 381 yards. The high plateau green has two deep bunkers at front right and then a steep fall-off at the right just a few feet from the edge of the green.

The par 5, 2nd comes back down the hill and bends right at the clubhouse. You must avoid the lush rough at Lahinch and on the 2nd there are also two large clusters of pot bunkers

that can add to your score. Just being on a Lahinch green in regulation is only part of the challenge as they are all a potential three putt.

You stand on the 3rd tee and face the prospect of a long drive into the wind, uphill and over a thirty feet high dune. Anything short, especially left, is in the rough on this hilly terrain. The fairway then becomes very narrow about 160 yards out from the exposed green with the edge of a cliff close to the left. Welcome to Lahinch!

After the 'Klondike' follows the equally celebrated par 3, 'The Dell'. The green is just 154 yards away but is almost

Photo courtesy Gary Prendergast

Par 3, 5th 'The Dell', side on from the 6th tee – from the 5th tee (right of picture) only a small section of the green can be seen

completely surrounded by large dunes. Only the right edge of the green can be seen from the tee. Whilst it is 37 yards wide, its depth varies between only 12 and 18 yards. Folklore, probably well founded, has it that this used to be the most holed in one par 3 in the world as enterprising caddies took advantage of the hidden green and changed the result of their players' shot in order to obtain a better tip at the end of the day.

The long par 4, 6th necessitates another blind drive followed by a rather scary second. There is a deep gully with a bunker in the centre of the fairway starting at 140 yards out from the green. Closer in there is a deep swale and two bunkers on the right.

The par 4, 7th starts off right on the shoreline and dog-legs left around coastal dunes to a small green that is back beside the sea. The 8th is a dramatic par 3 where you play across a valley of marram grass to a green higher up between two dunes. The two bunkers at the right are very much in play.

The tee at the 9th is the highest point at Lahinch. You can really go for the drive on this downhill par 4 but if you finish anywhere right of centre of the fairway then be prepared for a difficult second. The undulating green is 56 yards long and is set into the side of the dune on the right where there is a large bunker. Miss the narrow green to the left and you will roll down the very steep bank.

Ten is a tough par 4 of 441 yards and uphill as you approach the green. All the par 3's at Lahinch are good and the 11th is possibly the best of them. It can be a long 170 yards as you play into the wind straight back towards the ocean. A ridge of tall dunes runs along the left and there is a smaller mound followed by several deep hollows on the right. The green is very undulating, sloping from the back. The front and sides are guarded by three small but deep revetted straight faced bunkers.

One of the most photographed holes is the attractive 12th, a par 5 played from an elevated tee around the sandy beach towards Liscannor Bridge. Be careful not to take on too

The green at the 11th, possibly the best of the par 3's

View from the 9th tee looking across to the par 5, 12th with another rain squall about to arrive

There is no bail out area on the 195 yard 16th

much of the left hand corner with your drive. The green is in a delightful setting beside the estuary at the furthest point from the clubhouse.

By now you will have noted my liking for well designed short par 4's. The 13th is a wonderful example. It measures only 279 yards, slightly uphill, but this hole can be treacherous if you don't keep to the narrow fairway. The elevated green will test your putting skills.

Fourteen and fifteen are both good par 4's that are testing in both their length and need for accuracy. There is no bail out zone at the 16th, a downhill par 3 of 195 yards. Rolling mounds with long grass give way to a green guarded by bunkers everywhere except at the back. Club selection here can be rather difficult, especially with a helping breeze. For Lahinch, the background at the 16th is somewhat unusual with a row of white houses running along the other side of the road.

The 17th has a semi-blind tee shot over low dunes and a green with a dune at the right and three deep bunkers at the front. If there is a weak hole at Lahinch it is the18th – a relatively short and uninteresting par 5.

Lahinch is a big test of your golf. The blind drives can be tough but the shots into the green are a real feature of a difficult course with many memorable holes.

DOONBEG

DOONBEG IS HIDDEN AWAY ON THE COAST, SOUTH OF LAHINCH AND ABOUT 35 MILES WEST OF THE SHANNON INTERNATIONAL AIRPORT. THE LINKS COVERS AN ESTATE OF 400 ACRES BUT MOST OF THE HOLES ARE ALONGSIDE THE DUNES AND STRETCH FOR ONE AND A HALF MILES AROUND THE CRESCENT SHAPED DOUGHMORE BAY.

It is said that back in 1892 this location was the first choice of the officers of the Scottish Black Watch Regiment stationed in Limerick who wanted to have a golf course at their disposal. Instead they chose Lahinch which was less remote and was serviced by a railway.

This is Greg Norman's only work to date in the UK or Ireland. I first visited Doonbeg in 2003 when the course was not long open and the town was at best a small village. During my 2006 trip I had heard some negative comments about Doonbeg which surprised me because what I had seen three years earlier looked pretty good.

Having now played the course, albeit in fairly ordinary weather, I would rate it very highly especially the front nine where virtually all the holes are amongst the coastal dunes.

The 1st is an impressive par 5 which plays from an elevated tee to a wide fairway and then a green backed by a semi circle of large dunes. Make sure you avoid the pot bunkers in the middle of the fairway short of the green.

Above: 3rd green with out of bounds wall close by – the cars belong to the intrepid surfers who use the public walkway that runs across the course to access the beach
Below left: the 12th green was extended beyond the bunker which now lies in the middle

From the 3rd to the 6th are four very good holes. The 3rd is a short par 4 that is a birdie opportunity provided you don't stray right and over the stone boundary wall which is near the small raised green. The long par 5, 4th hole has six bunkers and an old grassed sod and rock wall that partly blocks access to the green.

The 5th is one of the best at Doonbeg. This shortish par 4 requires a very accurate blind uphill drive then a hard dog-leg right between the dunes. At this point the fairway runs downhill to a wind exposed green with the foaming breakers of the sea as the backdrop. Be careful with your tee shot as a large rough filled chasm awaits either a very long drive or a poor second shot. The 6th is a stunning hole of similar length (370 yards) to the 5th. The hole runs parallel with the beach at Doughmore Bay. The tee shot is very tight with thick marram grass beside the narrow fairway and out of bounds along the left of the fairway and then close to the left and back of the green. You need to avoid a fairway bunker and a greenside bunker on the right. The prevailing offshore breeze dictates a slight draw with your drive.

The first par 3 is at the 7th which is a less dramatic hole of 227 yards (195 from the white tee) downhill to a green at the foot of some dunes. The bunkers are at the sides so there is plenty of scope to run your ball onto the green. The 8th is

Photo David Worley

a very long and difficult par 5 that heads back to a huge green near the beach. The par 3, 9th (175 yards) is like a shorter version of the 6th hole. Out of bounds is frighteningly close to the left edge of the green, so much so that if you are playing out of the bunker at the right you could easily send your ball over the green and out of bounds.

Ten is a long par 5 (580 yards) rivalling the 8th. Those two holes are rated the hardest on the course. A hooked drive will be out of bounds and a hooked second or third shot will be in a wet ditch. The green at the 10th is in a slight dell in a semi circle of low dunes. The short 11th plays to an elevated green with a huge deep bunker at front right. There is also thick rough that will make recovery difficult if you go through the back of the green.

The two least attractive holes are the 10th and 12th which occupy flat ground lying near the boundary wall. The 12th green was originally built close to the out of bounds wall at the left and with a bunker at the right edge. It was later felt that this was too small a target so the extended green now encircles the bunker. I wonder how they react when someone chips on the green surface with a sand wedge.

The photogenic par 5, 13th requires an accurate blind drive to a fairway which dog-legs right to an elevated green in the dunes near the shoreline. The big danger is the extended area of rough that infiltrates across the upslope on the fairway from the right at about where your second shot would finish. Set into this upslope are five very severe natural looking

bunkers that are reminiscent of Norman's work at the course he designed at The National Golf Club one hour's drive south of Melbourne, Australia.

The short 14th is the hole you will never forget at Doonbeg. You will either love it or hate it. I loved it, perhaps because I was the only one on the green but one of my playing partners was over the large dune at the left and near the 6th green. It is only 111 yards but it is straight into the wind. The small green is cut into the side of a steep dune. There is no bail out area of any description. Anywhere short or right is in thick grass down a steep bank. If you are left you are on the side slope of the dune (or near the 6th green if you are way left) and if you are long then you will be out of bounds

Photo David Worley

Photo David Worley

Photo courtesy Gary Prendergast

and heading for the beach. I loved the fact that although it was cool, wet and windy, in the sea below was a large group of intrepid surfers. They probably thought we were just as silly to be playing golf in these conditions.

The 15th is another top quality par 4. The hole heads back towards the clubhouse with the beach along the right. The green has a narrow opening and is almost surrounded with low dunes at the front right and huge curved dune at the back which creates an amphitheatre atmosphere.

The long par 3, 16th is very similar to the 7th but with a little more room to run your ball on from the apron. Avoid the two small bunkers close to the left edge of the green.

The two closing holes are both tough par 4's to elevated and wind exposed greens. The drive at the 18th can take great courage as the prevailing offshore wind may require a shot that starts to the right of the out of bounds fence beside the beach. If you play safe with your second so as to stay away from out of bounds then you may finish down a bank or in one of the two fairway and three greenside bunkers on the left.

Opposite page: the 6th is a short par 4 that can ruin your card
Left: there is absolutely no margin for error at the wonderful par 3, 14th – the clubhouse and lodges are in the distance
Top: 15th with huge dunes behind the green
Above: daunting tee shot at the 18th in the heavy rain at Doonbeg

Design wise, there are a few holes where you have to cut across another fairway to get to the next tee but it seems to work quite well. Doonbeg has some really good holes, particularly the 1st, 5th, 6th, 9th, 14th and 15th and rates with the best courses in this part of Ireland.

BALLYBUNION – OLD COURSE

BALLYBUNION HAD ITS BEGINNINGS, OF SORTS IN 1893. AFTER FACING FINANCIAL PRESSURES IT RE-EMERGED IN 1906 AS A NINE HOLE COURSE LAID OUT BY LIONEL HEWSON, THE EDITOR OF 'IRISH GOLF'. THE LINKS WERE THEN EXTENDED TO EIGHTEEN HOLES IN 1926.

2nd green on the Old Course

Photo David Worley

Tom Simpson was called in to strengthen the course and in the following year (1937) Ballybunion hosted the Irish Amateur Championship. Much has been made of the fact that after Tom Watson first played here in 1981 he made the rest of the world acutely more aware of what the American writer, Herbert Warren Wind, described as "simply the finest seaside links in the world".

There is a feeling of great anticipation when you play Ballybunion for the first time. You expect something magical from the outset but you need to be patient because it is not until you reach the 7th that the Ballybunion you imagined begins to emerge.

The par 4, 1st features the sublime to the ridiculous. You need a slight draw to follow the shape of the fairway and to ensure you don't finish out of bounds to the right in the nearby cemetery. As you stand on the tee and look straight ahead yet another caravan park spoils the view.

The second hole, index number one, is a very good par 4 that gives false hopes that you are entering into the dunes. Only the longest of hitters will get on the green for two as the hole of 445 yards is uphill all the way. Two large dunes narrow the fairway at 68 yards from the plateau green which has a very steep incline at the front apron. There is a bunker

at the front on each side and anything right will run down a bank. This is a difficult target for your third shot let alone the second.

Although the 3rd is a long par 3 of 220 yards it is downhill. Three bunkers and numerous grassy swales are all around the green. From this elevated tee the caravan park completely spoils the aesthetics. The 4th and 5th are each testing par 5's into the wind. They bend left following the road which is out of bounds on the right hand side. At this stage you cannot help but ponder the whereabouts of the Ballybunion you have seen in all the brochures.

The tricky 6th is a par 4 of 364 yards. It dog-legs left and heads straight towards the sea. At around 50 yards short of the green the fairway is rather narrow and out of bounds is very close to the right. The long narrow green ends at the cliff edge with a grassy hollow on both sides.

The 7th is the first of four holes that run along the shore line along the right. The green here is also long and narrow with grassy hollows on the left. A fade will leave you on the rocks or the beach. Anything left is safe but then you have a more difficult angle across a low dune if you are to be on the green in two.

The 7th is the first of the holes along the shoreline – note the rockwall to reduce damage from the sea

The next three holes form a triangle with the par 3, 8th heading away from the sea. The green is across a valley and has four bunkers front and left and a tall mound at the back. The 9th is a very difficult long par 4 of 454 yards. The fairway bends right to a green with a mound at the right hand corner and a steep bank at the left side. If you miss to the right you will have a very delicate chip over the mound and on to the down slope.

On a windy day the short par 4, 10th hole can be a real handful. There is a carry of 157 yards needed to reach the fairway with dunes on the left and lower ground at the right. There is a deep hollow with rough ground immediately short and right of the green. You cannot run the ball on, you simply must land on the green from a high approach. If you pull your second long and left then you could finish down the cliff face.

If you have done your homework you will know that the marvellous 11th hole is rated one of the very best par 4's anywhere. The tee shot is a little similar to the one at the 7th with the sea at your right. In several places dunes then cut into the fairway until at 47 yards out there is only a very narrow opening to the small green. There is not much room at the right of the green before your ball descends down the cliff face but there seemed to be slightly more space here than was the case when I first visited in 2003. This area of the beach has been subject to damage from the sea so it may be that the cliff edge has been widened a little in order to fight against the erosion from the offshore winds. The 11th is also long at 453 yards so it is understandably rated index number two.

Three par 3's follow in the next four holes. Twelve is quite a challenge at 192 yards to a plateau green well above the tee. The view along the coastline from this green shows you the wonderful back nine in all its splendour.

Approaching the green at the marvellous 11th

The 12th, yet another great par 3 at Ballybunion

The par 5, 13th starts downhill but then heads uphill for the shot into the green. Be careful of the burn that runs right across the fairway about 80 yards short of the green.

Fourteen is a short par 3 of 131 yards over a valley to a green high up in the dunes. Whereas the 12th green is on a plateau, the 14th green is surrounded by dunes at the back and both sides.

Fifteen is my pick of the par 3's. From an elevated tee you hit downhill but usually into the wind coming off the sea. A very large dune blocks the front left of the green which has four small pot bunkers. The two at the front right are the biggest danger. The green is two-tiered and slopes from the back so you can afford to be aggressive on this 212 yard monster. This is another very photogenic hole with the green an oasis amongst the dunes.

The three closing holes are all dramatic tee shots with sixteen and seventeen featuring large dog-legs left at the point closest to the shoreline. At sixteen you need to watch how much of the corner you try to cut off by hitting over the dunes. Although this is a short par 5, the fairway becomes very narrow up a steep hill through large dunes. Seventeen is something of a par 4 version of the previous hole with a very attractive vista from the tee as you drive down to the edge of the beach before the fairway turns left. Setting aside the 11th, holes 15 to 17 are the best part of the course.

The par 4, 18th is all about position off the tee. A huge bunker occupies the whole width of the fairway starting at about 100 yards short of the green. The ideal drive is therefore just a straight hit of 250 yards. You then play up a steeper hill to a long green set amongst the dunes and in full view of the clubhouse to the right.

There are no quirky holes at Ballybunion, they are all a good but fair test of golf. The back nine is easily the best and is also lots of fun, which is how it should be.

Photo David Worley

212 yard, 15th – my pick of the par 3's on the Old Course

BALLYBUNION – CASHEN COURSE

IN THE LATE 1960'S BALLYBUNION GOLF CLUB WAS ABLE TO PURCHASE AN AREA KNOWN AS THE LOWER SANDHILLS. ROBERT TRENT JONES SENIOR WAS ASKED TO DESIGN A NEW COURSE WHICH EVENTUALLY OPENED FOR PLAY IN 1982.

Although somewhat shorter than the Old Course, the Cashen is considerably hillier with many narrow and severely undulating fairways. Given the difficult terrain and the fact that it is usually windy in this area, it is a legitimate criticism of the Cashen that the greens are perhaps a little too small.

The opening par 5 is well bunkered, particularly down the left side of the fairway. The green is anything but flat and drops away at the back. From the par 4, 2nd you first see the River Cashen after which the course is named. You have to land on the green at the 154 yard 3rd hole as there are two bunkers and a dune blocking the entrance to the triangular shaped green.

The main danger at the par 4, 4th hole is the three pairs of bunkers about 200 yards from the tee. Position for the second shot is the key to the short par 4, 5th hole. Six is a good looking par 3 of 155 yards with a ridge just short of the green and a bunker at the back that you cannot see from the tee.

The drive at the par 4, 7th must be dead straight. The beach is on the left and dunes and high marram grass lies to the right. The par 5, 8th is the longest hole at 605 yards. From an elevated tee it runs straight ahead with low dunes on either side. The 9th is a shorter par 5 of 478 yards but with a much more undulating fairway.

9th hole from behind the green

Photo: David Worley

The back nine is the more spectacular but more difficult of the two. The par 3, 12th plays even longer that its 210 yards would suggest as it is uphill all the way to a green that slopes from the back. Given the shape of the fairway, the bunker that is short of the right side of the green will catch many tee shots.

The holes from 13 to 17 are quite dramatic but also give you little margin for error. The fairways frequently narrow considerably in places where your ball is likely to land just short of the green. The par 4, 13th has a lovely green setting amongst the dunes. You cannot afford to miss this green on the right as there is a deep valley with thick rough. Many of the hillier holes make use of grassy hollows rather than bunkers.

The 15th is a short par 5 of 487 yards but is rated index number three. The fairway runs through an imposing line of dunes with a narrow landing area at the start of the steep incline just short of the green.

The 16th is the best of the short holes with its green perched right at the edge of the coastal cliff. Just a few feet left of the green is down the cliff and out of bounds. The short par 5, 17th requires a steady nerve as you play into a green that is just as close to the cliff edge as the previous hole.

The closing hole is somewhat similar in shape to the 18th on the Old Course. The second shot to the green needs to miss the two bunkers at the front and another two at the back.

Photos David Worley

Clockwise from above:
The par 5, 15th is not long but it is very challenging;
You can't get a much more dramatic setting than the par 3, 16th green;
The shot into the 17th green requires a steady nerve

The Cashen is not as good as the Old
but it is nevertheless a very good course.
It is not as easy to walk and
it does present some very small landing
areas and greens, especially on
the inward nine.

TRALEE

TRALEE GOLF CLUB CAN TRACE ITS BEGINNINGS BACK TO 1896. THE CLUB OF TODAY IS LOCATED ABOUT 20 MINUTES DRIVE AWAY AT BARROW WHERE THE ARNOLD PALMER DESIGNED COURSE OPENED FOR PLAY IN LATE 1984. THE THREE PREVIOUS LOCATIONS IN THE TOWN OF TRALEE WERE ALL IN AREAS WITH HIGH RAINFALL AND DID NOT HAVE THE SANDY SOIL OF THE PRESENT SITE.

Par 3, 3rd hole over the rocks and the remnants of a fourteenth century castle behind the green

Tralee consists of two completely contrasting nines. The outward nine is more gently rolling linksland with a number of very good holes beside the sea. The inward nine is mainly on higher ground amongst dunes and clifftops. The scenery is superb from anywhere on the course and the people here are the friendliest you could ever hope to meet.

The opening par 4 of 404 yards takes you immediately down to the golden sandy beach. An old stone wall runs along the left as you approach the green. So much for the gentle opening. The wonderful par 5, 2nd is 596 yards and follows the cliff edge with a dog-leg right. At the corner the cliff line eats into the fairway so you cannot take the short route. The green has bunkers on the left and the cliff close by at the right. It is no wonder this is rated the second hardest.

A hole you won't forget is the challenging and scenic 3rd, a par 3 of 194 yards. Rocky banks run in front of the tee almost all the way to the green. At the end of this narrow finger of land are the remains of a fourteenth century castle. A few yards beyond is Tralee Bay and the low-lying Fenit

Island. The only bail out area is to the left but from there you have to chip over two bunkers to a green sloping away from you.

The par 4, 4th runs away from the sea and the par 4, 5th then comes back to near the 4th tee beside the sea. The 6th then heads inland again before bending right and back towards the shoreline. Seven and eight run right beside the beach. The 7th is a short par 3 of only 157 yards but the green is on three different levels and has four pot bunkers at the sides.

The 8th is a lovely tranquil par 4 that runs along the beach on ground below the 6th fairway. Your tee shot must keep to the right side of the fairway otherwise you will be down the cliff face or on the beach itself. The view across to the left is almost as though you are on an island in the middle of the

ocean with no other noise other than the gentle lapping of the small waves and the echo of a well struck niblick. After the serene 8th, the 9th is a mundane par 5 uphill and back to the clubhouse.

The par 4, 10th dog-legs left into a pretty green setting amongst low dunes. The length of this hole from the back tee used to be 430 yards but an extra 44 yards has been added by a tiger tee on the other side of the road next to the clubhouse.

At the 11th, 'Palmer's Peak', the course climbs to its highest point. As you get closer to the green everything slopes down to the left so staying on this fairway can be difficult. The panoramic view from the green now looks across the ocean rather than the calmer waters that run by the first nine holes.

Peaceful setting of the 8th green and the low lying Fenit Island

Photos David Worley

The par 4, 12th is rated the hardest hole at Tralee – you can see why!

Par 3, 16th 'Shipwreck' from behind the green – the equally treacherous par 3, 13th green is set into the dune looking above the flag

The stretch from the 12th to the 17th features some really exhilarating holes in the dunes. The 12th is a tough par 4 that is rated index number one. The narrow neck approaching the plateau green is frighteningly thin with a huge chasm to the left.

The 13th is 159 yards with nothing but a deep grassy canyon between tee and green. Better to be long than short even if your ball does stay up the steep bank at the back of the green which is cut into the side of a huge dune.

The 14th gives you the driving option of two sections of a split level fairway. Fifteen is a short par 4 but you must stay on the fairway away from the long marram grass.

'Shipwreck' might be considered an appropriate name for the dangerous par 3, 16th, but in fact the name comes from the number of ships that have met their end on this stretch of coastline which is sometimes known as "the graveyard of the Spanish Armada". From an elevated tee you hit down to a green 199 yards away right at the edge of the cliff. The left bank is a safe line although there are two small bunkers at this side of the green. You only have a few feet at the right of the green before the out of bounds stakes are in play and three feet further on there is a long drop to the beach below. This hole is often into the wind so you need to be careful with club selection.

The short par 4, 17th runs above the beach used in the filming of "Ryan's Daughter". Like the short 15th, this green is elevated and exposed. Anything left or right here is in trouble but on both holes you have the option of being cautious with your second shot in the hope of a pitch and putt par or, at worst, a bogey. On the 17th you have the added danger of a scary drive across a deep gorge before you reach the fairway.

The 18th is a short par 5 that runs parallel with the 10th. This is a birdie chance provided you can stay out of the eight fairway and five greenside bunkers.

If you can place your drive in the right position then you can score well on the shorter back nine. However, if accuracy is not your forte then you may be reaching into your bag for replacement balls. I know there are some who don't like Tralee, mainly because of holes 12 to 17, but personally I rate it very highly with its mixture of the serene and the wild.

DINGLE

DINGLE IS LOCATED IN SOUTH WEST IRELAND NEAR THE SMALL TOWN OF BALLYFERRITER ON THE NORTH ARM OF DINGLE BAY. IT IS THE MOST WESTERLY COURSE IN IRELAND.

Although the club began in 1924, the course that is the Dingle Golf Club of today is the combination of design work of Eddie Hackett and Christy O'Connor Junior.

The day I played Dingle the weather was nothing short of diabolical. Even allowing for the inclement weather, the course was rather disappointing and I can only place it in the category of 'good holiday golf'. Much of the land is relatively flat and from what I could see through the torrential rain there was little or nothing in the way of dunes. The best view is not on the golf course but rather from the clubhouse which is on higher ground.

1st green and burn

The main hazard that is a feature at Dingle is the meandering burn which comes into play on no less than twelve holes. There is only one long par 5 (the 6th), but three of the four par 3's are quite long so the total yardage is a healthy 6737, par 71.

The par 4, 1st runs slightly downhill with a line of bunkers on the left which is the preferred side for your drive. For the first 200 yards there is out of bounds along the right. The burn cuts across not far in front of the green.

The 2nd is a long par 3 of 227 yards. Whilst the green is well bunkered at the sides, there is plenty of room to run your ball on from the apron. At the par 4, 3rd it is the second shot that poses the most difficulty. The last section of the fairway is rather narrow and the green is elevated.

The 4th is a good two shotter. Out of bounds is at your right and the slope into the burn starts at about 283 yards from the tee. There are three bunkers once you are over the burn. Heavy rough is also on the left.

Another long par 3 of 202 yards presents itself at the 5th. Out of bounds is close by at the right and there are four greenside bunkers. Provided you hit straight then the 6th is a relatively comfortable par 5. However, if you are inaccurate there is heavy rough and out of bounds on the right. There are four fairway bunkers along the left for those who steer too far away from the hazards on the right hand side.

The dog-leg 7th requires two very accurate strikes to reach the green which has three bunkers on the right and two bunkers plus a pond at the left side.

Index one is the 9th, a testing and long par 4 of 449 yards. The burn should not be in play for anything other than a duffed drive. The second shot is uphill with the approach area and the green itself shedding anything that is not hit perfectly straight.

Ten is another long par 3, of 197 yards. The green is very narrow at the front where there are three bunkers. A mound blocks the low approach to the left side of the green. At the par 5, 11th the burn is about 290 yards from the tee but is reachable downwind. The fairway then bends right just beyond where your second shot might land.

The 12th is the only short par 3 at 161 yards. The green is angled left so the entrance is more narrow. Three bunkers are along the left and one is at the back right. Thirteen may

Photo courtesy Gary Prendergast

Left: par 3, 5th with out of bounds on the right

Below: sign at the 5th tee

AS BAILE / NÍL CEAD ISTEACH
OUT OF BOUNDS / NO TRESPASSING

be a short par 5 but the burn is a real menace here. The hole dog-legs right where the burn first runs across the fairway at around 210 yards at the right hand corner. If you try to cut too much off the corner you may finish out of bounds. The burn runs along the right side and then runs back through the fairway again just short of the green.

Fourteen is the easiest hole at Dingle. It is a downhill par 4 of only 342 yards with just two fairway bunkers. The next three holes are all par 4's. Fifteen has out of bounds very close to the left, sixteen has the burn and seventeen has the burn and a well bunkered fairway just short of the green.

The par 5, 18th requires a drive over the burn. The fairway then has a broken area with two bunkers about 100 yards short of a very tricky green. By now you probably feel you have seen more than enough of the burn.

Dingle is pleasant enough but is just not in the same league as its neighbours such as Ballybunion, Tralee, Dooks and Waterville.

DOOKS

GOLF WAS INTRODUCED AT DOOKS AS LONG AGO AS 1889 BY THE OFFICERS FROM THE ROYAL HORSE ARTILLERY WHO WERE ATTENDING TRAINING AT THE GLENBEIGH ARTILLERY RANGE. THE COURSE WAS ORIGINALLY NINE HOLES UNTIL THE LATE 1960'S WHEN THE MEMBERS WERE ABLE TO PURCHASE THE FREEHOLD. ON A SHOE STRING BUDGET A COMMITTEE DESIGNED THE SECOND NINE WHICH OPENED IN 1970.

Photo David Worley

Dooks commences with a lovely par 4

I was fortunate to play Dooks in August 2006 by which time the new work by Martin Hawtree had been completed. In a bold move, the members agreed to have 16 holes redesigned – it has worked brilliantly. The members, committee and Martin Hawtree should be congratulated for producing what is now a really beautiful links.

You can't imagine a more wonderful setting than Dooks near Glenbeigh on the south side of Dingle Bay. Almost all the holes have panoramic views across the water to the sand dune peninsulas of Rossbeigh and Inch and then to the north are the imposing Dingle Mountains and Slieve Mish. The course itself is links with a heathland feel on a number of the holes.

Dooks commences with a lovely par 4 that starts uphill to a green set between two dunes. Watch for the hidden bunker set in a hollow just short of the green. Through the gap in the dunes the green has the backdrop of fir trees, sea and mountains. The 18th is a very similar hole and runs parallel to and in the same direction as the 1st. The 2nd is a shorter par 4 of 318 yards but it is up a steep hill to a very exposed plateau green.

The 1st green exemplifies Martin Hawtree's recent work on all the greens at Dooks

Photo courtesy Donal Brosnan/Dooks GC

The par 4, 3rd runs back toward the sea and the 2nd tee. The 4th is a delightful par 3 of 174 yards running along side the shoreline. Thick rough is on both sides and there are out of bounds stakes at the left and only a few yards from the fairway at about 30 yards short of the green. This will tempt you to play to the right where the only bunker is located.

Five is a long par 4 which is uphill. A slight draw is needed to the narrow fairway that bends left through grassy mounds. Six is a lovely short par 5 that dog-legs right in the opposite direction to the 5th. The raised tee will tempt you to really go for a big drive but you need to avoid the mound with two bunkers and then the thick gorse that is at the right hand corner. The tilted green is higher up as you head back to the sea. Thick rough awaits you if you are long or left of the green.

The 7th is rated index number two. It is a par 4 of 469 yards uphill through some attractive dunes on both sides of the fairway. Two bunkers on the right and short of the elevated green are in play for all other than big hitters.

The new 8th is a pretty par 3 of 183 yards to a green on lower ground. Bunkers are on both sides of the green and thick rough will catch a duffed tee shot. This hole tends to play shorter than its yardage would suggest.

Nine and ten are back to back par 5's where you must stay on the fairway and avoid the rough and heather that is very close by. The 11th is an intimidating looking par 3 of 173 yards and uphill. There is an eroded waste area in front of the tee. You need to hit almost over the edge of the out

of bounds fence which runs at an angle in to the left side. The plateau green has one bunker at the left and the out of bounds fence very close to the back.

The par 4, 12th is a potentially dangerous hole. It is a dog-leg left, 368 yards uphill. The shape of the hole pretty much dictates that you hit a slight draw but all along the left side is thick scrub and gorse.

Thirteen is a par 3 of 171 yards up a steep hill with the fairway flanked by heather. Three bunkers are at the sides and a steep bank lies at the back of a very undulating green.

The 14th is a very attractive par 4 of 406 yards but I am rather surprised it is rated the hardest at Dooks. The fairway

Photo courtesy Donal Brosnan/Dooks GC

Photo David Worley

Above: 3rd green and par 3, 4th hole Below: long par 4, 7th through the dunes

Above: the 6th is a lovely short par 5 that dog-legs right Below: the new par 3, 8th

runs downhill and slopes to the right. Heavy gorse is in play if you pull your second shot left and heathery rough is along the right. The green is well guarded with four bunkers toward the front and grassy hollows at the rear.

The 15th used to be a par 3 but now it is a tricky short uphill par 4. There is a fair carry over rough before the fairway commences. The green cannot be seen and is around to the right in line with two bunkers set into a mound. Long hitters need a fade from the tee otherwise you will run out of fairway.

The par 4, 16th is quite different to the other holes at Dooks. The tee shot is over a pond to a fairway that bends right with a tall stand of conifers running along the right hand side. The drive is the key to this hole.

Seventeen plays longer than its 395 yards. The hole is uphill with a real heathland feel. Thick bracken is in front of the tee and heather is at the right. A hooked drive will be in serious trouble amongst heavy scrub.

The par 4, 18th is similar to the 1st hole but is slightly longer at 426 yards. There are no bunkers but only the centre of the green is visible through two very large mounds or dunes. The view from near the 18th green looking across the course towards the 3rd, 4th and 6th greens is one of great natural beauty.

Photo courtesy Gary Prendergast

Dooks is an enchanting place that you are bound to enjoy. Apart from the scenery, it is a fun course that can also bare its teeth with some pretty tight fairways and areas of thick rough and gorse. It also has an indefinable unspoilt, natural charm that is a prerequisite for genuine links golf.

Photo courtesy Donal Brosnan, Dooks GC

WATERVILLE

ALTHOUGH GOLF WAS PLAYED ON A VERY BASIC 9 HOLE COURSE AT WATERVILLE IN THE 1880'S, ITS BEGINNINGS REALLY DATE TO THE 1960'S WHEN JOHN MULCAHY, AN IRISH BORN AMERICAN, BOUGHT THE LAND AND GAVE THE DESIGN TASK TO EDDIE HACKETT AND CLAUDE HARMON, THE 1948 US MASTERS CHAMPION.

The new Waterville opened in 1973 as one of the longest courses in the Republic – today it measures a very long 7331 yards from the back and 6783 from the white tees.

The Waterville I played in August 2006 was brilliant – immeasurably improved upon from my visit in 2003 when apparently renovation works had just started and it was in poor condition. After John Mulcahy died in 2002, the syndicate which then owned Waterville appointed Tom Fazio to improve a few things, particularly the first hole. His report recommended a number of additional alterations including new holes at the 6th and 7th. Thankfully his proposals were implemented with stunning results.

The opening hole has plenty of thick rough, mounds to the left and a wet ditch on the right, but if you keep to the fairway it is straightforward needing two good strikes.

You are aware that this is a long course as soon as you survey the 2nd, a par 4 of 464 yards and rated index number one. The hole bends right but there are plenty of bunkers if you try to cut the right hand corner. The green is in a pretty setting located very close to a wet ditch at the right and the River Inny estuary.

Par 4, 9th hole requires two accurate shots to the green

The par 4, 3rd hole is almost as difficult. It is a little shorter at 417 yards but the fairway dog-legs hard right just before the green. Anywhere too far right from the tee will be in the water and if you are too far left there is a line of four fairway bunkers. To the right or through the back of the green will leave you in the water of the estuary while too far left and you will be lost in the spiky reeks. A good straight drive can make this a much easier hole.

Waterville possesses four of the best par 3's that you will ever find on the one golf course. The 4th is 179 yards through thickly grassed dunes to a green with one deep pot bunker at the very front. The fairway slopes from the left so you have very little chance of running on through the narrow gap between the dunes on the left and the bunker.

Above: the superb par 5, 11th as seen from near the 18th tee
Right: the 17th, 'Mulcahy's Peak', is probably the best of the short holes

The long 5th (595 yards) needs a good straight drive over gorse just to reach the start of the fairway which then dog-legs left. Six and seven, the two new holes each feature a ditch or burn that is very much in play at the right edge of the fairway. The 6th is a par 3 of 194 yards. The ditch and a bunker are at the right and even though you will be in grassy hollow there is a little more room if you miss just left of the green. The 7th is a really tough par 4. The fairway slopes to the right and bends right with a burn running along this side. Once the burn disappears the fairway narrows at about 120 yards short of the green.

The 8th and 9th are both long par 4's bending left and right respectively. The 9th is an attractive looking hole from a tee amongst low dunes. The green is raised and has an extremely narrow opening between two pot bunkers.

The 10th tee is elevated and is close by the clubhouse. Although this seems incredibly long for a par 4 at 475 yards (450 yards white tee) it does not play quite as long. You need a solid drive and then an accurate second along the narrow fairway. There are no greenside bunkers so you can run your ball on from the flat ground.

Above: long par 3, 12th, 200 yards over a deep valley
Below: plaque beside the 12th tee

View from behind the 16th green where the River Inny estuary runs into Ballinskelligs Bay

"THE 'MASS' HOLE"

IN THE 18TH CENTURY, THE CELEBRATION OF MASS WAS PUNISHABLE BY DEATH IN IRELAND FORCING THE LOCAL POPULATION TO USE THE SECLUDED VALLEY IN FRONT OF THIS GREEN TO HOLD THEIR SERVICES. THE ORIGINAL LINKS DESIGN CALLED FOR A GREEN TO BE PLACED IN THIS HIDDEN VALE. HOWEVER, THE LOCAL WORKMEN DECLARED THE AREA SACRED GROUND AND REFUSED TO DISTURB THE SITE. A COMPROMISE WAS REACHED WITH THE GREEN BEING RELOCATED ON THE HILL OVERLOOKING — THE MASS HOLE.

The par 5, 11th 'Tranquility' is close to being the best hole at Waterville. The drive is semi blind through the dunes to a fairway that turns right near the 260 yard mark from the tee. You need to keep your first two shots down the left side which is slightly higher. The circular green is up a steep slope with two bunkers just off the fairway short and left of the green. To the back left is a high dune whilst a grassy hollow lies at the right.

The 12th is named the 'Mass' hole as it was here that Catholics celebrated Mass during times of persecution in the 18th century. This is a long par 3 of 200 yards from a raised tee over a deep valley to a green at the same height as the tee. Rough ground is everywhere except for a small area below the steep bank at the front of the green.

Thirteen is a par 5 and is rated the easiest hole on the course. It seemed harder to me as although it is a short par 5 it has thick rough and gorse if you hook and bunkers line the edge of the fairway which dog-legs left.

Fourteen is another long par 4 that is made even more difficult by being uphill to an angled green. Fifteen is a good looking par 4 that is downhill with a snaking fairway over the last 160 yards.

The 16th is a beautiful par 4 of 386 yards that dog-legs left around the beach. 'Liam's Ace' is so named as some how or other Liam Higgins holed in one here. This is almost a different hole with the spiky vegetation that blocked the sea views now removed and planted lower down the bank

Photo David Worley

where it should still help reduce the soil erosion. The green is not an easy target as it is kidney shaped with grassy hollows at the sides. Dunes are further left and the rocks and beach are not far from the right edge of the green that affords stunning views, especially looking back across the water to the mountains.

Hole seventeen, 'Mulcahy's Peak', is probably the best of all the par 3's. It is 194 yards across the valley to an exposed plateau green with a wonderful backdrop of sea and mountains. There is no safe place to miss but anywhere a little right will suffer the worst fate as you will be on the beach.

Waterville concludes with a tough par 5. From the elevated tee you might need to start your drive over the rocks near the beach if the wind is offshore. The fairway is noticeably narrow with spiky bushes at the right and a ridge of mounds or low dunes on the left. The green is angled to the left and is tucked away behind a dune that blocks the left side. There are also plenty of bunkers and grassy hollows so your third shot will need to be a slight draw to the right of the green assuming you are lucky enough to be approaching from the centre of the fairway.

18th is a tough final hole, especially into the wind

The greens and fairways at Waterville are first class. In fact, like Turnberry, the fairways are almost too lush for a links course but, knowing how wet it can be in Ireland, this may be something they really can't control. Waterville is an enjoyable 'monster' but make sure you bring your 'A' game with you.

OLD HEAD

THE CLIFFTOP LINKS AT OLD HEAD IS ON A SPECTACULAR PROMONTORY A FEW MILES FROM KINSALE IN COUNTY CORK, SOUTHERN IRELAND. THE TOTAL AREA OF THE SITE IS 220 ACRES OF WHICH 180 IS TAKEN UP BY THE COURSE.

Old Head Golf Links opened in 1997. The design and routing is a combined effort from Ron Kirby, Paddy Merrigan, Eddy Hackett, Joe Carr, Liam Higgins and Haulie O'Shea. A large stone wall and a gate keeper at the narrow entrance to the site ensure that this extraordinary location is reserved exclusively for golfers.

More than half the holes feature tees and greens at the edge of 250 feet high cliffs. I would not want to be standing on some of the tees, such as the 12th and 18th, on a windy day. There are no fences or barriers – you just stare straight down the steep cliff face as you prepare to hit. The whole course is very well maintained but it must be expensive to keep it at such a high standard as, for example, about three or four greens have to be replaced every year because of the salt in the air and the lack of sunlight hours.

I thought some of the clifftop holes at Nefyn in Wales were spectacular but nothing can prepare you for the amazing, if not audacious, holes at Old Head.

Above: 2nd hole from behind the green
Opposite page: the intimidating view from the 18th tee below the lighthouse – a long carry is needed to reach the fairway at top right of photo – the 17th green is to the left

There are five tees, including the ladies, on each hole. Although the black tees are the longest, these are rarely used so I have taken the blue tees as the bench mark.

The opener is a good par 4 with a generous fairway to get the field away. Make sure you keep away from the two bunkers at the right hand corner 233 yards from the tee. The walk to the second tee brings you to the cliff edge and the challenge begins. This is a scenic but dangerous par 4 of 388 yards. The fairway turns sharply to the left around a ravine with out of bounds stakes down the bank just before the start of the steep cliff. The fairway slopes left so your drive should be down the right. The green is higher up for your second shot and is perched beside the cliff on the left. Keep right and your ball should feed down to the green.

The third is a par 3 of 176 yards to a green close to the edge of the cliff. There is thick rough between tee and green but there is room to miss on the right. This hole does not need any further hazards by way of bunkers.

Most of the holes are extremely photogenic and the 4th is one of the best. Appropriately named, 'Razor's Edge', it is like a more dramatic version of the second hole. The par 4 of 423 yards has 300 feet cliffs along the left all the way to the green with the lighthouse behind. Two large fairway bunkers should deter you from cutting off too much of the left hand corner. There is absolutely no margin for error with the shot into the green. Anywhere left or long is down the cliff and a rocky wall runs along the right.

Photo David Worley

Photo courtesy Old Head GC

The 5th is also a long par 4 (409 yards) which dog-legs right and is then uphill. The fairway slopes left to right but if you go too far left there is a high stone wall and out of bounds. The elevated green can be quite a tricky putting proposition. The par 5, 6th is a longer version of the 5th. The green is two-tiered and is heavily bunkered especially on the right from 60 yards out.

Even the walk from the tee can be a little scary at the par 3, 7th which is perched at the cliff edge. Anywhere right is down the cliff and if you miss left you will then be chipping back to a green running away from you. The 8th is a par 5 of 520 yards which bends left around a nest of five bunkers. The rough here is quite heavy even in close proximity to the green. Nine is a similar shape but instead of being a comfortable par 5 it is a very tough par 4 of 451 yards. Three bunkers are strategically placed on the left approximately 240 yards from the tee.

Probably the only weak holes are the 10th and 11th. At the par 5, 10th the fairway dog-legs at almost 90 degrees to the right about 220 yards from the tee. The green is uphill with a stone wall and gorse plantation intruding on to the fairway 75 yards short of the green. The 11th is the only one of the

Left: clubhouse entrance
Above: 4th hole 'Razor's Edge' with the 3rd green bottom right

five par 3's that is not alongside a cliff. This hole plays longer than its 178 yards as it is uphill and often into the wind. One big bunker lies at the left but down the grassy hollow further left is not as bad as it looks.

There are countless memorable holes at Old Head but the 12th has to be one of the most challenging. This par 5 starts with a tee that is frighteningly close to the cliff. The drive is uphill to a fairway which you cannot see but there is a

marker stone indicating its starting point 214 yards away. (The markers at Old Head are known as 'Stones of Accord' and are the club's logo.) Slightly left of this line will see your ball tumbling down the steep cliff face. Once you climb to the fairway you are confronted initially with a wide expanse that then quickly becomes a very narrow entrance to the green. The second shot is downhill but with the cliff only a few yards from the left of the green you may be better to play down the right side to about 50 yards short and then

Par 5, 6th with its tricky two-tiered green

Above: you will never forget the 12th hole – the marker stone (right of photo) is a carry of 214 yards uphill
Below: start of the fairway at the 12th

chip on. Low dunes run along the right but that is a better option to lost ball down the cliff. If you play this hole conservatively it is not quite as hard as it first appears. On the other hand you could easily lose a ball with all three shots if you pull everything to the left.

Thirteen is by far the most difficult of the short holes although it is not so short at 227 yards uphill (258 from the back tee). The biggest danger is left where there are thick shrubs and then out of bounds stakes with the entrance road just below. A really wild hook into the wind could see your ball over the road and heading down the cliff.

Fourteen is a testing par 4 of 428 yards and is rated index number one. The uphill drive is made more difficult by three bunkers that leave only a narrow space on the left side. The green is a little further away than it seems. Two bunkers are at the right and although there is room to the left if you go too far you will encounter the spiky plants that are around the rear of the green. This is a high and exposed area of the course where you will often be hitting into the off shore breeze.

The last four holes are first class as you resume play alongside the spectacular cliffs that are now at your right. The short par 4, 15th is only 328 yards downhill so this can be birdied provided your drive is on the correct line down the left side

The short par 4, 15th can be eagle, birdie, or lost ball

The 16th is the most exciting of the short holes – the green is re-laid almost yearly due to wind and salt spray damage

Aerial photograph of Old Head Golf Course

of the fairway. A mound with bunkers is left of the green and at the right there are two more bunkers and then the cliff edge. The land on this promontory was originally very rocky so when the course was being built thousands of tons of soil had to be brought in. levelling areas for some of the cliff-side greens was a dangerous occupation with the man responsible, Haulie O'Shea, having on one occasion to jump from an earth mover as it careered down the cliff face into the sea two hundred feet below. This area may have been the location as the 15th is called 'Haulie's Leap'.

The 16th is the most exciting of the par 3's. Only a thin pathway connects the tee and the green 183 yards away. A line of seven pot bunkers runs from the front and then around the bank at the left of the green. A narrow ridge a few feet from the right of the green is all that stops you from going down the cliff. For safety reasons, out of bounds stakes run along the right but with a strong off shore breeze you might have to start your ball along this line. The wind is a real factor here as I was advised that this green has to be re-laid almost yearly because of wind damage.

On paper the par 5, 17th looks to be an absolute monster at 606 yards (632 from the back) with yet another green at the cliff edge. With a slight tailwind my playing partner was on the green in two mighty hits. The key is to keep your second in the middle of the fairway so you can then run your third straight down the hill where just the one bunker guards the left side of the green. On the par 5, 12th three pulled shots would result in three lost balls and here at the 17th three sliced shots will achieve the same result.

The next time I play Old Head I want an experienced Sherpa from Tibet to assist me along the narrow ledge, that they call a walkway, to the 18th tee. I cannot imagine how dangerous this would be on a really windy day which is perhaps part of the reason why the course is closed from November to March each year. The tee is set on the side of the cliff directly below the lighthouse.

The lighthouse stands some 150-200 feet above the sea at the very end of the promontory. There is a photograph in the clubhouse that was taken during a storm just a few years ago

and the waves are crashing over the bottom of the lighthouse! Many ships have been wrecked here over hundreds of years but probably the most infamous was the Lusitania which sank here in 1915, not due to the rocks but at the receiving end of a German torpedo.

But back to the 18th, a very strong finishing hole of 419 yards (460 back tee) and uphill all the way to the green. After you conquer your fear of falling down the cliff from the small teeing ground you need a strong drive – preferably a slight draw around the right side of the fairway which slopes across to the left side. The fairway bends left with a large bunker on the left side about 90 yards before the green. There is one more bunker just below the green which slopes from the back and with a steep incline at the very front.

The low rise stone clubhouse sits above the 18th green and provides a fabulous panorama. Old Head is a really memorable experience that is quite unlike anything you will have ever encountered.

ROSSLARE

Photo David Worley

ROSSLARE IS THE ONLY LINKS COURSE
OF ANY NOTE IN THE SOUTH EAST OF
IRELAND. WHEN GOLF BEGAN HERE IN
1905, ROSSLARE WAS NOTHING MORE
THAN A SMALL FISHING VILLAGE.

The club was founded by James Farrall an architect and engineer from Dublin. Farrall first noticed the land in 1904. Within a year an eighteen hole course had been squeezed into a very small area, hence it was rather short. Partly due to the cost of establishing the links, Farrall was declared bankrupt in 1906. By 1908 a new club was formed which this time had the long term lease of the land owned by the members. The re-opened course was reduced to a more practical nine holes.

In 1925 a resolution was passed to buy land for an extra nine holes. Fred Hawtree and J H Taylor were engaged to design a new eighteen hole links which was formally opened in 1928.

The quality of Hawtree and Taylor's work was such that by 1934 Rosslare was chosen to host the Irish Close Championship.

The History of Rosslare has been very much one of its constant battles with the elements. Between 1930 and 1960 six greens were lost to the sea. The seaside dunes are low and the course is particularly vulnerable to south easterly and north easterly storms. This is made even more dangerous due to the tidal range in Wexford Bay of nearly six feet.

The coastal holes were buffered by railway sleepers in 1983 and then, after parts of the course was submerged in 1990, a huge rock revetment wall 460 yards long was built.

The short par 4, 13th – you may be better to lay up rather than try to drive the green

Rosslare is a genuine seaside links although there are no dunes in play. It is a very tight course with some thick rough, gorse and nasty patches of sea buckthorn introduced from England in order to help with the erosion problem.

The par 4, 1st is a good starting hole that requires a slight draw through the trees with the tee shot to set up the hole. The 2nd is a long par 3 of 198 yards through gorse and back towards the clubhouse. There are bunkers at the sides and back of the green but the front is open for a run on shot.

The 3rd can be a tricky par 5. The hole dog-legs left with thick rough and scrub all down that side. Three bunkers protect the front and left of the slightly raised green and there are grassy mounds at the right.

There are some tough par 4's at Rosslare with six being over 400 yards from the back tee. The 5th is 455 yards and rated the second hardest hole on the course. You need to miss the fairway bunkers and then watch for the broken ground and hollow just short of the green.

Photo David Worley

you are in long grass or gorse. Your long second shot needs to be dead straight to miss the two bunkers almost hidden at the front sides of the green.

The 18th is a tough finishing hole where you need to be very thoughtful with each shot. The drive is uphill over rough to a fairway that bends left. There is one bunker at the left but a wall of six with high sleepered faces at the right. If you managed a good drive onto the fairway there is then only a narrow gap between dunes and further on a burn which runs in front of the green and into a pond on the left. This hole is 477 yards (425 white) so unless you hit a very good drive you would be wise to lay up with your second. The burn juts out into the fairway in a V shape so judging distance for your lay up is made a little more difficult.

It probably helps at The European if your normal drive is a slight draw. There is a good variety of holes, some with wonderful views. The course is beautifully maintained and, as a matter of policy, is never too crowded. This area is also blessed with a lower rainfall and sunnier climate than most of Ireland.

Above: green at the 14th, the best of the par 3's
Left: plaque at the 14th tee

THE EUROPEAN CLUB

The hole you are about to play was named as one of the
WORLD'S 500 GREATEST GOLF HOLES
in January 2000 by a global alliance of major golf magazines

This hole is named in honour of the skills of
GENE SARAZEN

*If your trip to the Emerald Isle
only allows time for half a dozen adventures
on the links then The European should be added
as a "must play" on your list.*

Seven is a par 5 of 554 yards. The fairway is narrow and provides some tight landing areas before you reach the elevated green with three bunkers towards the front. This is the longest distance from the clubhouse. The next holes are all more inland until the 14th returns to near the beach. The 11th is deservedly index one. It measures 481 yards and dog-legs right. A long straight drive is essential with the next shot over the marker post.

The 13th is one of the best holes at Rosslare. It is a par 4 of just 282 yards but there is danger at the right which eventually leads to out of bounds. The green is raised up with steep banks on all sides and two pot bunkers at the left. You may be better to lay up rather than try to drive the green.

The par 3, 14th (172 yards) heads straight back towards the sea and is somewhat more difficult than it first appears. Club selection is important as the bunker at the front dictates that you can't run your shot on.

The 15th, 16th and 17th are all good par 4's of 400 yards or more. Each hole runs along the shoreline so a hook will put you in long grass in the low dunes or possibly even on the beach.

The closing hole is a short par 5 of 482 yards that requires very straight hitting. Trees run along the left hand boundary. At 86 yards from the green there is a wall that runs at 90 degrees on the left. On the right at this point there are also trees and another wall which runs behind the trees and then at the rear of the green. There are also plenty of fairway bunkers, mainly along the right side.

Photo David Worley

Par 4, 16th at Rosslare

Rosslare drains well as any true links course should. It is a very good test of your ability to hit the ball straight. It probably suffers from the lack of spectacular holes and as there are no other links courses nearby it is not usually on the golfing tourist's itinerary.

ARKLOW

Photo David Worley

The large greens are exceptionally good at Arklow

THE LINKS AT ARKLOW ARE LOCATED JUST OUT OF THE TOWN IN SOUTH WICKLOW AND ABOUT 10 MILES SOUTH OF THE EUROPEAN AT BRITTAS BAY.

From a golfing perspective, J H Taylor is credited with having discovered the site. He and Fred Hawtree designed the eighteen holes which opened for play in 1927.

There was a period when some holes were lost to the sea and some to encroaching industrial development but by the 1970's Arklow was again restored to an eighteen hole links. The present layout also reflects work from Eddie Hackett and more recently E B Connaughton.

There are burns and ditches running across parts of the course and coming into play on six or seven holes.

Some of the best holes are the 2nd, 3rd, 6th and 15th. The remodeled 3rd is a par 3 of 198 yards from the back tee. You are usually into the wind so a solid tee shot is needed through the dunes to a well bunkered and undulating green.

Whilst Arklow is not long at 6383 yards, it has some very attractive holes amongst the low dunes. The large greens are exceptionally good, many with interesting mounds and swales.

THE EUROPEAN

Par 5, 3rd hole at The European

PAT RUDDY DISCOVERED THE DUNELAND AT BRITTAS BAY IN THE EARLY 1980'S WHILST SURVEYING THE EAST COAST OF IRELAND BY HELICOPTER IN SEARCH OF LINKS LAND SUITABLE FOR A COURSE OF HIS OWN. THE EUROPEAN OPENED FOR PLAY CHRISTMAS 1992.

Photo courtesy The European GC

Picturesque 8th green set amongst the dunes

Par 4, 11th hole

The 12th is my favourite hole at The European

I fell in love with The European when I first played it in 2003. On my return game in 2006 I kept noticing bunkers that I did not remember from before only to be later informed by Pat Ruddy that sixteen new sleepered bunkers were added prior to the hosting of the Irish Amateur in June 2006.

There are only two par 5's, as Pat Ruddy points out, it is hard to find long stretches amongst dunes that are suitable for a par 5. But there are many demanding par 4's and three totally different par 3's. If you are feeling energetic then you can play 20 holes as there are two additional par 3's, 7a and 12a.

Three tee choices are available and from the very back you will be playing 7355 yards. The white tees are still a very solid test at 6720 yards. There are no weak holes at The European but some of the best are the 3rd, 6th, 7th, 10th, 11th, 12th, 13th, 14th, 15th and 17th.

The 1st is an ideal opening par 4 of 424 yards (363 white). A good drive is necessary if you are to get a shot at the green with two bunkers at the front and one at the right. Be warned that the sleepered bunkers at The European are meant to be penal so you need to think your way around the course.

The par 3, 2nd hole plays back towards the farmland in the distance and is one of the few holes that does not have a real links feel. The 3rd is probably the last of the easier holes. This is a lovely par 5 of 499 yards that runs downhill through the dunes and towards the sea. Take care with your second shot as the fairway slopes to the right where there are some almost hidden bunkers.

The 4th is the first of a number of very tough par 4's. It is 470 yards (426 white) to an elevated green that slopes from the back. Two bunkers are at the front sides and anything left will run down a bank. The fairway is quite narrow about 130 yards out from the green. The 5th is a shorter par 4 that dog-legs left. You need to be careful to avoid the two sets of bunkers along the left side of the fairway.

Six is a very challenging downhill par 3 of 210 yards (177 white). A river bordered by thick rough runs along the left and a large kidney shaped bunker is beside the right edge of the green. On a windy day this is the first of two consecutive holes that may easily reduce your stock of golf balls.

The long par 4, 7th (470 yards blue, 449 white) is rated index number one. It is probably a much harder hole when you are not familiar with the course. A river and dense rough runs all the way along the right. The drive needs a carry of about 200 yards just to reach the fairway. There is a marshy swamp on the left that appears in play from the tee but it is actually about 300 yards away even from the white tees. If you play too far to the left on the fairway with your drive then your second is over the swamp to a green with two bunkers on the left side and the river at the right. I have no doubt that this hole has ruined many a stroke round.

Eight and nine are two moderate length par 4's with the 8th featuring a picturesque green set amongst the dunes.

Photo David Worley

Photo courtesy The European GC

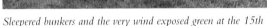

Sleepered bunkers and the very wind exposed green at the 15th

Narrow fairway of the demanding 17th, a par 4 of 432 yards

Then follows the 10th – a very good par 4 that heads uphill and back toward the Irish Sea. This is a testing 466 yards from the blue tees but somewhat easier at 397 yards from the white. The fairway narrows between the dunes and then bends right just before the green with one deep bunker at the front left.

At the par 4, 11th your drive has to avoid four bunkers including a wide cross bunker about 225 yards out. The green is the reverse of the 10th with the one bunker at the front right.

It is the 12th, 13th and 15th alongside the sea that I remember most fondly. The holes themselves are wonderful but so is the peaceful feeling of isolation with the gentle lapping of the waves on the deserted beach.

From the elevated tee on the par 4, 12th you need a slight draw with your drive. There are nine bunkers to stay clear of and then you can have fun trying to two putt on the 127 yard long green that is seven yards longer than the biggest double green on the Old Course at St Andrews.

It is a pity that the par 3, 12a is not normally in play. The green is in a wild setting with tall rugged dunes at the back and right. There is no fairway, only rough and a nasty pot bunker short of the green.

The 13th is by far the longest hole but a draw from the tee on higher ground will set up a potential birdie opportunity on this 596 yards (503 white) par 5 along the beach. Be careful to stay out of the nest of five bunkers on the right at the dog-leg left corner at 285 yards from the tee. There is another well placed bunker to avoid at the front right of the very wide green. The green is kidney shaped with a bunker eating into the back so you could find yourself unable to putt directly to the flag if you are on the wrong section of the green.

Fourteen is the best of the short holes. The tee shot is 195 yards (165 white) uphill to a green that slopes from the back. There are three bunkers around the green and a large dune that will hold anything that is pulled left. Elsewhere is long grass or bracken.

The par 4, 15th is the last of the seaside holes. A slight draw is needed from the tee as long as you avoid the four bunkers at the left corner of the slight dog-leg left. The second shot is uphill to a very wind exposed green. Don't be too strong here otherwise you will finish in some spiky rushes that are very close by and presumably were planted to help with wind erosion.

Sixteen has out of bounds on the right and a very narrow fairway for the last 130 yards. The 17th runs downhill with its narrow fairway winding between a line of dunes on either side. From the tee the hole looks at first glance like a par 5 but it is a testing par 4 of 432 yards. If you spray your drive

ROYAL DUBLIN

ROYAL DUBLIN BEGAN AS A NINE HOLE COURSE AT PHOENIX. IT THEN BRIEFLY MOVED TO SUTTON BEFORE SETTLING UPON THE PRESENT SITE AT NORTH BULL ISLAND IN 1889. BY 1891 THERE WERE 250 MEMBERS AND THE CLUB WAS GRANTED THE ROYAL PREFIX.

Bull Island is connected to the mainland by way of a wooden bridge and now a proper road over reclaimed soil which runs by the far end of the course. Bull Island is a wildlife and nature reserve which creates an unusual contrast to the foreboding tall industrial chimneys in the distance.

The club received substantial compensation after the military had rendered the course and clubhouse almost unrecognisable by the end of the First World War. This enabled them to engage E S Colt to partly restore and also redesign the course. Not much changed until 2003 when Martin Hawtree was brought in to upgrade the links, particularly holes six to twelve.

The 5th fairway runs like a ribbon through the low dunes

When I played Royal Dublin in late August 2006 most of Hawtree's work was completed. Aprons and greens have been substantially remodeled with the greens now smaller but more undulating. By the time the clubhouse and course improvements are completed they will have spent a tidy sum of 8 million Euros on these works.

Low lying links such as Royal Dublin are at the mercy of global warming and rising sea levels. In 2002 a combination of events led to a king tide which flooded the clubhouse and parts of the course. As a result of this a large earthen retaining wall is being built along the right hand side of holes 10, 11, 12, 13, 16 and 17.

Royal Dublin has firm fairways but little in the way of dunes or panoramic vistas. It is an old style out and back layout. The outward nine is some 500 metres shorter (yes, just to confuse all of us, they use metres) and has, in my opinion, the most interesting holes. A feature of the front nine is the tight fairways, numerous bunkers and plenty of small grassy mounds and low dunes.

The round begins with a good well bunkered par 4 followed by a short par 5 of 445 metres. Out of bounds runs along the right on both holes and with a wet ditch on the left of the 2nd. The 3rd is not an overly long par 4 at 373 metres but there is a carry of 184 metres just to reach the fairway. An out of bounds area lies just short of the left hand side of a green protected by a semi-circle of five pot bunkers at the front.

The prevailing wind is usually with you at the start so perhaps deliberately the short par 3, 4th hole turns back in

The par 4, 8th is the best hole at Royal Dublin

The par 3, 7th at Royal Dublin is 196 metres

10th green

the opposite direction. There is little in the way of fairway anywhere here so you must land on the green which starts at 152 metres from the tee. Two sets of industrial chimneys dominate the skyline in the near distance.

The long par 4, 5th (446 metres) is a beautiful looking narrow fairway that runs like a ribbon through a line of low dunes running along both sides. Out of bounds again is along the right as with the equally attractive par 5, 6th which measures a healthy 543 metres.

The par 3's at seven and nine and the first half of the par 4, 18th are the only holes that run across the course. Into the wind the 7th is quite a challenge at 196 metres from the back tee and 171 from the white. A poor shot that is short and right will find either gorse or a pond. Short left may leave you amongst several conifers. Anywhere short and straight is safe with then a simple chip to the green which slopes from the back.

The par 4, 8th is my pick as the best hole at Royal Dublin. This is a very tight par 4 of 375 metres with a slight bend left at around 190 metres from the tee. Like the 5th hole, the fairway is flanked by a line of low dunes, particularly on the right hand side. The green is a difficult target with a fall off on the left and mounds with rough on the right.

The turning point back towards the clubhouse comes after the short 9th. There is long grass all the way to the apron of the green which has four bunkers at the front and sides and a fall off at the back.

The 10th is a long par 4 that is now stretched to 422 metres from the back. Apart from its sheer length, made longer by the prevailing wind, there is a narrow burn or wet ditch that angles across just in front of the green. The par 5, 11th features out of bounds and the burn on the right and another burn nearer the green on the left side. The fairway is well bunkered and is rather narrow commencing at 85 metres from the green.

Either a very solid straight hit or a slight draw is needed at the 188 metre 12th. A large mound and then a bunker are at the left of the green whilst another bunker is at the front right. The rough is quite thick if you miss this green by more than seven or eight metres.

Thirteen is a long and narrow par 4 with a wet ditch and out of bounds the danger for any drive with a hint of fade. A burn meanders along the fairway starting at about 70 metres out on the right at the par 5, 14th. Anything too strong may finish in gorse that lies in a semi-circle behind the green.

A long par 4 at the 15th is followed by an interesting short par 4 of 278 metres (258 white). Out of bounds runs along the right of the 15th but is only in play for a horrible slice. This should be an easy four by way of drive and pitch but beware the numerous bunkers that leave you with a very limited landing area. The green falls off on the right and has two more bunkers at the back if you pull a chunky pitch to the left.

Out of bounds is very much in play at the right edge of the par 4, 17th fairway. Four bunkers are in place to catch a tee shot that is not perfectly straight and just left of centre.

The 18th is not a classical finishing hole but by its very shape it has decided many events. The fairway turns 90 degrees to the right at about 340 metres and then there is a further 90 metres to the centre of the fairly open green. A burn and then out of bounds occupies all the area to the right so it is a brave decision to try to head straight for the green. A straight drive will leave you with an easy second but the fairway narrows the further you hit and there are bunkers if you pull your tee shot a little left.

Royal Dublin is also synonymous with Christy O'Connor who became the professional there in 1959. Many famous names have won tournaments here starting right back at 1894 when John Ball successfully defended his Irish Open Amateur title.

17th green

Photos courtesy Owen O'Connor/Royal Dublin GC

18th green and clubhouse from the 90° bend in the fairway about 90 metres out

Photos courtesy Owen O'Connor/Royal Dublin GC

This is an old fashioned links that now has a little more challenge and variety as a result of the new greens. It will also test your ability to hit the ball straight, especially on the front nine.

PORTMARNOCK

The opening hole at Portmarnock, described by Donald Steel as being "neither difficult nor straightforward"

ON CHRISTMAS EVE 1893 W C PICKEMAN AND HIS FRIEND GEORGE ROSS ROWED THE SHORT DISTANCE TO THE PENINSULA OF PORTMARNOCK LOOKING FOR LAND THAT COULD MAKE A SUITABLE GOLF LINKS. THIS IDEAL LINKS LAND WAS FIRST USED AS A PRIVATE NINE HOLE COURSE BY THE JAMESONS, OF WHISKY DISTILLERY FAME.

Index 1 at Portmarnock is the 4th, a long par 4 of 474 yards

The 3rd is another par 4 of around 400 yards that also bends left. The estuary is along the right which is the preferred side for the second shot into the green. A larger bunker in the centre of the fairway is 36 yards out but makes the green look a little closer than it really is.

Index one at Portmarnock is the par 4, 4th hole which measures 474 yards from the back tee. This is a lovely looking hole that curves left through the first line of dunes. You need to drive to the right side but beware of the two sets of bunkers at 240 yards and 304 yards respectively from the tee. The fairway is very narrow at the approach to the green set at the base of the low dunes and with a stand of pine trees at the back right.

The par 4, 5th is nearly as difficult. It is slightly shorter at 442 yards but it requires a blind tee shot – a rarity at Portmarnock. The line from the tee is the two tall chimneys in the distance. You need a drive that will carry 211 yards just to reach the fairway.

The longer outward nine is really showing its teeth by the par 5, 6th which measures 603 yards from the back tee. This narrow fairway also bends left. The second shot should remain just short of two fairway bunkers, the first of which is 83 yards out. A pond is in the rough on the left beside where you should be playing your third to the elevated green.

Seven is a great little par 3 that plays shorter than its notional 184 yards. A duffed shot is in long grass or a small pond. The ball tends to kick from left to right on this tricky green. Two tough long par 4's bring you back to the clubhouse. The 8th is another hole bending left but the 9th finally provides for the reverse. Be careful with the shot into the green on the 9th as there are gorse bushes everywhere.

The back nine is virtually a separate loop with the 12th to 18th holes on the other side of the clubhouse.

John Jameson agreed to a 25 year lease and by 1894 the first nine holes were laid out by Pickeman with Mungo Park, the 1874 Open Champion, acting as consultant greens architect. The second nine was completed in 1896 and in 1899 the club was honoured with the Irish Open Amateur which was won by John Ball.

Portmarnock has now hosted numerous Irish Opens, the Dunlop Masters, the Canada Cup in 1960 and the Walker Cup in 1991. In 1949 the British Amateur Championship was held at Portmarnock – the first time it had been played outside the United Kingdom.

Donald Steel succinctly describes the opening hole of 405 yards as being "neither difficult nor straightforward, an ideal way to start".[1] Rough and then water, by way of the estuary, runs the whole of the right hand side. The green is long and narrow with three bunkers at the front and one at the left edge.

The 2nd is of similar length but bending slightly left. There are two bunkers on the right that can trap your drive and then three short of the green. The entrance is open but there are a further four around the two-tiered green.

The 14th, described by Henry Cotton as "the best par 4 in the world" – the green is in the distance just left of centre

The 14th green has a steep slope and is well bunkered

A good drive over the intimidating gorse at the par 4, 10th will then set you up for a possible birdie. The second shot won't be long but needs accuracy as the slightly built up green falls away to grassy hollows on all sides. Surprisingly, this is rated the eighth most difficult hole.

The 11th is a long par 4 where any one of the eight nasty little pot bunkers can add at least one to your score. Twelve is a par 3 of 160 yards that is slightly uphill to an elevated green with seaside dunes at the rear. If your tee shot finishes in any of the four small but very deep and straight faced revetted bunkers then you may have no option other than to be playing away from the green.

The long par 5, 13th is riddled with fairway bunkers. There are seven that may trap the drive and a further eight

to catch the approach to the green. The two holes that follow are amongst the very best at Portmarnock.

The 14th tee is set amongst pine trees. One lone conifer stands as sentinel on the right of the fairway which starts about 180 yards out from the tee. This is a superb par 4 with two lots of bunkers dominating the landscape. The first starts at 124 yards from the green. The second group of three is around the front section of the elevated green which has a very steep slope from back to front. Henry Cotton described the 14th as "the best par 4 in the world".

Fifteen is a brilliant par 3 of 190 yards running alongside the sea. The out of bounds fence and beach is just a few yards to the right where there is also scrub and buckthorn nearer the green. Anything short is in thick rough, left of the green is a

deep swale and there are three small but deep bunkers at the front corners of the rectangular shaped green.

The par 5, 16th has three pot bunkers in a line across the fairway 154 yards from the green. The entrance to this green is made even more narrow by three bunkers at the right and one at the left. Seventeen is a very long par 4 of 472 yards. The hole requires two straight shots with bunkers on the right very much in play for your long second. As you glance through the pine trees on your left you will see the small island known as Ireland's Eye which rises from the silhouette of the coastline like a snow capped mountain.

The 18th is a great finishing hole with a stadium atmosphere formed by the raised green with gorse, buckthorn and low trees at the sides and the stately clubhouse standing at the

The 15th is a brilliant par 3 of 190 yards

Ireland's Eye from the 17th fairway

rear. It may be a relatively modest 411 yards from the back tee but plenty of trouble is lurking close by. From the tee you feel as though you need a slight fade with the fairway angling a little right. However if you are too far right there are three bunkers, rough and then gorse waiting to spoil your round at the worst possible place. The safer strategy is to drive to the left side of the fairway. This hole will usually play longer as you will be into the prevailing wind so take at least one extra club for your second into the green.

In addition to the Championship Course, Portmarnock also has another nine holes of comparable quality. The newer nine was designed by Fred Hawtree and opened in 1971.

Just as Christie O'Connor is synonymous with Royal Dublin so too is Harry Bradshaw with Portmarnock. Bradshaw took over the role as the club's professional from Eddie Hackett in 1950 and remained there for forty years.

Portmarnock has no weak holes. Everything is very natural which makes for a great links experience. The greens are large and fast running. Several styles of bunkers appear on the course but the revetted ones are by far the toughest due to their depth and small diameter.

1. *Classic Golf Links of Great Britain & Ireland* – Donald Steel

Following the staging of the Irish Amateur Open Championship in May 2006, Portmarnock has now hosted no less than 75 major championship events. That alone should be testimony to its qualities.

PORTMARNOCK – HOTEL & GOLF LINKS

Photo David Worley

From the 16th tee, across the 8th green, to the par 3, 9th

FORMING PART OF THE LAND WHERE THE JAMESON WHISKEY FAMILY ORIGINALLY HAD THEIR OWN NINE HOLE COURSE ONE HUNDRED YEARS AGO, THE BERNHARD LANGER LINKS DESIGN COVERS AN AREA OF 180 ACRES.

The course is a healthy 6255 metres from the back tees and opened for play in 1996. The hotel is built on the site that includes the original Jameson family home. It is in a lovely setting beside the sea with views to the islands of Lambay and Ireland's Eye.

The course features some wonderful seaside dunes, elevated tees and greens and beautifully presented but very penal revetted pot bunkers. Good use is made of dog-legs and, perhaps not surprisingly, the four hardest holes are all par 4's of over 400 metres.

The stunning par 4, 18th and hotel

Apart from the 10th, almost all of the last eleven holes make maximum use of the nearby dunes.

The par 4, 1st is an interesting hole of 320 metres which dog-legs right, just past an old private cemetery on the right hand side which is out of bounds. A burn runs across the fairway about 100 metres out from the green. The 7th is a fine looking par 4 of 412 metres. A burn crosses the fairway about 70 metres out, just where your second shot might land. Three large pot bunkers are around the green with low dunes at the rear.

It is not until the dog-leg 8th that the holes enter the duneland. This is a good par 4 of 374 metres with a green amongst seaside dunes. The par 3, 9th is one of the best holes. It measures 145 metres and runs parallel with the shoreline. This must be one of the very few par 3's you will ever play that has no bunkers. The green is on a plateau with a deep hollow in front. If you miss short and right it will be extremely difficult to make par. You may need to take one more club to reduce the chances of landing short of the green.

Index number one is the 11th, a par 4 of 419 metres. The fairway curves right with plenty of bunkers along the left side. Another good hole is the par 4, 16th. The tee is amongst the dunes with a long carry required to reach the fairway before it dog-legs right. There are deep pot bunkers at the right hand corner of the dog-leg. The second shot needs to land on the green as the front and sides are littered with bunkers. The par 3, 17th runs away from the clubhouse in a similar fashion to the short 9th. The raised green is in a most attractive setting with just the one bunker at the front left.

The 18th is a visually stunning par 4 that runs along a valley between some impressive seaside dunes. The tee is elevated with panoramic views across the course and down the fairway. The green is set in an amphitheatre below the dunes with the hotel as a further back drop. You will be doing well to avoid all of the bunkers that make this an excellent but rather demanding finishing hole.

The 17th, a par 3 of 185 metres

Above: 18th hole from behind the green – the small island 'Ireland's Eye' is at the far left
Far left: sign on the 1st fairway

With larger dunes and plenty of marram grass, Portmarnock Hotel & Golf Links has a slightly wilder look than its older and more esteemed neighbour. Some years ago I had heard reports that the Langer design was not a true links course. I would beg to differ. This is the real thing and there are some very good holes, especially on the back nine.

THE ISLAND

"IN SEPTEMBER 1887 FOUR MEN ROWED ACROSS THE CHANNEL WHICH SEPARATES THE NORTH DUBLIN VILLAGE OF MALAHIDE FROM THE SPUR OF LAND TO THE NORTH KNOW LOCALLY AS THE ISLAND. THEIR MISSION WAS TO SURVEY THE WILDERNESS AND ASSESS ITS SUITABILITY AS A GOLF LINKS." [1]

Photo courtesy The Island GC

The club that started in 1890 today has a links measuring 6236 metres from the back tees. In 2006 some upgrading of the course was being undertaken by Martin Hawtree.

This is an attractive looking links with some very large dunes, plenty of rough and bracken, revetted bunkers and excellent greens.

The opening hole is an impressive par 4 of 397 metres with large dunes in play right from the outset. If you block your second shot right you will be in serious trouble in the dunes. The par 4, 2nd has a very narrow crumpled fairway that runs downhill. The 3rd is a slightly longer par 4 that runs uphill on the coastal side of the second. Thick rough on both sides helps contribute to this being rated index number two.

The 4th is a great little par 4 of 318 metres. The fairway runs between dunes to a narrow and very undulating green. The 5th to the 8th are par 4's that run back and forth parallel to each other. Five is another wonderful looking hole requiring a blind drive with large dunes at the right and a dell green at the foot of some more tall dunes. The Island is not over endowed with bunkers but those that are there are very well placed.

The 6th is just 299 metres but three bunkers at the start of the dog-leg left need to be avoided with your drive. Seven is the second longest of the par 4's (412 metres). A forest of sea buckthorn around the green will mean an almost certain lost ball for any errant approach. Eight is a short par 4 (278 metres) that needs a slight fade through the narrow gap in the dunes that encroach onto the fairway.

After eight successive par 4's each of which is quite different, comes the first par 3 at the 9th. There are two bunkers short of the green on the right and two beside the green at the left. You can run your shot on but if you miss to the right you are in heavy scrub. Left or long will find long grass.

The back nine is on the other side of the clubhouse with the first eight holes all running east or west.

Photo David Worley

Top: the 5th starts with a blind drive and ends in a tranquil setting in the dunes
Bottom: the tide may be out but the par 3, 13th is always an extremely difficult proposition

The fairway is very narrow for the first two shots at the 515 metre par 5, 15th

The 16th is the last of the short holes. It is only 139 metres but the green can be an elusive target. There are no bunkers but if you miss the narrow fairway the rough is thick. The green is on a plateau with a steep run-off on all sides.

From above the tee of the par 4, 17th you will see Ireland's Eye in the distance. This is a tricky hole with water, especially at high tide, at the right. The landing area just short of the green is very bumpy with a ridge running in the direction of the green in the middle of the fairway.

With the exception of the 1st, 13th and 18th, all holes run more or less east or west. The 18th is a long par 4 of 421 metres. It is, however, rather odd that from a matchplay perspective it is rated index number 1. The tee is elevated overlooking a fairway that is extremely undulating for the first 200 metres. A straight drive through the valley is essential. There is just the one very well positioned bunker that is front left of the raised green.

The Island is a really top links course that is relatively unknown outside of Ireland. Apart from being a wonderful test of golf it possesses the important quality of having a most natural and authentic links charm.

1. *A Century of Golf on the Island*

The 10th is a par 5 that is uphill and dog-legs right for the last 90 metres. Two bunkers protect the left of the green. Anything short will kick right down a swale or into a deep pot bunker.

Eleven and twelve are tight par 4's with no bunkers. The 12th green is elevated amongst the dunes. Anything that misses the green left or right is in trouble.

There are some great holes on this part of the course. The par 3, 13th is likely to stay in your memory – possibly for all the wrong reasons. Into a headwind it can play much longer than its 192 metres. Anything pushed right will be in the buckthorn or lower down on the water's edge. There is a large hollow between tee and green so it is just about carry all the way. This hole is a real potential card wrecker. Left is initially a safer option but then you have a tricky chip with a steep drop on the right of the green.

The 14th is in a narrow valley fairway which runs alongside more water at the right. From the raised tee you can go for your drive at the wonderful par 5, 15th (515 metres), however watch for the three bunkers on the left. The last half of the undulating fairway features a huge dune formation that runs along the left and then behind the green. The view from above the back of the 15th is superb.

Par 3, 16th from behind – the tee is at the right hand corner, the green is on a plateau with a steep run-off on all sides

LAYTOWN & BETTYSTOWN

TOM GILROY MADE A PRIMITIVE START TO GOLF AT THE PRESENT SITE BACK IN THE 1880'S. IT WAS HOWEVER NOT UNTIL 1909 THAT ANOTHER GOLFING FANATIC, GEORGE DALY ORGANISED A MEETING TO FORM WHAT WOULD BE KNOWN AS LAYTOWN & BETTYSTOWN GOLF CLUB.

A nine hole course was laid out initially and then extended to eighteen at the end of World War I.

A number of well known players have emerged from the club, most notably Des Smyth and Philip Walton.

The course is not demanding in terms of its total length of 5862 metres, but it does place an emphasis on accurate shot making and the wind is a constant factor. Despite the relatively short length, it achieves a par rating of 71 by having just three par 3's. The two par 5's are not long but the par 4's provide for plenty of variety.

One of the best holes is the 7th, a par 4 of 361 metres. The fairway winds through low dunes which form a narrow entrance along with one bunker, to the lovely large green.

Index 1 is the par 4, 12th. This hole relies primarily upon length for its rating and at 421 metres is by far the longest of the two-shotters.

Laytown & Bettystown is located about 30-40 minutes north of Dublin near Drogheda and ten miles from County Louth. It is beside the Irish Sea near the mouth of the River Boyne.

Photo courtesy Laytown & Bettystown GC

Par 4, 7th hole – if you want to know the prevailing wind direction just look at the shape of the two trees

You will not find it as difficult as nearby County Louth but it has some interesting holes through low level dunes and the greens are of a very high quality.

SEAPOINT

Photo courtesy Photoscheu

Seapoint – 18th fairway

The home hole is a challenging par 5 (505 metres) that bends left as you approach the green.

SEAPOINT IS A RELATIVELY NEW LINKS BUT IT IS RAPIDLY MAKING A NAME FOR ITSELF AS A COURSE THAT SHOULD NOT BE LEFT OFF THE ITINERARY.

Founded in 1993, the design is the result of the combined work of Des Smyth and Declan Branigan. Recent upgrades took place in 2004/5.

Seapoint is located at the mouth of the River Boyne at Termonfeckin, just north of County Louth at Baltray. The layout measures a very healthy 6473 metres from the back tees. There are dunes, marram grass and a variety of indigenous plants. Some of the front nine has a heathland feel but the last four holes alongside the Irish Sea are amongst classic duneland.

A stream runs in front of the first two greens and then along the right hand side of holes three, four and five. New bunkers have been added to the par 4, 4th hole and part of the lake is now in play at the front right of the green. You need to keep left off the tee for the best line for your second shot.

The fifth is the most difficult hole at Seapoint. At 385 metres it is a little shorter than the 4th but water is in play for both the drive and the shot into the green which is surrounded by water. Out of bounds is all along the right hand side so accuracy is absolutely essential.

Holes six, seven and eight continue on the inland part of the course with one last water challenge at the 186 metre par 3, 9th.

The back nine is on the sea side of the layout. Ten is a shortish par 5 of 490 metres and presents a birdie chance provided you manage to avoid the fairly deep bunkers that are close to the green.

This section of the course features low dunes and a number of well placed revetted bunkers. At the eleventh the bunkers are mainly for those who attempt to cut across the right hand corner of the dog-leg.

Twelve, thirteen and fourteen are each par 4's in excess of 400 metres. The 12th has a raised, two-tiered green. The 13th has gorse for those who stray from the fairway and four new bunkers have been added to protect the green. Be careful also of the bunkers at the left hand corner of the bend in the fairway.

The par 4, 14th turns to the right with the green hidden behind some mounds. You can't see the bunkers that are at the edge of this green.

The par 3, 15th heads towards the sea so it is usually into the prevailing wind and plays longer than its 154 metres. Anything pushed to the right is likely to be in serious trouble.

The 16th is a lovely short par 4 of 342 metres with the inviting fairway running parallel to the shoreline. Seventeen is a most picturesque par 3 (171 metres) with the sloping green set amongst low dunes and the sea very close at hand.

The home hole is a challenging par 5 (505 metres) that bends left as you approach the green. Again, accuracy is needed particularly to avoid the punishing rough in the dunes along the right.

Scenic and challenging – Seapoint is well worth investigating.

COUNTY LOUTH

COUNTY LOUTH, OR BALTRAY AS IT IS OFTEN KNOWN, IS A LITTLE DIFFICULT TO FIND ON A WINDING COASTAL ROAD ABOUT FIVE MILES SOUTH OF DROGHEDA. DON'T LET THAT DETER YOU AS THIS IS ONE OF IRELAND'S FINEST LINKS.

The 4th green needs no bunkers – the ridge in front will kick balls away from the target

The club started in 1892 but the present course, designed by Tom Simpson, did not open until 1938. There really aren't any weak holes although the rather flat par 3, 17th probably relies upon length as its main defence.

The greens at Baltray are second to none. The revetted bunkers are in plentiful supply but are larger and perhaps therefore a little less severe than those at Portmarnock. Parts of the course contain thick rough and bracken which will punish any shots wide of the target.

You won't get many tougher starts than the 1st at County Louth. It is the second longest of the par 4's at 454 yards and furthermore it is uphill. The fairway has a continuous bend left with patches of thick bracken amongst the rough on both sides. The tee shot is made more difficult by two bunkers on the left starting at 241 yards and two on the right at about 295 yards from the tee.

The 2nd is a par 5 with a similar shape to the 1st hole. The three-tiered green will test your putting skills. The 3rd is also a par 5. There are no bunkers which is rather unusual for a long hole but the fairway is very tight especially at 70 yards out from the long but narrow green. This hole is pretty much unchanged from Tom Simpson's original design.

The 4th is also devoid of bunkers. This is a lovely par 4 with a very bumpy fairway running amongst low dunes. A grassy ridge just short of the green will tend to kick balls away from the target.

A wonderful par 3 of 173 yards follows at the 5th. The raised green runs off on the left and at the right there are two pot bunkers. Bracken and rough await if you over club with your tee shot. The 6th is yet another par 5 which dog-legs left and, like the second, has a narrow neck just short of the green.

Seven is a very good short hole. Two bunkers lie at the front of the elevated green which runs off on all sides. It is only 163 yards from the back tee but is rated index number ten so this will give you an idea as to the difficulty of hitting and then holding the green. Holes 8, 9 and 10 are all solid par 4's of over 400 yards. The 9th is particularly well bunkered, especially for the drive.

Index number one is the par 4, 11th which measures 470 yards and used to be played as a short par 5. The shape of

Photo courtesy County Louth GC

The narrow and bumpy entrance to the green helps compensate for lack of length at the par 4, 14th

The 15th is an excellent par 3

the hole and positioning of the bunkers dictates that the drive needs to keep to the left side of the fairway. The narrow green has two bunkers at front left and another two at the right.

The 12th is a wonderful looking par 4 that curves left through dunes which form a narrow pass just short of the green. The par 4, 13th is slightly uphill with an impressive line of dunes at the right. Like so many of the holes at County Louth, the fairway narrows just before the green.

The raised tee is on the shoreline for the short par 4, 14th. Mounds and swales make the approach area very tight for those capable of driving the 332 yards to the equally tricky tiered green.

A number of the holes were lengthened for the Irish Open which was held at County Louth in 2004 (and won by the Australian, Brett Rumford). The 15th is a first class short hole that is now 15 yards longer at 167 yards. The green is angled to the left. There is a steep slope at the front with a very deep

bunker. A fade may end up in either of the other bunkers that are at the right edge of the green.

The par 4, 16th features an entrance barely 10 yards wide through grassy mounds to a sloping green higher up on the hill. A dune runs to the very edge of the green on the right.

The rather mundane par 3, 17th is followed by a good par 5 of 559 yards to finish. The 18th has deep rough and bracken all the way along the right. Three bunkers lie at the left to catch the drive. There are another two bunkers that are in the centre of the fairway 97 and 50 yards out respectively.

County Louth is a classic links that will punish bad shots and will certainly test your ability to avoid any three putt greens.

ACKNOWLEDGEMENTS

There are so many people I must thank and I apologise for any inadvertent omissions.

My sincere thanks and appreciation to Peter Thomson for contributing the Foreword, there is surely no-one on the planet more qualified to comment on Links golf.

Peter Thomson's photo is courtesy of Eagles Nest Publishing (Ross Perrett and Kimbal Baker).

To the Club Secretaries who assisted with tee times, I thank you. Many also gave me a copy of their club history and others also assisted with photographs. Whilst any photos not taken by myself have been specifically accredited, I have attempted to also list contributors on this page.

Alan Birch has been simply marvellous with his help by way of photos of many courses in the Liverpool area, particularly Royal Birkdale and Royal Lytham & St Annes. I look forward to one day showing him our great courses in and around Melbourne.

Duncan Martin, my dear friend from Glasgow, as always provided help in many ways with his intimate knowledge of the golf industry.

The 2006 trip was an arduous 3 months which would not have been possible to complete without the great company and assistance from Gary Prendergast during our month in Ireland.

My love and appreciation to my wife, Irene, for helping in so many ways during the trips of 1996, 1998, 2003 and the first 2 months of the 2006 Journey. Irene also typed the draft for *Journey through the Links* and assisted with the proof-reading.

Particular thanks to the following Golf Clubs (in the geographical order of the Journey):

West Kilbride (and Jane Young from South West Scottish Golf)
Dundonald (Guy Redford)
Royal Dornoch (John Duncan)
Tain
Brora
Moray (Steve Crane)
Carnoustie
Monifieth
Lundin Links (Alistair McDonald)
Craigielaw
Muirfield (Alastair Brown)
Luffness New (Tony Yeates)
Dunbar
Berwick-upon-Tweed
Seaton Carew
Seacroft
Royal West Norfolk
Felixstowe Ferry (Richard Tibbs)
Princes (Bill Howie)
Royal Cinque Ports
Royal St George's
Littlestone (Charles Moorehouse)
Hayling (special thanks to Ray Gadd, the Professional)
Burnham and Berrow
Royal Porthcawl
Pennard
Tenby (David Hancock)
Nefyn (Barry Owens)
Conwy (Aled Jones)
Western Gailes (Ian Sproule)
Royal County Down (James Laidler)
Royal Portrush (Wilma Erskine)
Castlerock (Mark Steen)
Rosapenna (special thanks to Frank Casey)
Donegal
Enniscrone (Michael Staunton)
Carne (Mary Tallot)
Doonbeg
Lahinch
Ballybunion
Dingle
Dooks
Waterville (Noel Cronin)
Old Head
The European (special thanks to Pat Ruddy Snr)
Royal Dublin (Paddy Walshe, Hon.Sect.)
Portmarnock (John Quigley)
County Louth

Photo acknowledgements to Club or photographer, if known:
Archerfield (Lindsay Scott)
Ashburnham (Ian Church)
Ballyliffin – photos by Larry Lambrecht
Carnoustie (Colin Mcleod) – photos by Darren J Kirk at Scratch Design
Castlerock (Mark Steen) – photos by www.brsgolf.com
Conwy (Aled Jones)
County Sligo (Hugh O'Neill)
County Louth (Michael Delaney)
Dooks – photos by Donal Brosnan
Dunbar (Shirley Fairbairn)
Dundonald (Guy Redford) – photo by Iain Lowe
Inverallochy (James Buchan)
Kilmarnock Barassie (Donald Wilson)
Laytown and Bettystown
Muirfield – photo by Alastair Brown
North Wales (Gren Jones)
Old Head
Pennard
Perranporth (Martin Philp)
Portmarnock Hotel and Golf (Moira Cassidy)
Princes – photo by Richard Kimber
Rosapenna – photos by Aidan Bradley www.golfcoursephotography.com
Royal Dublin – photos by Owen O'Connor
Royal Guernsey
Royal Troon – photos by Kenneth Ferguson www.photoscot.com
Saunton
Seapoint – photo by Photoscheu
Silloth (John Hill)
Skibo Castle (Claire Bruce)
Southerness
St Annes Old Links – photo by Stuart Hogg
St Enodoc (Tuck Clagett) – photos Phil Inglis
The European
The Island (Louise McAuley)

Plus additional photos from:
Gary Prendergast, Alan Birch, John Cornish, Ian Gust and Ian Stanley.

SPIRITS OF THE LINKS

No niblicks clicking,
no plus fours of red, green or blue.
Shadows stretch across the green,
fairways show their changing hue.

All is quiet from the sounds of 'fore,'
Summer evenings breathing life anew.
One last circle from the gulls offshore,
oh the pity these days so few.

Each hour they guard the hallowed turf
protecting now what they once made
along with God, this near untouched earth
of J.H., Old Tom and James Braid.

David Worley

Muirfield at dusk